The First Book of
Quicken® 6

The First Book of
Quicken® 6

Paul McFedries

alpha
books

A Division of Prentice Hall Computer Publishing
11711 North College, Carmel, Indiana 46032 USA

To Jan, Lorraine, Gregg, Iain, and Paul: a small circle of friends.

© 1992 by Alpha Books

All rights reserved. No part of this book shall be reproduced, stored in a retrieval system, or transmitted by any means, electronic, mechanical, photocopying, recording, or otherwise, without written permission from the publisher. No patent liability is assumed with respect to the use of the information contained herein. Although every precaution has been taken in the preparation of this book, the publisher and author assume no responsibility for errors or omissions. Neither is any liability assumed for damages resulting from the use of the information contained herein. For information, address Alpha Books, 11711 N. College Ave., Carmel, IN 46032.

International Standard Book Number: 1-56761-020-X
Library of Congress Catalog Card Number: 92-73563

95 94 93 92   8 7 6 5 4 3 2 1

Interpretation of the printing code: the rightmost number of the first series of numbers is the year of the book's printing; the rightmost number of the second series of numbers is the number of the book's printing. For example, a printing code of 92-1 shows that the first printing of the book occurred in 1992.

Screen reproductions in this book were created by means of the program Collage Plus from Inner Media, Inc., Hollis, NH.

Printed in the United States of America

Publisher
Marie Butler-Knight

Managing Editor
Elizabeth Keaffaber

Acquisitions Editor
Stephen R. Poland

Development Editor
Seta Frantz

Staff Writer
Joe Kraynak

Production Editor
Annalise N. Di Paolo

Copy Editor
Howard Peirce

Cover Design
Susan Kniola

Designer
Jay Corpus

Indexers
Loren Malloy
John Sleeva

Production Team
Tim Cox,
Terri Edwards,
Mark Enochs,
Tim Groeling,
John Kane,
Carrie Keesling,
Phil Kitchel,
Tom Loveman,
Angie Trzepacz,
Suzanne Tully,
Julie Walker,
Kelli Widdifield

Special thanks to Hilary Adams
for ensuring the technical accuracy of this book.

Contents

1 What Is Quicken? — 3

Monitoring Your Money with Categories 4
    Including More Detail
        with Subcategories and Classes 7
Producing Reports 8
The Process of Using Quicken 6 8
Other Financial Tools 10
Knowing the Terminology 12
About the Examples Used in This Book 12
    The Home Example 12
    The Business Example 13

2 Getting Started with Quicken — 15

Starting Quicken 15
    Did Quicken Start Properly? 16
Running Quicken for the First Time 18
Using the On-Line Help System 19
    Context-Sensitive Help 19
    The Help Table of Contents 20
    The Help Index 20
    Scrolling Through the Help Screens 21
    Viewing Related Topics 21
    Searching for Help Topics 22
Moving Around in Quicken 25
    A Note About Menu Styles 25
Using Quicken Menus 26
    Quicken Pop-Up Menus 26
    The Main Menu 28
    Quicken Pull-Down Menus 29
    Bypassing the Pull-Down Menus 30
Other Screen Elements 31
Using a Mouse with Quicken 32
Setting Quicken Preferences 33
    Customizing Screen Settings 33
Exiting Quicken 35

3 Working with Quicken Accounts — 37

- Types of Accounts 37
- Setting Up Accounts 39
- Working with Accounts 43
  - Selecting Accounts 43
  - Editing an Account 45
  - Deleting an Account 46
- Working with Account Files 47
  - How Many Account Files Do You Need? 48
  - Adding a New Account File 49
  - Specifying the Location of Your Account Files 51
  - Selecting an Account File 52
  - Editing an Account File Name 53
  - Deleting an Account File 54
  - Copying an Account File 55
- Backing Up and Restoring Account Files 57
  - Backing Up Account Files 57
  - Setting the Backup Reminder Frequency 59
  - Restoring Backed-Up Account Files 61
- The Book Examples 62

4 Using Categories and Classes — 65

- About Categories 66
  - Standard and Custom Categories 66
- Viewing the Categories 67
  - Navigating the Category List 69
- Working with Categories 70
  - Editing Categories 70
  - Deleting a Category 72
  - Printing the Category List 73
- Adding Your Own Categories 74
  - Practicing with Category Suggestions 77
- Using Subcategories 78
  - Adding, Editing, and Deleting Subcategories 80
  - Practicing with Subcategory Suggestions 82
- Using Classes 82
  - Adding Classes 84
  - Modifying Classes 86
  - Deleting a Class 87
  - Using Subclasses 87

5 Working with the Register — 91

Using the Register Screen 92
   Navigating the Register Screen 93
The Register Fields 95
   The Date Field 95
   The Check Number Field 97
   The Payee Field 98
   The Memo Field 98
   The Category Field 98
   The Payment Field 99
   The Cleared Field 99
   The Deposit Field 99
   The Balance Field 100
Adding a Transaction to the Register 100
Editing a Register Transaction 104
Deleting a Transaction 104
Copying a Transaction 105
Voiding a Transaction 106
Transferring Funds Between Accounts 107
   Editing Transfers 109
Printing the Register 110
Using Quicken's Basic Math Calculator 111

6 Writing and Printing Checks — 115

Using Quicken Checks 115
The Write Checks Screen 118
The Check Fields 118
   The Date Field 118
   The Amount Field 119
   The Address Field 120
   The Memo Field 120
   The Check Number Field 120
Writing a Check 121
Reviewing Your Checks 124
Editing Checks 124
Deleting a Check 125
Voiding a Check 126
Setting Up Your Printer 127

Getting Ready to Print 128
    Setting Vertical Alignment on a
      Daisywheel or Dot-Matrix Printer 129
    Setting Vertical Alignment on a Laser Printer ... 131
    Setting Horizontal Alignment 133
Printing Checks 133
    Fixing Printing Problems 136

7 Splitting, Memorizing, and Automating Transactions   139

Splitting Transactions 140
    Editing a Split Transaction 143
    Deleting Transaction Splits 143
Memorizing Transactions 144
    Memorizing a Transaction 144
    Recalling Memorized Transactions 146
    Memorizing Split Transactions 147
    Editing Memorized Transactions 148
    Deleting Memorized Transactions 150
Using QuickFill to Automate Your Work 150

8 Reconciling Your Accounts   155

The Reconciliation Process 155
Reconciling Your Account with Quicken 156
Starting the Reconciliation 157
Marking Cleared Transactions 160
    Marking a Range of Uncleared Transactions 161
    Searching for Uncleared Transactions 162
When Your Account Balances 163
When Your Account Doesn't Balance 165
    Changing Uncleared Transactions 167
    Entering Missing Transactions 168
    Adjusting for Unresolved Differences 168

9 Your Finances with Other Quicken Accounts   173

Recording Cash Transactions 173
   Using a Cash Account...............................174
   Updating Your Cash Balance.............................174
   Tracking Cash in a Bank Account 176
Recording Credit Card Transactions 177
   Should You Create a Separate
     Credit Card Account? 177
   Setting Up a Credit Card Account 178
   Reconciling Your Credit Card Accounts 179
   Tracking Credit Cards in a Checking Account ...182
   Using IntelliCharge 183
Recording Other Assets and Other Liabilities 184
   Setting Up Asset and Liability Accounts 185
   Entering Asset and Liability Transactions 185
   Updating Asset and Liability Values 186
   Marking Closed Assets and Liabilities 187
   Amortizing Your Loan Payments 188
Recording Investment Transactions.......................191

10 Creating and Printing Reports   193

The Reports Menu 193
Personal Reports...194
   Cash Flow Report 195
   Monthly Budget Report 197
   Itemized Categories Report................................197
   Tax Summary Report 199
   Net Worth Report 199
   Missing Check Report..202
   Tax Schedule Report...202
Business Reports 205
Investment Reports 205
Creating a Predefined Report 206
   Viewing the Report on the Screen 207
Customizing Reports 209
Printing Reports 212
   Printing Wide Reports 213
   Printing to a Disk File 213

11 Budgeting and Financial Planning with Quicken — 217

Setting the Groundwork 218
Setting Up a Quicken Budget 218
    Setting Budget Amounts 220
    Copying Budget Amounts to Other Months 221
    Budgeting Items that Recur
      Every Two Weeks 223
    Using Historical Income and Expense Data 224
    Budgeting Amounts for Transfers 226
Producing Budget Reports 227
    The Monthly Budget Report 227
    Custom Budget Reports 230
Printing Your Budget Report 231
Using Quicken's Financial Planning Calculators ... 232
    The Loan Calculator 233
    The Investment Planning Calculator 234
    The Retirement Planning Calculator 235
    The College Planning Calculator 236
    The Refinance Calculator 237

12 Graphing with Quicken — 239

Types of Graphs 240
The View Graphs Menu 240
    Income and Expenses 243
    Net Worth 244
    Budget and Actual 245
    Investment 246
Creating a Graph 247
Changing Display Options
  for the Graph Feature 248
Graphing Selected Data 249

13 Using Quicken at Tax Time — 253

Planning for Taxes 253
Using Tax-Related Categories 255
    Setting Up Tax-Related Categories 259
    Marking an Existing Category as Tax-Related ... 260

Searching for Additional Categories 261
Using Classes 262
Setting Up Tax-Related Accounts 262
Creating Tax Reports 265

14 Setting Up a Business Accounting System — 269

Cash Versus Accrual Accounting 269
Completing Your Chart of Accounts 270
Tracking Accounts Receivable—Cash Method 272
    Setting Up an Accounts Receivable
      Asset Register 273
    Entering Invoices 273
    Entering Payments 275
Tracking Accounts Payable—Cash Method 277
Tracking Accounts Receivable—Accrual Method ... 278
    Setting Up an Accounts Receivable
      Asset Register 278
    Entering Invoices 279
    Entering Payments 279
Tracking Accounts Payable—Accrual Method 281
    Setting Up an Accounts Payable
      Liability Register 281
    Entering a Bill 282
    Entering Your Payment 282
Producing Business Reports 283

15 Quicken Applications — 287

Preparing Payroll 287
    Setting Up a Payroll System 288
    Writing Payroll Checks 291
    Memorizing Payroll Checks 294
    Paying Payroll Taxes 295
    Producing Payroll Reports 295
Tracking Business Inventory 296
    Some Inventory Examples 298
Managing Rental Properties 300
    Entering Transactions 301
    Producing Property Management Reports 303

Tracking Personal Belongings 304
Tracking Home Repairs and Improvements 306
The End 308

A Installing Quicken   311

What You Need to Run Quicken 311
Quicken Installation 312

Index   317

Introduction

The decade of the 1980s was one of tremendous financial excitement: record stock prices, corporate takeovers, and massive consumer spending. Along with excitement, however, came excess: overvalued shares, junk bonds, and record consumer-debt levels. Finally, as the decade neared its end, these excesses took their toll: the stock market crash, the savings and loan crisis, and record numbers of bankruptcies. Now, with the 1990s well under way, there is a new mood. The lessons of the past decade have been learned, and financial responsibility is the order of the day.

The 1980s also saw the emergence of the personal computer. The IBM PC was introduced in 1981, and the idea of the desktop computer gained immediate respectability. Since then, there have been relentless, often spectacular, improvements in the technology of both hardware and software. Perhaps more important, millions of people have learned that computers can help increase productivity and enhance creativity.

When you combine the recent trend toward financial responsibility with the productivity of the personal computer, is it any wonder that a financial management program like Quicken has an installed base of over one million users? People from all walks of life have found that Quicken can help them take control of their finances quickly and effortlessly.

Although Quicken is an easy program to learn and use, there are features of the program that can confuse first-time users. *The First Book of Quicken 6* is designed to teach you the fundamentals of using Quicken and lead you through the more complex capabilities of the program. With *The First Book of Quicken 6,* you'll get the most out of your software investment.

Some of What's New in Quicken 6

Quicken 6 is a major upgrade with many new features. If you've used a previous version of Quicken, you'll learn these new features as you go along. For now, here's a summary of some of the enhancements found in Quicken 6:

- *Financial Graphs.* In addition to creating reports, you can now create and view graphs of your financial data. You can use these graphs to analyze income and expense or your net worth, create more accurate budgets, and even see a price history of your investments.

- *QuickFill.* With the new QuickFill feature, you start typing an entry, and Quicken fills in the rest of the transaction for you, using either a memorized transaction or a transaction from the two most recent months. You can then edit the transaction as needed.

- *Amortization for loans with variable interest rates and prepayments.* Quicken 6 comes with an enhanced loan amortization feature that can handle loans with variable interest rates and can account for any prepayments you make on the loan.

- *Financial calculators.* Quicken 6 offers five calculators designed to help you plan your finances and meet your financial goals: a loan calculator, an investment calculator, a retirement calculator, a college planning calculator, and a refinance calculator.

- *IntelliCharge—electronic charge card service.* With Quicken and a Quicken charge card, you get your credit card statements on disk or via CompuServe.

- *New electronic payment features.* If you subscribe to the CheckFree electronic payment service, you can now set up fixed payments instead of entering the payment each time. You can also send and receive mail from CheckFree electronically. Because electronic payments are a slightly more advanced topic, they are not covered in this book.

- *Pop-up calendar.* The pop-up calendar shows the days of any month. You can quickly go to a transaction in the current account by selecting the date of the transaction from the calendar. You can also cut and paste dates from the calendar into your transactions.

- *Cutting and pasting transactions.* With Quicken 6, you can now copy a transaction on one date to another date to save time entering duplicate information. You can then edit the new transaction as desired.

- *New assistants.* Quicken has added four new assistants to help lead you through some of the more complicated tasks: Amortized Loan, Investment Account, Investment Transactions, and Export Tax Information.

- *Importing stock prices from Prodigy.* With Prodigy, you can save stock price information from the Dow Jones service to an ASCII text file that you can import into Quicken. This advanced topic is not covered in this book.

Who This Book Is For

This book is for anybody who is considering purchasing a financial management program such as Quicken for their home or business. It is also for those who have already installed Quicken and need to know where to go from there.

This book is for people who don't want to learn accounting theory to manage their finances. *The First Book of Quicken 6* covers Quicken with an intentionally brief, concise, and easy-to-follow approach. There are numerous examples throughout the book to show how Quicken works in the real world.

This book does not assume that you're an expert DOS user or that you've used a previous version of Quicken. First-time Quicken users are led carefully through each of Quicken's major features. If you've used Quicken before, this book points out many of the enhancements introduced in Version 6. It also provides you with numerous tips and ideas that you can put to use immediately.

Conventions Used in This Book

This book offers several features that will make learning Quicken as simple as possible and allow you to access information quickly and easily. Following are some of these features:

- Numerous examples from both home and business situations show the ways that Quicken can be used.

- Messages that appear on-screen are printed in `computer type`.

- Text you type appears in **`bold, color computer type`**.

- You can select an option by using your mouse or by pressing the highlighted letter in the option's name. In this book, the highlighted letter appears in **B**old type.

- Menus, commands, or options you select or keys you press appear in color. These items are appropriately capitalized.

- Keys that you press appear as special keyboard characters. For example, "Type Y and press Tab or Enter."

> **QUICK STEPS** — This icon introduces Quick Steps that provide you with step-by-step instructions for performing everyday tasks, such as writing a check. Many of the Quick Steps procedures are listed alphabetically on the inside front cover of this book.

VERSION 6 — This icon points out features that are new to Quicken 6. If you're already familiar with Quicken, look for these icons to learn about the new features.

This icon introduces you to practical ideas for using Quicken in real-world situations.

NOTE: This icon points out extra information on Quicken features that you may need to know.

TIP: This icon offers tips and techniques that make Quicken easier to use.

This icon indicates special situations where caution is required.

Acknowledgments

Robert Pirsig, in *Zen and the Art of Motorcycle Maintenance,* tells us that a person who sees Quality and feels it as he works is a person who cares. If this book is a quality product, it's because the people at Alpha Books editorial cared enough to make it so.

For the first edition, I'd like to thank Mary-Terese Cozzola Cagnina for pulling the project together and for having one of the best names in publishing. Special thanks go to Senior Development Editor Lisa Bucki for recommending me to write this book and for being the most pleasant slave driver an author could hope to have. Thanks, also, to Production Editor Chuck Hutchinson for his insightful comments and unfailing good humor, Copy Editors Judy Brunetti and Sara Black for their uncanny ability to find my dumb mistakes, Technical Editor Herb Feltner for making sure that what I said was supposed to happen actually did, and to

Development Editor Faithe Wempen for her excellent late-inning relief. Thanks, finally, to Sharon Severn at Maxwell Macmillan Canada for the last-minute administrative support.

For the second edition, I owe special thanks to Seta Frantz for carefully guiding the revision of the book, to Howard Peirce for tightening the language, and to Liz Keaffaber for coordinating the production of the book.

Trademark Acknowledgments

All terms mentioned in this book that are known to be trademarks or service marks are listed here. In addition, terms suspected of being trademarks or service marks have been appropriately capitalized. Alpha cannot attest to the accuracy of this information. Use of a term in this book should not be regarded as affecting the validity of any trademark or service mark.

Lotus and 1-2-3 are trademarks of the Lotus Development Corporation.

Quicken is a registered trademark of Intuit.

QuickPay is a trademark of Intuit.

TurboTax is a registered trademark of ChipSoft, Inc.

In This Chapter
What Is Quicken?
The Check Register
Categories and Classes
Generating Reports
The Four Stages of Using Quicken

Personal Finances

- Quicken is a personal finance program that helps you keep track of income, expenses, and investments.
- As you write checks, Quicken automatically updates the balance in your check register.
- Quicken allows you to generate various reports, such as a tax summary, that present your financial data in a meaningful form.

A Four-Stage Process

To use Quicken, you must follow a four-stage process.

- Stage 1: Set up.
- Stage 2: Enter transactions.
- Stage 3: Reconcile accounts.
- Stage 4: Generate reports.

Other Financial Tools

- Quicken 6 can graph your financial data. For example, you can view a graph of your income and expenses.
- Quicken's loan amortization calculator can tell you how much the loan will cost you and how much of each payment will go toward the principal and interest.
- The financial planning calculators help you plan for major expenses, determine how your investments will grow, and help you plan for retirement.
- With CheckFree, you can issue check payments by phone.
- With IntelliCharge, you get a credit card statement on disk.

Chapter 1

What Is Quicken?

Quicken is a financial management software package suitable for the home, home office, or small business. Quicken is powerful enough to handle just about any financial task: recording transactions, writing and printing checks, budgeting, preparing tax information, and creating business or personal financial reports. Quicken is flexible, too; you can customize various aspects of the program to suit your financial situation. Yet for all this, Quicken is remarkably easy to learn and use.

At its most basic level, Quicken is a record-keeping device. You enter all your transactions in an electronic equivalent of your paper check register, as you can see in Figure 1.1. There are fields for the date, a check number, the payee, the amount, and the running balance. The big difference, of course, is that the entries in the Quicken register are always neatly arranged, and the balance is calculated automatically.

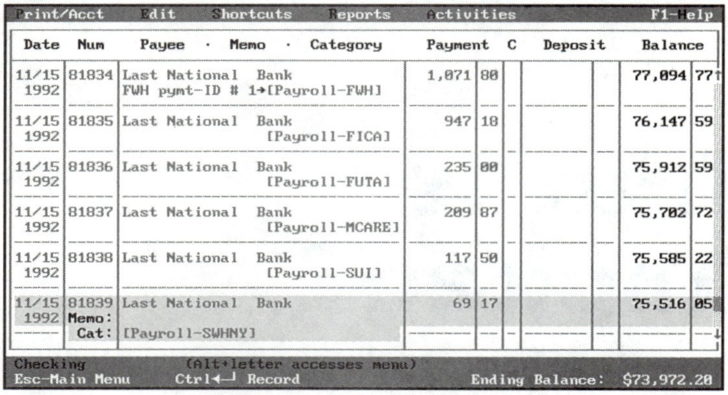

Figure 1.1
Quicken's Check Register screen showing sample transactions.

```
Print/Acct    Edit    Shortcuts    Reports    Activities           F1-Help
Date   Num    Payee  · Memo  · Category    Payment  C  Deposit    Balance
11/15  81834  Last National  Bank            1,071 88             77,094 77
1992          FWH pymt-ID # 1→[Payroll-FWH]
11/15  81835  Last National  Bank              947 18             76,147 59
1992                         [Payroll-FICA]
11/15  81836  Last National  Bank              235 88             75,912 59
1992                         [Payroll-FUTA]
11/15  81837  Last National  Bank              289 87             75,702 72
1992                         [Payroll-MCARE]
11/15  81838  Last National  Bank              117 50             75,585 22
1992                         [Payroll-SUI]
11/15  81839  Last National  Bank               69 17             75,516 05
1992   Memo:
       Cat:  [Payroll-SWHNY]
Checking              (Alt+letter accesses menu)
Esc-Main Menu    Ctrl↵ Record                Ending Balance:  $73,972.28
```

Each account you set up in Quicken (you can set up an account for each of your bank accounts, your credit cards, your mortgage, and so on) has its own register. These registers record all your transactions, including transfers between accounts. The information contained in these registers becomes, in effect, your personal financial database. You can use Quicken to summarize and extract information from this database for things like budgeting and tax preparation.

Monitoring Your Money with Categories

It is no secret how Quicken helps you get a handle on your finances. Put simply, Quicken shows you how much money is coming in and where that money is going. In short, Quicken makes you *aware* of your financial situation.

Consider a simple case. Suppose you use Quicken to record all your personal cash flow transactions for one month. At the end of the month, Quicken can add up all the inflows and outflows and give you a basic report like the one shown in Figure 1.2.

Figure 1.2
A sample report showing monthly inflows and outflows.

```
                          CASH FLOW
                  10/ 1/92 Through 10/31/92
      HOME-Bank,Cash,CC Accounts
      Page 1
      11/ 1/92
                                              10/ 1/92-
                         Category Description  10/31/92

                         INFLOWS
                            Inflows - Other    2,266.29

                         TOTAL INFLOWS         2,266.29

                         OUTFLOWS
                            Outflows - Other   2,466.69

                         TOTAL OUTFLOWS        2,466.69


                         OVERALL TOTAL          -200.40
```

As you can see in the figure, for this particular month, expenses exceeded income by about $200. This is useful information that can alert you to cut back on spending. But cut back where? How was the money spent? You need more *detail*.

To display more detail, you can sort your income and expenses into meaningful groups, called *categories*. For example, you can set up categories for each source of income you have: salary, account interest—even a trust fund. You can set up expense categories for your automobile, groceries, clothing, utilities, entertainment, and mortgage interest. Whenever you write a check or use your credit card, you simply tell Quicken which category to assign the payment to. Quicken keeps track of the totals in each category.

Then, at the end of the month (week, year—whatever), you can get Quicken to list your income and expenses by category. Compare the category-based report in Figure 1.3 to the one presented in Figure 1.2. Both reports are based on the same transactions. As you can see, however, the category report is much more useful.

Figure 1.3

A sample report with inflows and outflows listed by category.

```
                                    CASH FLOW
                            10/ 1/92 Through 10/31/92
         HOME-Bank,Cash,CC Accounts
         Page 1
         11/ 1/92
                                                      10/ 1/92-
                               Category Description   10/31/92

                               INFLOWS
                                  Salary Income        2,266.29

                               TOTAL INFLOWS           2,266.29

                               OUTFLOWS
                                  Automobile Expenses    404.09
                                  Clothing               221.10
                                  Entertainment          631.11
                                  Groceries              323.17
                                  Motgage Interest Exp   887.22

                               TOTAL OUTFLOWS         2,466.69


                               OVERALL TOTAL          -200.40
```

With Quicken, you can set up as many or as few categories as you require. The program even comes with a list of predefined categories you can use as is or modify to suit your needs.

Including More Detail with Subcategories and Classes

You can see even more detail about your finances by using *subcategories*. Subcategories enable you to break down a category into smaller groups. For your computer, for example, you know that you spend money on hardware (a modem, a printer, extra memory), software (Quicken, utilities, games), and miscellaneous supplies (disks, paper). In your Quicken account, you could establish a general Computer category and several subcategories for each of these types of expenses as follows:

Category	*Subcategories*
Computer	Hardware
	Software
	Supplies

At any time, Quicken can give you a summary report for each of these subcategories.

Quicken also lets you group your transactions by *classes*. While categories tell you the *what*s of a transaction, classes provide a different perspective—the *who*s, *where*s, and *when*s. For example, if you run a home office, you might pay for both business and personal expenses from the same account. You can tell Quicken to divide all your expenses into two classes: Business and Personal. In doing so, each category you create can be split between these two classes. For example, the Computer category would look like this:

Category	**Classes**
Computer	Business
	Personal

Classes provide a real advantage at tax time when you're calculating your deductions. You can run a class-based report that will give you separate totals for business expenses—just plug these in the tax form.

Producing Reports

Many people are satisfied using Quicken just to record their transactions and to write and print checks. However, as the examples in the preceding section showed, if you want to use Quicken for tax preparation or in any kind of business, you'll need to extract and summarize the information contained in your registers. In Quicken, you do this by generating reports.

For example, suppose you run a home-based business and you want to prepare information for your tax return. You need a report that will summarize all your business income and expenses for the year. With Quicken, all it takes is a few keystrokes (or mouse clicks) to produce a tax summary report like the one shown in Figure 1.4.

Quicken provides a number of predefined reports for personal, business, and investment use. Quicken generates each of these reports using a predefined format. If you don't like the defaults Quicken uses, you can create a custom report. (For example, you can change the row and column headings, the items to subtotal, or the accounts to use.) You can also restrict the transactions used in the report to certain dates, categories, or classes.

The Process of Using Quicken 6

You will get the most out of Quicken if you learn the program in stages, using a systematic approach such as the one in this book. Here are the four basic stages in the Quicken process:

Stage 1: Set up. In this stage, you prepare Quicken for your own use by setting up files, accounts, categories, and classes.

Stage 2: Enter transactions. In this stage, you write and print checks and enter your deposits, withdrawals, transfers, and any other transactions that affect your accounts.

Stage 3: Reconcile accounts. When you get your bank or credit card statement each month, you'll use it to reconcile your Quicken bank or credit card accounts and correct any discrepancies.

Stage 4: Generate reports and graphs. Once you have some transactions and you've checked their accuracy, you can begin to generate reports and graphs to help you learn more about your finances.

```
                          TAX SUMMARY REPORT
                        1/ 1/92 Through 12/31/92
CHECK-Checking
Page 1
1/ 5/93
                                              1/ 1/92-
                          Category Description    12/31/92
                          ─────────────────────   ─────────

                          INCOME/EXPENSE
                            INCOME
                              Gross Sales         57,898.01
                                                  ─────────
                          TOTAL INCOME            57,898.01

                            EXPENSES
                              Freight                678.33
                              Legal Fees           2,122.65
                              Office Expenses     1,555.72
                              Travel Expenses     4,672.21
                                                  ─────────
                          TOTAL EXPENSES           9,028.91
                                                  ─────────
                          TOTAL INCOME/EXPENSE    48,869.10
                                                  ═════════
```

Figure 1.4
Quicken can produce a tax summary report in just a few keystrokes.

Figure 1.5 illustrates this four-stage process.

Figure 1.5

The four-stage process of using Quicken.

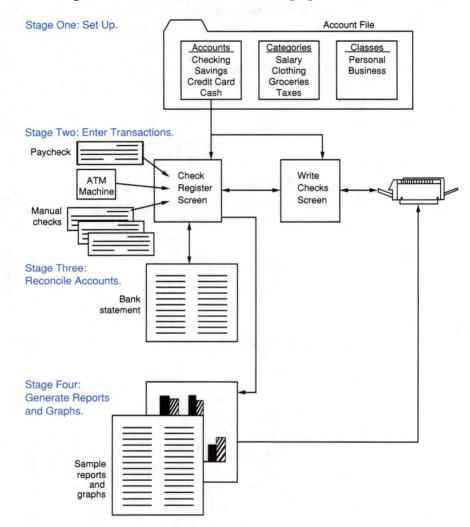

Other Financial Tools

In addition to a basic accounting system, Quicken offers several very useful accounting tools. The following list provides a brief description of each tool:

What Is Quicken?

Graphs With Quicken's new graph feature, you get a clearer picture of your finances. For example, you can view a graph that compares your income to your expenses. However, you cannot print graphs.

Loan Amortization Calculator With this calculator, you enter the amount of money you want to borrow, the interest rate, and the term (the amount of time you have to pay off the loan). Quicken determines how much you will actually pay over the life of the loan and how much of each payment goes toward principal and interest. The calculator can amortize loans with fixed or variable interest rates and prepayments.

Financial Planning Calculators These calculators help you plan for major expenses, such as car loans and college costs, and prepare for your retirement. For example, you can tell Quicken how much money you have invested and the annual yield, and Quicken will tell you how much your investment will be worth in 10 years.

Electronic Bill Paying If you have a modem, you can subscribe to an electronic bill-paying service called CheckFree. CheckFree can handle electronic transfers to any company that can handle electronic transfers. If the company or individual cannot handle such transfers, CheckFree mails the person a printed check two or three days before the payment due date.

Electronic Credit Card You can get a Quicken credit card from Intuit and use it just like a Visa or American Express card. Intuit sends your statement on disk each month, or you can connect to the service through CompuServe.

Knowing the Terminology

Although Quicken is an accounting program, you don't have to be an accountant to use it. This book uses only basic financial terms and expressions, most of which will be familiar to you. However, if you come across an unfamiliar word or phrase, please see the inside back cover of this book.

About the Examples Used in This Book

By its very nature, Quicken is a program designed to work in the real world: checking accounts, credit cards, mortgages, money—things you deal with every day. As a result, Quicken is best taught using real-world examples, and it is best learned through extensive hands-on practice.

To illustrate Quicken's concepts and techniques, this book uses two practical examples: one for the home and one for a business. The following sections describe these two examples in a bit more detail.

The Home Example

Quicken is the ideal home-accounting system, no matter how simple or complex your personal finances. In this book, you will follow the financial exploits of the Johnson family. The Johnsons are typical in many ways: they have two children, a house with a mortgage, and a car loan. They pay bills, they make improvements to their house, and they have some investments. Mrs. Johnson runs a desktop publishing business from their home and teaches computer courses at the local college, and Mr. Johnson is a manager in a large corporation. The Johnsons' example will illustrate the many ways that Quicken can help you manage your household finances.

The Business Example

While Quicken is not powerful enough to handle the accounting needs of a large corporation, it can easily satisfy the modest demands of a small business. To demonstrate this, you will follow the Book City Bookshop as an example throughout this text. Book City is a general-purpose bookstore that is typical of many small businesses. It has a payroll (a staff of 15), inventory (all those books), accounts payable (all those books), and accounts receivable (book returns to publishers). You will follow Book City to examine these and other small business concerns such as budgeting and taxes.

In This Chapter

Starting Quicken

Getting On-Line Help

Moving Around the Quicken Screens

Using a Mouse with Quicken

Using the Quicken Calculators

Starting Quicken

1. Turn on your computer.
2. Type **Q** and press `Enter`.

Choosing Menu Options

You can choose menu options in any number of ways:
- Type the highlighted letter in the option's name.
- Use the arrow keys to highlight the option and press `Enter`.
- Move the mouse pointer over the option and click the left mouse button.
- To open a pull-down menu, click on its name in the menu bar, or hold down `Alt` while typing the highlighted letter in the option's name.

Getting Help

- Press `F1` for help on the task you are currently performing.
- Press `F1` twice to see the Help Table of Contents.
- Press `Ctrl`-`F1` to use the Help Index.
- To search for a help topic, press `Ctrl`-`F`.

Quitting Quicken

1. Press `Esc` until the Main Menu is displayed.
2. Select **Exit**.

Chapter

2

Getting Started with Quicken

In this chapter, you'll learn how to start Quicken on your computer and how to navigate the Quicken screens using either your keyboard or mouse. You'll also learn how to get on-line help. You will use the techniques you learn in this chapter throughout this book.

Starting Quicken

> **CAUTION**
>
> You must run the Quicken installation program before using Quicken for the first time. The disks that come with the Quicken package contain files that have been compressed to save space. You cannot use these files until they are expanded by the installation program. If you haven't installed Quicken on your computer, see Appendix A, "Installing Quicken," for installation instructions.

To run Quicken, perform the following Quick Steps:

Starting Quicken

1. Turn on your computer if it is not on already. — The DOS command prompt appears as C> or C:\>.
2. Type **Q** and press [↵Enter]. — Quicken starts.

Did Quicken Start Properly?

If you installed Quicken correctly and followed the proper start-up instructions for your computer, you should see one of the following two screens:

- *The Welcome to Quicken 6.0 screen.* Figure 2.1 shows the Welcome to Quicken 6.0 screen that appears if you're starting Quicken for the first time. (Refer to the next section, "Running Quicken for the First Time," for instructions on how to proceed.)

- *The Quicken Main menu.* Figure 2.2 shows the menu screen that appears if you've installed Quicken 6 over Quicken 5. Quicken assumes that if you worked with version 5, you won't need the basic help that the tutorials provide.

If you see the DOS error message Bad command or file name instead of either of these screens, DOS may not know where the Quicken files are stored. Try changing to the drive and directory that contains the Quicken program files—for example, C:\QUICKEN. Then type **Q** and press [↵Enter].

Getting Started with Quicken

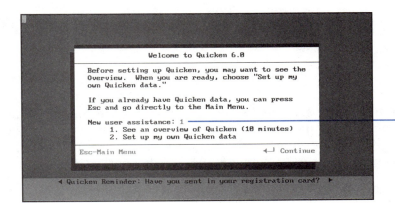

Figure 2.1
The Welcome to Quicken 6.0 screen.

Enter your selection here.

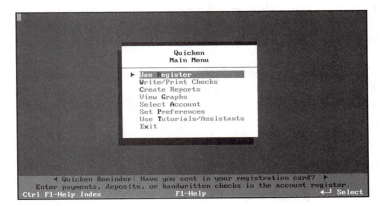

Figure 2.2
This Quicken Main menu appears if you've installed Quicken 6 over a previous version of Quicken.

TIP: If you find that the screen is unreadable when you start Quicken, the reason could be that you set up Quicken for a color monitor, but you're trying to run it on a monochrome monitor. From the Main menu choose Set **P**references, **S**creen Settings, Screen **C**olors, **1** Monochrome (or simply press P S C 1) to change the Quicken setup to a monochrome monitor.

Running Quicken for the First Time

If you're not upgrading from a previous version of Quicken and you're starting Quicken for the first time, the Welcome to Quicken 6.0 window appears (see Figure 2.1). The Welcome window is designed to help new Quicken users become familiar with the program. The window gives you the following options:

```
1. See an overview of Quicken (10 minutes)
```

This overview is a self-contained tutorial, which shows you several of the main Quicken screens and some of the program's basic functions. Follow the instructions on-screen.

```
2. Set up my own Quicken data
```

This tutorial takes you step-by-step through the process of setting up your own data file, categories, and bank account. See Chapter 3, "Working with Quicken Accounts," for instructions on setting up Quicken data files and accounts, and Chapter 4, "Using Categories and Classes," for a complete discussion of Quicken categories.

To choose one of these options, simply type the option number in the New user assistance field. For now, follow these steps to skip the tutorials and start Quicken:

1. Press Esc. Quicken displays a window asking you if you're sure you want to quit the tutorials.

2. Press Esc. Quicken displays the Main menu as shown in Figure 2.2.

> **TIP:** You can return to the Welcome to Quicken 6.0 screen and run the tutorials at any time. Simply go back to the Quicken Main menu and select Use Tutorials/Assistants.

Using the On-Line Help System

If you're using Quicken and you get confused or don't know what to do next, you can access Quicken's on-line Help system, which comes in the following three forms:

- Context-sensitive Help
- The Help Table of Contents
- The Help Index

Context-Sensitive Help

When you press F1 anywhere in Quicken, a *context-sensitive* Help screen appears. Context-sensitive means that the Help text relates to the specific task you're working on. For example, if you were at the Main menu and you pressed F1, you would see the Help screen shown in Figure 2.3. (Notice that the text of the Help screen deals only with the Main menu options.)

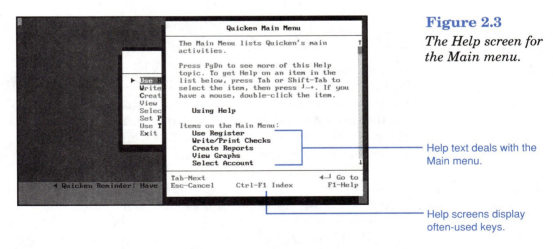

Figure 2.3
The Help screen for the Main menu.

Help text deals with the Main menu.

Help screens display often-used keys.

The Help Table of Contents

If you press F1 twice, the table of contents for the Help topics appears (see Figure 2.4). This provides you with a list of Help topics organized by task. This feature is especially useful when you're learning how to use Quicken, because you can see at a glance the things that Quicken can do. For example, if you want to access the Help information related to working with checks, select the Writing and printing checks topic from the Table of Contents.

Figure 2.4
The Table of Contents screen.

Organized by task

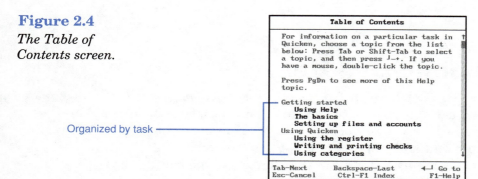

The Help Index

You can access the Help system's index by pressing Ctrl-F1 (see Figure 2.5). The Index is organized alphabetically and contains a complete list of Quicken functions and features. The Index entries are divided into first-level entries (in Figure 2.5, Accounts, Amortization, and so on) and second-level entries (Assigning tax schedules to, Deleting, Editing, and so on).

> **NOTE:** The Help Index you see on your screen may differ from the one shown in Figure 2.5. The creators of Quicken regularly add topics to the Index in response to user suggestions.

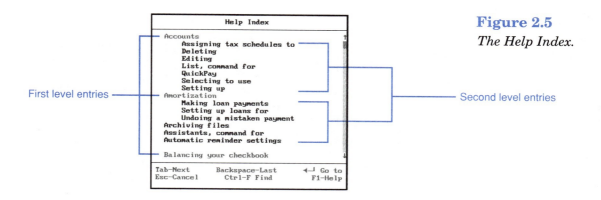

Figure 2.5
The Help Index.

Scrolling Through the Help Screens

Many Help topics contain more than a screenful of information. You can move through these screens by using PgDn and PgUp to move a screenful at a time. You can also use ↑ and ↓ to move a line at a time.

If you have a mouse, you can use the scroll bars at the side of the Help window to move through the list. See the section "Using a Mouse with Quicken" later in this chapter for more information on Quicken mouse techniques.

Viewing Related Topics

Most of the Help windows contain phrases shown in bold type or in a different color. These are called *hypertext links* (or simply *links*), because they provide a connection to other related Help topics. Use Tab to move down through the link names (use Shift-Tab to move up the list), and select the link you want by pressing Enter. Figure 2.6 shows the Quicken Main menu Help window with the link to the Use Register topic selected. When you press Enter, Quicken displays the Use Register command Help window, as shown in Figure 2.7.

Figure 2.6

The Use Register link.

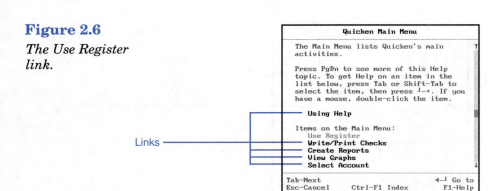

Figure 2.7

The Use Register command Help window.

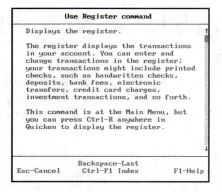

Searching for Help Topics

Wherever you are in the Help system, you can quickly find the topic you want by using either of two search methods. The first is an alphabetical search for the first letter of a topic's name. Simply press any alphabet key on your keyboard, and Quicken jumps to the first topic or subtopic that begins with that letter. In the Help Index, this search applies only to the first-level entries. For example, press P in the Help Index to go to the first-level entry Passwords.

The second search method is Quicken's Find feature, which enables you to search for a topic that contains a specific word or phrase. For example, to find Help topics that deal with checks and check writing, you would ask Find to search the Help Index for the

Getting Started with Quicken — 23

word *check*. This feature works from any Help screen and finds both first- and second-level index entries. The following Quick Steps describe how to use the Find feature in Help.

Finding a Help Topic

1. From any Help window, press Ctrl-F.

   Quicken displays the Find window, as shown in Figure 2.8.

2. Type the word or phrase you want to find and press Enter.

   Quicken moves to the first topic that contains the word you entered.

3. Press Ctrl-N to search for the next occurrence of the word or phrase or Ctrl-B to search backward.

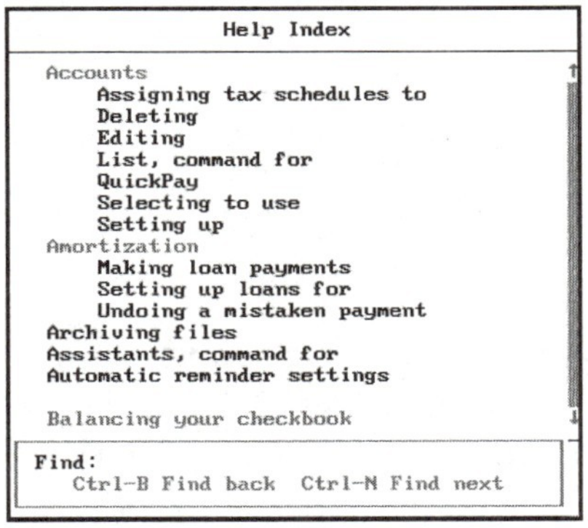

Figure 2.8
The Find window.

TIP: To save keystrokes, you can enter a partial word or phrase. For example, if you want to find the topic *Account information,* you could enter `acc` or even `inf` in the Find window.

You can refine your search by using special *wild-card characters*. In poker, you can designate a card as *wild;* that card can then take the place of any card during the game. Quicken's Find feature has borrowed this concept and has designated two symbols, the question mark (?) and the double period (..) as wild-card characters.

? Use the question mark to substitute for a single character. You can place the question mark anywhere in a word or phrase, and you can use more than one.

.. Use the double period to substitute for a group of characters. You can place the periods within or on either side of a word or phrase.

Table 2.1 shows how you can use these wild cards when searching for Help topics (the examples are from the Help Index).

Table 2.1
Using Wild Cards to Search for Topics

Example Search Entry	Finds
memor..	**Memor**ized transactions **Memor**izing **Memor**y
?al	B**al**ancing your checkbook C**al**culator
??port..	Ex**port**ing Im**port**ing Re**port** settings

To return to the previous Help window, press **←Backspace**. To leave the Help system, press **Esc**. Table 2.2 summarizes the special keys that you can use to navigate the on-line Help system.

Getting Started with Quicken

Key	Effect
PgDn	Moves down one screenful.
PgUp	Moves up one screenful.
↓	Moves down one line at a time.
↑	Moves up one line at a time.
Tab	Moves to next link name.
Shift-Tab	Moves to the previous link name.
Any alphabet key	Moves first to the topic that begins with the letter pressed (first-level topics only with Help Index).
Ctrl-F	Activates the Find feature.
Backspace	Returns to the previous Help window.
	Exits the on-line Help system.

Table 2.2
Special Keys Used with On-Line Help

Moving Around in Quicken

Quicken is a fast and flexible financial program for the home and office. However, one of its strongest features has nothing to do with finances—it's the way you move around in the program. Quicken's intuitive and consistent interface enables you to maneuver quickly and easily through the various screens and commands. In this section, you will learn how to navigate the Quicken menus and screens using the keyboard and mouse.

A Note About Menu Styles

By default, Quicken uses a menu style, called the Alt-keys menu style, which is used in many other programs. This style assigns each menu option a *selection key* (usually a letter in the option's name). To select the option quickly, you press the key that corresponds to the highlighted letter in the option's name (or press that key in conjunction with another key, such as Ctrl or Alt).

If you don't see such highlighted letters, Quicken may be set up to use a different menu style. You can switch to the Alt-keys menu style by performing the following steps:

1. From the Main menu, select Set **P**references. Quicken displays the Set Preferences menu.

2. Select **S**creen Settings. Quicken displays the Screen Settings menu.

3. Select Menu **A**ccess. The Menu Access dialog box appears.

4. Press [2] to select the Alt-keys menu style, and press [↵Enter]. A message box appears, telling you that the new menu style will take effect the next time you start Quicken.

5. Quit Quicken and then restart it to use the new menu style. (Refer to the end of this chapter for information about quitting Quicken.)

Using Quicken Menus

You can access most Quicken commands and functions easily by using the Quicken menus. There are two types of menus: *pop-up menus* and *pull-down menus*.

Quicken Pop-Up Menus

Unlike an activated pull-down menu, which is attached to the menu bar at the top of a screen, pop-up menus appear anywhere on the screen. The Quicken Main menu, shown in Figure 2.9, is a typical pop-up menu. The selected option (Use **R**egister) is indicated by the selection bar and a small arrow to the left of the option. Notice that each option contains one highlighted letter. This letter corresponds to the selection key you can press to select the option quickly. For example, in the Main menu, press [A] to execute the Select **A**ccount option.

Getting Started with Quicken   27

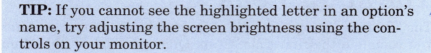

TIP: If you cannot see the highlighted letter in an option's name, try adjusting the screen brightness using the controls on your monitor.

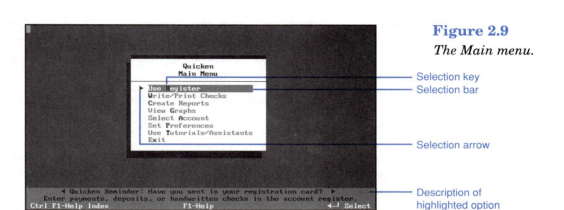

Figure 2.9
The Main menu.

— Selection key
— Selection bar

— Selection arrow

— Description of highlighted option

If you've forgotten what an option does, highlight the option and look at the bottom of the screen. Quicken displays a description of the option, as shown in Figure 2.9. This short description may be enough to jog your memory. If not, press F1.

Table 2.3 summarizes the keys you can use when working with the pop-up menus.

Key	Effect
↓	Moves the selection bar down one item.
↑	Moves the selection bar up one item.
↵Enter	Executes the highlighted option.
Selection key	Executes the option without highlighting it.
´	Removes the menu from the screen (does not work with the Main menu).

Table 2.3
Pop-Up Menu Keys

The Main Menu

The Main menu is an example of Quicken's pop-up menus. After you complete the first-time setup, Quicken displays the Main menu every time you start the program. This menu serves as a bridge to all of Quicken's features, so it's a good idea to become familiar with its options. You can return to the Main menu from any Quicken screen by pressing Esc. However, depending on where you are in the program, you may need to press Esc several times to return to the Main menu.

The Main menu contains eight options. This section introduces you to each of these options and tells you where you can find more information about them in this book.

- *Use **R**egister*   Takes you to the register for the account you're currently working in. A Quicken register is much like the paper register you use to record your checking account transactions. For more information on registers, see Chapter 5, "Working with the Register."

- *Write/Print Checks*   Lets you write and print checks. See Chapter 6, "Writing and Printing Checks," for more information.

- *Create Reports*   Displays the Reports menu, where you can choose from various types of financial reports. Reports are discussed in Chapter 10, "Creating and Printing Reports."

- *View **G**raphs*   Displays the Graphs menu, where you can choose to view various types of graphs. Graphs are discussed in Chapter 12, "Graphing with Quicken."

- *Select **A**ccount*   Selects the Quicken account you want to work with or lets you create a new account. See Chapter 3 for an introduction to accounts.

- *Set **P**references*   Displays the Set Preferences menu, which presents you with several customization choices, such as customizing your screen colors, printer settings, and other options. See "Setting Quicken Preferences" later in this chapter.

- *Use Tutorials/Assistants* This option displays a menu of tutorial programs that can help you get started with Quicken and learn about its features. The first-time setup tutorials were discussed briefly earlier in this chapter. Quicken 6 comes with four new assistants for setting up amortized loan payments, setting up an investment account, entering investment transactions, and exporting information to a tax program. To start one of these assistants, choose Use Tutorials/Assistants from the Main menu. Then choose More Assistants and select the assistant you want to run.

- *Exit* Saves your files and returns you to DOS.

Quicken Pull-Down Menus

The other type of Quicken menu is called a pull-down menu. Many Quicken screens contain a menu bar that runs along the top of the screen. Selecting one of the options in the menu bar pulls down the hidden menu attached to that option. For example, in the register screen in Figure 2.10, the Edit menu has been pulled down. Notice that each menu bar option contains a highlighted letter (the selection key letter). You select the pull-down menu by holding down [Alt] while pressing the key that corresponds to the highlighted letter in the menu's name. For example, to open the Edit menu, press [Alt]-[E].

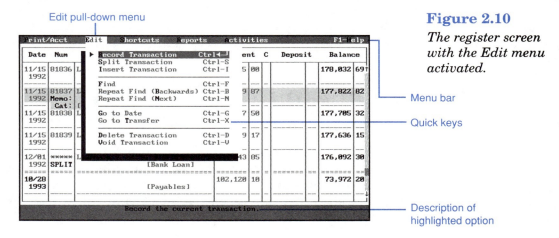

Figure 2.10
The register screen with the Edit menu activated.

Once you've activated the menu you want, you can select options from the menu just as you can from a pop-up menu. In addition, you can use `←` and `→` to open adjacent menus.

Table 2.4 summarizes the keys you can use when working with pull-down menus.

Table 2.4
Pull-Down Menu Keys

Key	Effect
`Alt`-key	Pulls down the menu with the highlighted letter in its name.
`↓`	Moves the selection bar down one option.
`↑`	Moves the selection bar up one option.
`←`	Closes the current menu and opens the menu to the left.
`→`	Closes the current menu and opens the menu to the right.
`↵Enter`	Executes the selected menu options.
Selection key	Executes the option with the highlighted letter in its name.
`Esc`	Closes the current menu.

NOTE: Throughout this book, I will tell you only to enter a command; it's up to you to decide how you want to do it. You can use the arrow keys to highlight the option and then press `↵Enter`, or type the option's selection key, or use the mouse to click on the option.

Bypassing the Pull-Down Menus

Notice that to the right of each option on the Edit menu is a keystroke that starts with Ctrl-. Quicken calls these keystrokes *Quick Keys*. They enable you to bypass the menu altogether and immediately enter many of the most commonly used menu options. For example, instead of pulling down the Edit menu and selecting Split Transaction, you can press Ctrl-S.

Other Screen Elements

In addition to the menu bar, the Quicken screens contain a number of other features that you should be aware of. Look at the register screen in Figure 2.11. The bottom two lines of a Quicken screen usually provide some extra information. The register screen, for example, tells you the name of the account you are currently working in and the account balance. (You'll learn how to set up your own accounts in the next chapter.) In addition, Quicken lists frequently used key combinations. For example, you can press Esc to return to the Main menu.

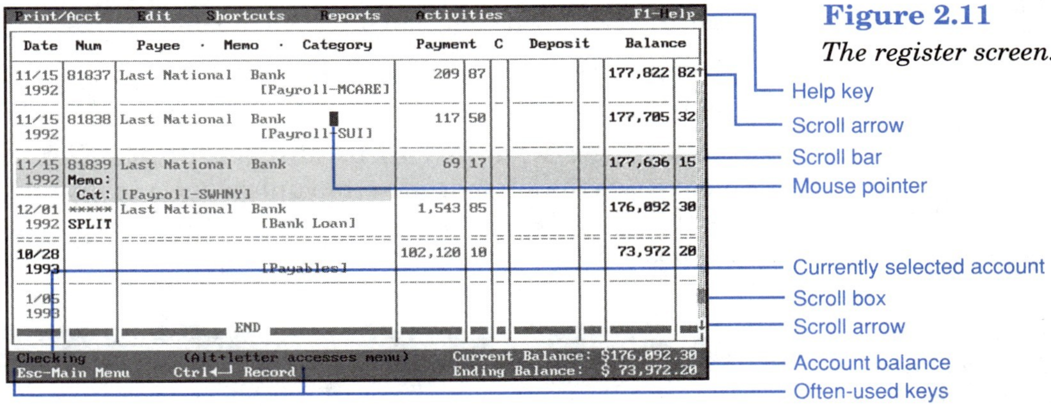

Figure 2.11
The register screen.

- Help key
- Scroll arrow
- Scroll bar
- Mouse pointer
- Currently selected account
- Scroll box
- Scroll arrow
- Account balance
- Often-used keys

On the right side of the screen, you will see the scroll bar. The scroll box inside the scroll bar tells you where you are in your list of register entries. For example, if the scroll box is halfway down the bar, you are looking at the entries in the middle of the register. You'll learn more about using the scroll bar in the next section.

Using a Mouse with Quicken

Quicken works with any Microsoft-compatible mouse. If you are unfamiliar with using a mouse, here are some basics. Quicken displays the mouse pointer on your screen as a small rectangle (see Figure 2.11). The pointer moves on the screen as you move the mouse on your desk. You use the following techniques with a mouse:

Point Move the mouse pointer to a specific screen location.

Click Press and release the left mouse button without moving the mouse.

Double-click Quickly press and release the left mouse button twice without moving the mouse.

Drag Press and hold down the mouse button while moving the mouse.

In this book, when you are told to click, double-click, or drag the mouse, use the left mouse button unless specifically told to use the right button. Table 2.5 summarizes the mouse equivalents for the keyboard techniques discussed so far.

Table 2.5
Quicken Mouse Techniques

Action	Effect
Clicking on a Help topic	Highlights the topic.
Double-clicking on a Help topic	Opens the Help topic window.
Clicking on a pop-up menu option	Executes the option.
Clicking on a menu bar option	Pulls down the associated menu.
Clicking on a displayed key combination	Executes the command key combination.
Clicking on F1-Help	Accesses context-sensitive help.
Clicking on a scroll bar arrow	Moves up or down one item in the direction of the arrow.
Clicking on a scroll bar arrow and holding down the button	Moves rapidly through the list in the direction of the arrow.

Action	Effect
Clicking above or below the scroll box inside the scroll bar	Moves up or down one screenful.
Dragging the scroll box	Moves up or down to a different position in the list.
Clicking the right mouse button	Has the same effect as pressing Esc.

Setting Quicken Preferences

After you install Quicken, it is ready to go. However, Quicken does provide a number of customization options so you can set up the program to work exactly the way you want it to. This section shows you how to customize your screen and summarizes the other preferences discussed throughout this book.

Customizing Screen Settings

Quicken allows you to modify the following screen settings:

Screen Colors   The colors or shades of gray that the Quicken screens use.

Screen Patterns   The background patterns that appear behind the various windows that Quicken displays. Quicken 6 offers several new patterns.

EGA/VGA 43-line Display   The number of lines that are displayed. This option is available only if you have an EGA or VGA monitor.

Monitor Display   The speed at which Quicken displays its screens. If the Quicken screens are displayed too fast, you'll see "snow" on your screen. In such a case, you will need to use the slow setting. EGA and VGA monitors always use the fast setting.

Menu Access   The style of menu option access. You can use either the [Alt]-key or Function key method. The [Alt]-key method was discussed earlier in this chapter. With the Function-key method, Quicken displays the name of a menu or option preceded by a function key or number; to make your selection, you press the appropriate key or number. This book assumes you are using the [Alt]-key method.

VERSION 6

Screen Graphics   When you view graphs, Quicken typically displays larger graphics and smaller type. This option lets you display larger type or view the graphs in black-and-white mode.

VERSION 6

Register View   You can choose to display three text lines for each transaction (the default) or only one line (compressed).

To change the display settings, perform the following steps:

1. From the Main menu, select Set **P**references. Quicken displays the Set Preferences menu as shown in Figure 2.12.

2. Select Screen Settings. Quicken displays the Screen Settings submenu.

3. Select the screen setting you want to change.

4. Enter your changes.

5. Press [Esc] as many times as needed to return to the Main menu.

NOTE: Quicken offers various other customization options through the Set Preferences submenu. These options are discussed in greater detail in the chapters where they apply.

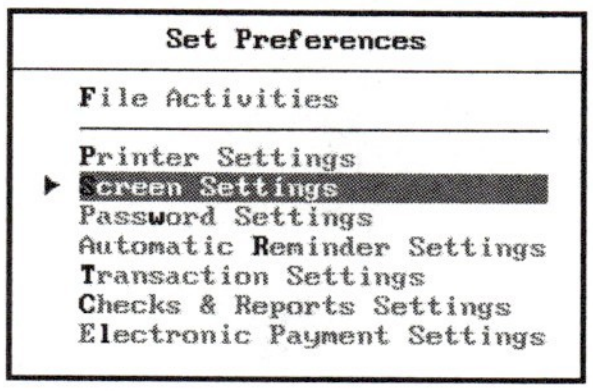

Getting Started with Quicken

Figure 2.12
The Set Preferences menu.

Exiting Quicken

Quicken automatically saves your data when you exit the program. Ideally, you should make backup copies of any files you changed during your Quicken session. (See Chapter 3 to learn how to use Quicken to back up your data quickly and easily.) The following Quick Steps summarize how to exit Quicken.

Exiting Quicken

1. Press Esc or click the right mouse button until you reach the Main menu.
2. Select Exit. Quicken saves your data and exits to DOS.

Always leave Quicken by using the **Ex**it option from the Main menu. If you exit in any other way (by turning off your computer, for example), Quicken has no chance to save your files, and you risk losing some or all of your data.

In This Chapter

Identifying Quicken Account Types

Setting Up Accounts

Modifying Accounts

Using Account Files

Maintaining Account Files

Creating an Account

1. Choose Select Account from the Main menu.
2. Press Ctrl-Ins.
3. Select an account type.
4. Enter a name for the account.
5. Enter the starting balance and date of the starting balance.
6. Enter a brief description of the account, if you want.
7. Select the source of the starting balance.

Selecting an Account

1. Choose Select Account from the Main menu.
2. Highlight the account you want to use and press ↵Enter.

Editing an Account

1. Choose Select Account from the Main menu.
2. Highlight the account you want to edit.
3. Press Ctrl-E.

Adding an Account File

1. Select Set Preferences from the Main menu.
2. Select File Activities.
3. Choose Select/Set Up File.
4. Select <Set Up New File> or press Ctrl-Ins.
5. Enter a name for the file.
6. Select the category list you want to use.

Chapter 3

Working with Quicken Accounts

Now that you've learned some Quicken basics, you're ready to start using Quicken to keep track of your financial affairs. In this chapter, you'll learn how to set up and work with Quicken accounts and account files.

Keep in mind that Quicken stores all your financial records in a single account file. This account file can contain up to 255 separate accounts, such as savings, checking, and credit. In each account, you enter your transactions. If you have a separate business, you can create an additional account file that stores financial data for all the accounts used by the business.

Types of Accounts

Quicken can handle all sorts of accounts, including checking and savings accounts, investments, and just about any other asset or liability you may have. Quicken is designed to work with six specific types of financial accounts, as listed in Table 3.1. You are free to use any of these account types for other purposes.

> **FYI IDEAS**
>
> If you have an inventory that has large quantities of a few items, for example, you can set up an account for each item to keep a rough running inventory total. Or, if you have a service business and bill in hour, half-hour (.5), or quarter-hour (.25) increments, a Quicken account will track hours per job.

Table 3.1
The Quicken Account Types

Account Type	Examples
Bank account	Checking account Savings account Money market fund Certificate of Deposit Payroll Regular income (alimony, royalties, grants, and so on)
Credit Card	VISA, American Express, and so on Department store cards Personal line of credit
Cash	Petty cash Spending cash
Other Asset	House and other real estate Personal belongings (antiques, jewelry, and so on) Accounts receivable Business inventory Trust fund Personal loan (paid to you) Lease (paid to you) Whole life insurance
Other Liability	Mortgage Accounts payable Personal loan (paid by you) Lease (paid by you) Income tax payable
Investment	Stocks Bonds IRAs Mutual funds

Table 3.2 gives some general guidelines to help you select the best Quicken accounts to take care of your financial matters.

Table 3.2
Some Quicken Account Guidelines

Term	Explanation
Bank Account	If the money is in the bank and you can write checks or make withdrawals to get it out, it's a bank account.
Cash	Usually considered liquid (easy to get at) money. This money is not in a bank account, but rather can be readily found; for example, in your wallet or in a petty cash box at the office. Quicken is designed to treat the money in a cash account as dispensable—you can spend some and just list it under miscellaneous.
Asset	Something you own.
Liability	Something you owe.
Other Assets	Money that belongs to you or property (real estate or personal belongings) you own. You can, with varying degrees of difficulty, withdraw the money or sell the property and receive money for it.
Other Liabilities	Money you've borrowed or property you're still paying for. If you sell the property, some or all of the money you get may have to be paid back to the lender.

Although you use each of these account types to handle vastly different transactions, you set up each one in a similar way. For each account, Quicken needs to know the account type, its name, the starting balance and date, and an optional account description.

Setting Up Accounts

Before you can do any work in Quicken, you must first set up an account. In this section, you'll create a basic checking account for a home office by following these steps:

1. Start Quicken if it's not already running, and go to the Main menu. Refer to Chapter 2 for details.
2. Choose Select Account. Quicken displays the Standard Categories dialog box, as shown in Figure 3.1.
3. Type 3 to select Both Home and Business and press Enter or click on Continue. (For more information about categories, refer to Chapter 4.) A help box appears, telling you what to do next.
4. Read the information in the help box and then press F10. Quicken displays the Set Up New Account dialog box, as shown in Figure 3.2.
5. Type 1 to select Bank Account. Press Tab↹ or Enter to move down to the Name for this account field.
6. Type a name for the account. The name can be up to 15 characters long and can include any combination of letters, numbers, spaces, and other characters except [ ] : or /. For your checking account, the name "Checking" is usually sufficient.

> **TIP:** If you have similar accounts in different banks, differentiate them by using an abbreviation of the bank name together with the account type. For example, if you have checking accounts at both First Federal and Metropolitan Savings, you could name them 1st Fed Check and Metro Check, respectively. If you have a similar account type at the same bank, use the bank abbreviation with the account number. For example, 1st Fed 270131 and 1st Fed 890865.

7. Press Enter or click on Continue. The Starting Balance and Description window appears as in Figure 3.3.
8. Type an opening balance for your account. The best place to get this balance is from a bank statement. Press Enter or click on the as of field.

Working with Quicken Accounts

9. Type a date to reflect the date of your last bank statement. The format to use is month/day/year. Press `Enter` or click on the *Description* field.

10. Type a description of the account if you want, and then press `Enter` or click on *Continue*. The Source of Starting Balance dialog box appears, prompting you to specify where you obtained the balance information.

11. Type the number that represents the source of the balance information and press `Enter`.

12. Press `Enter` twice. The Select Account to Use window appears.

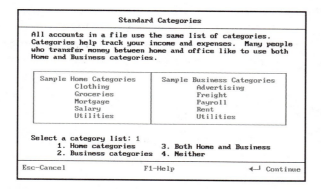

Figure 3.1

The Standard Categories dialog box.

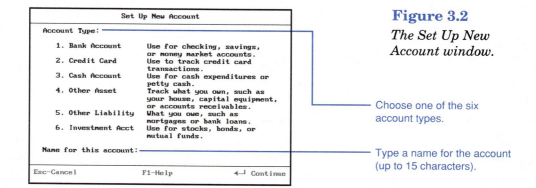

Figure 3.2

The Set Up New Account window.

Choose one of the six account types.

Type a name for the account (up to 15 characters).

Figure 3.3

The Starting Balance and Description window.

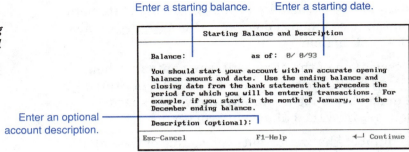

Now that you've set up your first account, you can create additional accounts by following essentially the same procedure. Before doing so, however, you should read Chapter 9, "Your Finances with Other Quicken Accounts." This chapter gives you important tips and suggestions for such things as opening balances and initial entries. Use the following Quick Steps to set up other accounts.

Setting Up a Quicken Account

1. From the Quicken Main menu, choose Select Account.

    Quicken displays the Select Account to Use dialog box.

2. Press Ctrl-Ins (if you press Ctrl-Ins, you don't have to press Enter) or select <New Account> and press Enter.

    Quicken displays the Set Up New Account dialog box.

3. Select the Account Type you want to create and press Tab or Enter.

    The cursor moves to the Name for this account field.

4. Type a name for the account, and press Tab or Enter.

    The Starting Balance and Description dialog box appears.

5.	Type the starting balance for the account, and press `Tab` or `Enter`.	The cursor moves to the as of field.
6.	Type the starting date for the account in the form *mm/dd/yy*, and press `Tab` or `Enter`.	The cursor moves to the Description field.
7.	Type a brief description for the account, and press `Enter` or click on Continue.	The Source of Starting Balance dialog box appears.
8.	Type the number that represents the source of the balance information, and press `Enter`.	A message appears, indicating whether or not Quicken thinks you've made a wise choice.
9.	Press `Enter` twice.	The Select Account to Use window appears.

Working with Accounts

Quicken gives you tremendous flexibility when working with your accounts. Whether it's selecting accounts to use, editing existing accounts, or deleting accounts that you no longer use, Quicken makes the task fast and easy.

Selecting Accounts

Before you can enter a transaction in an account, you must tell Quicken which account you want to work with. For example, if your savings account is currently active but you want to enter a transaction in your checking account, you must first change to the checking account. Use the following Quick Steps to select an account.

Chapter 3

Selecting an Account

1. From the Main menu, choose Select Account.

   Quicken displays the Select Account to Use window, as shown in Figure 3.4.

2. Use the arrow keys to highlight the account you want to use and press ⏎Enter. Or, double-click on the account to select it with the mouse.

   Quicken takes you to the register associated with the account. The account name appears in the lower left corner of the screen.

Figure 3.4
The Select Account to Use window.

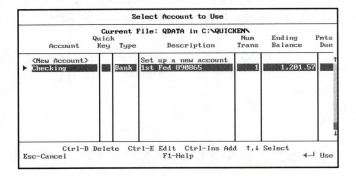

TIP: From most Quicken screens, you can access the Select Account to Use window quickly by pressing Ctrl-A.

TIP: As you work with Quicken, your list of accounts may grow quite long. Quicken provides a shortcut method for finding accounts in the Select Account to Use window. Type the first letter in the name of the account you want to select, and the selection bar moves to the first account beginning with that letter. For example, if you press C, Quicken highlights the first account beginning with the letter *C*; for instance, Checking.

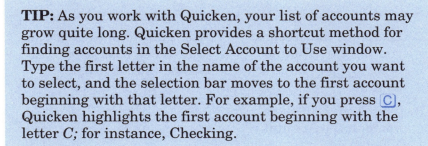

Editing an Account

Quicken allows you to edit the names and descriptions of existing accounts. This is useful, for example, if you made a mistake when you set up the account originally. You may also want to edit the name or description of an account if you transfer the account to a new account number or to another bank branch. Quicken does not, however, allow you to change the account type or current balance. To do that, you must delete the account and start over.

You can also edit an account to assign it a Quick Key (1–9). Whenever you want to select the account, hold down Ctrl and press the number assigned to that account. For example, if you've assigned the Quick Key number 1 to your checking account, you can press Ctrl-1 from any Quicken screen to go to the checking account register. To remove a Quick Key from an account, assign it the number 0. The following Quick Steps tell you how to edit an account.

Editing an Account

1. From the Main menu, choose Select Account. Quicken displays the Select Account to Use window.

continues

continued

2. Highlight the account you want to edit and press Ctrl-E or click on Edit.

   The Edit Account Information dialog box appears, as shown in Figure 3.5.

3. (Optional) Edit the name in the Account Name field.

4. (Optional) Press Enter or click on the Description field. Edit the account description.

5. (Optional) Press Enter or click on the Quick Key assignment field. Type the Quick Key number and press Enter.

Figure 3.5
The Edit Account Information dialog box.

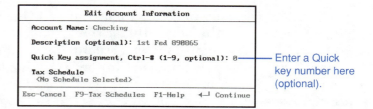

Enter a Quick key number here (optional).

Deleting an Account

If you close an account or if you decide an account is not worth tracking any longer, you can delete the account.

Working with Quicken Accounts

Once you've deleted an account, you cannot restore it. Be absolutely certain you want to delete an account before doing so.

Use the following Quick Steps to delete an account.

Deleting an Account

1. From the Main menu, choose Select Account.

    Quicken displays the Select Account to Use window.

2. Highlight the account you want to delete.

3. Press Ctrl-D or click on Delete at the bottom of the window.

    A message box appears showing the account you selected and warning you that you are about to remove an account permanently.

4. Type yes to confirm that you want to delete the account and press Enter or click on Delete. To cancel the deletion, press Esc or click the right mouse button.

    Quicken deletes the account.

Working with Account Files

The accounts you create in Quicken are stored together in an account file. Quicken is designed so that you never have to copy, rename, or delete these files manually (at the DOS prompt); you can and should perform these functions from within the program.

When you set up your first account earlier in this chapter, Quicken automatically created an account file called QDATA and stored the account in this file. This is the only account file most users will ever need. However, Quicken allows you to set up as many account files as you want. In addition, you can edit, copy, and delete these files as needed.

How Many Account Files Do You Need?

The number of account files that you can set up is limited only by the amount of disk space on your computer. Each file can store up to 255 accounts, so you may be wondering why anyone would want more than one account file. In most cases, one file is sufficient, but there are times when you'll need extra files:

- You run a business that is completely separate from your home finances. In this case, you would want to ensure that your finances stay separate by setting up two account files—one for your business and one for your home.

- You run two or more separate businesses. You need at least three account files in this situation—one for each business and one for your home.

- You're using Quicken to track other peoples' finances. In this case, set up an account file for each person.

- You could create a practice file for learning Quicken.

On the other hand, there are advantages to having all your accounts in one file:

- You can transfer funds only between accounts that are in the same file (for example, between your savings and checking accounts).

Working with Quicken Accounts

- The reports Quicken generates consolidate data from accounts in the same file but not from different files.
- All the accounts in a file share the same Category List. You cannot copy changes or additions you've made to the Category List to another file. (See Chapter 4 for a discussion of categories.)

As a general rule, stick to one account file unless you have enterprises that have totally separate finances.

Adding a New Account File

If you decide that you need more than one account file, use the following Quick Steps to create the new file.

Adding a New Account File

1. From the Main menu, select Set **P**references. — Quicken pops up the Set Preferences menu.
2. Select **F**ile Activities. — Quicken displays the File Activities menu, as shown in Figure 3.6.
3. Choose **S**elect/Set Up File. — Quicken displays the Select/Set Up New File window, as shown in Figure 3.7.
4. Select <Set Up New File> or press Ctrl-Ins. — Quicken displays the Set Up New File window, as shown in Figure 3.8.
5. Type a name for the new file. The name you use must be a legal eight-character (or fewer) DOS file name.

continues

continued

6. Press `Tab` or `Enter`.	The cursor moves to the Location for file field.
7. If you want to store the file in a different drive or directory, type a path to the drive and directory.	
8. Press `Enter` or click on Continue.	The Standard Categories dialog box is displayed.
9. Select the Category List you want to use for this file and press `Enter` (see Chapter 4).	The Select/Set Up New File window appears showing the name of the new account file.
10. To add another account, repeat steps 4 through 9.	
11. Press `Esc` or click the right mouse button until you return to the Main menu.	

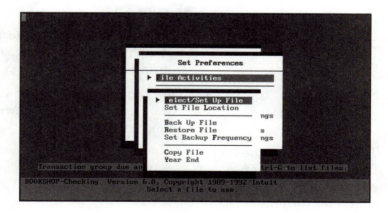

Figure 3.6
The File Activities menu.

Working with Quicken Accounts 51

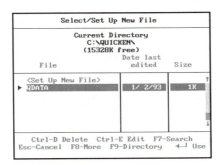

Figure 3.7
The Select/Set Up New File window.

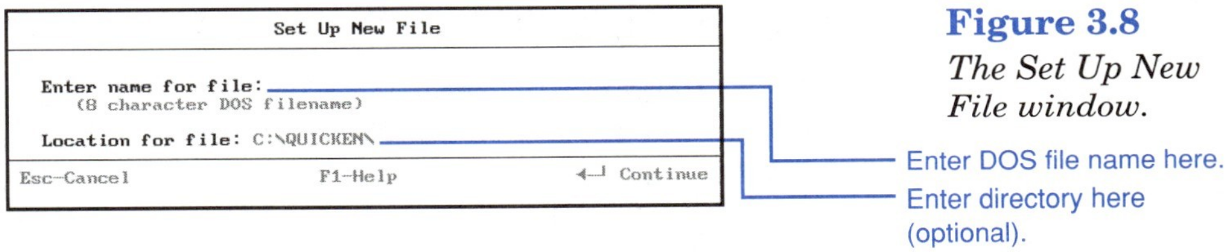

Figure 3.8
The Set Up New File window.

Enter DOS file name here.
Enter directory here (optional).

To follow the examples presented in this book, you'll need to set up a couple of account files. For the home example, create an account called HOME. In the Category List, press 3 to select Both Home and Business. For the business example, create an account called BOOKSHOP, and press 2 in the Category List to select Business categories.

Specifying the Location of Your Account Files

By default, Quicken stores your account files in the QUICKEN directory. If you've worked with a previous version of Quicken and have stored your account files in a different directory, you must tell Quicken where those files are stored. You may also need to specify a location for the account files if you keep different account files in separate directories. To specify the location of your account files, follow these steps:

1. From the Main menu, select Set Preferences. Quicken pops up the Set Preferences menu.

2. Select **File Activities**. Quicken displays the File Activities menu.

3. Choose **Set File Location**. Quicken displays the Set File Location dialog box.

4. Type a path to the directory that contains the account files you want to use.

5. Press `Enter` or click on **Continue**.

Selecting an Account File

If you're using more than one account file, you must take care that you're using the correct file. If you enter transactions in the wrong file, you'll have to delete the erroneous entries and re-enter them in the correct file. When you start Quicken, the program assumes you want to work with the file that was active the last time you used Quicken. If this is not the file you want to work with, use the following Quick Steps to select another file.

Selecting an Account File

1. From the Main menu, select **Set Preferences**.	Quicken pops up the Set Preferences menu.
2. Select **File Activities**.	Quicken displays the File Activities menu.
3. Choose **Select/Set Up File**.	Quicken displays the Select/Set Up New File window.
4. Highlight the file you want and press `Enter` or double-click on the file.	Quicken loads the account file and prompts you to select the account you want to use.

Working with Quicken Accounts 53

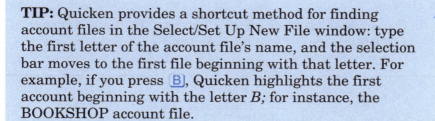

TIP: Quicken provides a shortcut method for finding account files in the Select/Set Up New File window: type the first letter of the account file's name, and the selection bar moves to the first file beginning with that letter. For example, if you press B, Quicken highlights the first account beginning with the letter *B;* for instance, the BOOKSHOP account file.

Editing an Account File Name

You can change the name of a Quicken account file. You might want to do this, for example, if you made a mistake when you created the file. You might also want to change the file name if the nature of your business changes. Use the following Quick Steps to change a file name.

Editing an Account File Name

1. From the Main menu, select **Set P**references.
   Quicken pops up the Set Preferences menu.

2. Select **F**ile Activities.
   Quicken displays the File Activities menu.

3. Choose **S**elect/Set Up File.
   Quicken displays the Select/ Set Up New File window.

4. Highlight the name of the file you want to edit and press Ctrl-E or click on Edit.
   Quicken displays the Rename A File dialog box, as shown in Figure 3.9.

5. Delete the old file name (use Del) and type the new file name.

continues

Chapter 3

continued	
6. Press Enter or click on Continue.	The new file name appears in the Select/Set Up New File window.

Figure 3.9

The Rename A File dialog box.

Enter new file name here.

Deleting an Account File

You can use Quicken to delete a file you no longer use. This is a drastic step because all the accounts stored in the file are lost. Delete a file *only* if you are no longer tracking any of the accounts in the file. For example, if you set up a practice file to learn Quicken, you can delete the file when you no longer need it. Similarly, if you sell a business, you can delete the account file associated with that business. (However, you may want to copy the files to a floppy disk for safekeeping.)

CAUTION Once you've deleted an account file, you cannot restore it unless you have a backup copy or a utility program that can undelete files. Be certain you want to delete an account file before doing so.

Use the following Quick Steps to delete an account file.

Deleting an Account File

1. From the Main menu, select **Set Preferences**.	Quicken pops up the Set Preferences menu.

Working with Quicken Accounts

> 2. Select **F**ile Activities.
>
>   Quicken displays the File Activities menu.
>
> 3. Choose **S**elect/Set Up File.
>
>   Quicken displays the Select/Set Up New File window.
>
> 4. Highlight the file you want to delete and press `Ctrl`-`D` or click on **D**elete.
>
>   Quicken displays the Deleting File window. The box shows you which file you've selected and asks if you are sure you want to delete the file.
>
> 5. Type **yes** and press `↵Enter` to confirm the deletion, or press `Esc` or click the right mouse button to cancel.
>
>   Quicken removes the file name from the Select/Set Up New File window.

Copying an Account File

With Quicken you can copy all or part of an account file. You would do this, for example, if you wanted to send a copy of your Quicken records to your accountant or save a copy of the file to archive before deleting it. Use the following Quick Steps to copy an account file.

> ### Copying an Account File
>
> 1. Select the file you want to copy, and then press `Esc` to return to the Main menu.
>
> 2. Select **S**et **P**references.
>
>   Quicken pops up the Set Preferences menu.
>
> *continues*

continued

3. Select **File Activities**.	Quicken displays the File Activities menu.
4. Choose **Copy File**.	Quicken displays the Copy File window, as shown in Figure 3.10.
5. Type a file name for the new Quicken file. The new name must be a legal eight-character (or less) DOS file name.	
6. Press `Enter` or click on the **Location of new file** field.	The cursor moves to the Location of new file field.
7. Type the drive and directory where you want the copy stored, and press `Enter`.	The cursor moves to the Copy transactions from field.
8. To copy only a portion of the file, type the transaction dates you want to copy and press `Enter`. To copy the entire file, press `Enter`.	The cursor moves to the next field.
9. Type **Y** and press `Enter`, or click on **Continue** to have Quicken copy prior uncleared transactions.	Quicken copies the file. When the copy operation is complete, Quicken asks if you want to work with the original file or the new copy.
10. Highlight the appropriate option and press `Enter`, or click on the file you want to use.	Quicken returns you to the Main menu.

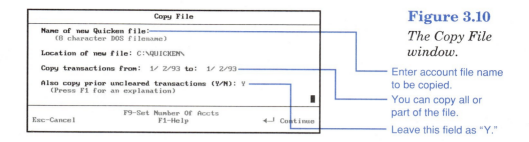

Figure 3.10

The Copy File window.

- Enter account file name to be copied.
- You can copy all or part of the file.
- Leave this field as "Y."

Backing Up and Restoring Account Files

As with all your data, you should save copies of your Quicken files on floppy disks. This procedure, known as *backing up* your files, enables you to restore your records with a minimum of data loss if your original files become lost or damaged.

> **NOTE:** How often should you back up your Quicken files? If you find that you're entering transactions every day, you should back up your data on a daily basis. If you use Quicken less often, once a week should be fine.

When you back up your files for the first time, make two backup copies, Backup 1 and Backup 2. The next time you back up, use only the Backup 1 disk. The time after that, use the Backup 2 disk. By alternating the backup disks in this way, your data will still be safe should a problem arise with one of the disks. In addition, you should store your backup copies in a safe place. Try to keep one of the copies in an off-site location. Then, in case of fire or theft, you'll still be able to restore your files.

Backing Up Account Files

You don't need to use a specialized backup program to save your Quicken files. Quicken can perform your backups for you. Use the following Quick Steps to back up an account file.

QUICK STEPS: Backing Up an Account File

1. Place a formatted floppy disk in drive A or B.

2. From the Main menu, select **Set Preferences**.

   Quicken pops up the Set Preferences menu.

3. Select **File Activities**.

   Quicken displays the File Activities menu.

4. Choose **Back Up File**.

   Quicken displays the Select Backup Drive window, as shown in Figure 3.11.

5. Enter the letter of the drive that contains the floppy disk and press ⏎Enter or click on **Continue**.

   Quicken displays the Select File to Back Up window, as shown in Figure 3.12.

6. Highlight the file you want to back up and press ⏎Enter or click on **Continue**.

   Quicken backs up the file to the floppy. A message box appears to tell you that the operation was successful.

7. Press ⏎Enter or click on **Continue**.

   Quicken returns you to the Select File to Back Up window.

8. To back up another file, repeat steps 6 and 7.

Figure 3.11
Select a backup drive.

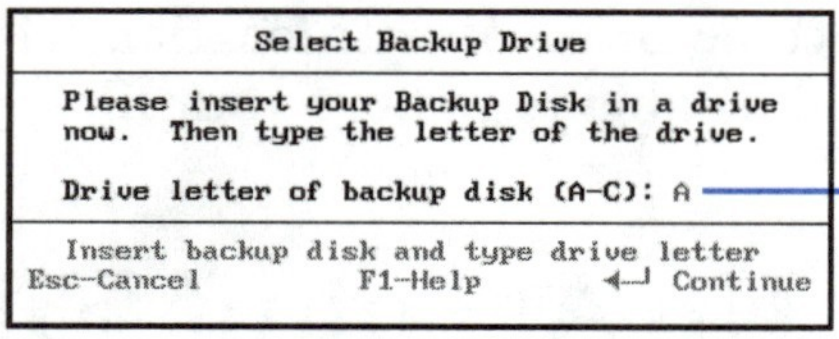

Enter the letter of the drive that contains the backup floppy disk.

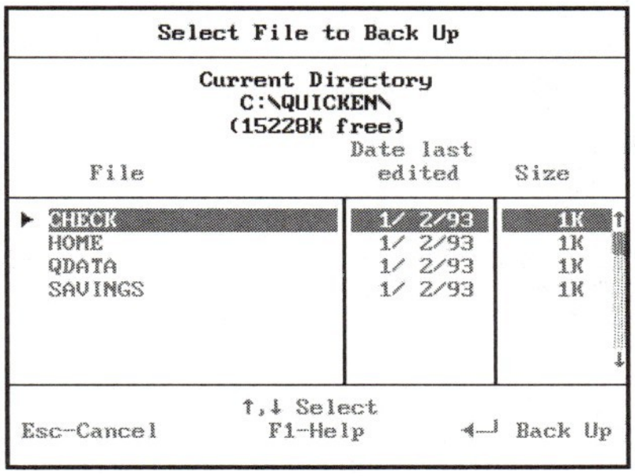

Working with Quicken Accounts

Figure 3.12
The Select File to Back Up window.

```
          Select File to Back Up
           Current Directory
              C:\QUICKEN\
              (15228K free)
                         Date last
     File                 edited      Size
  ► CHECK                 1/ 2/93      1K
    HOME                  1/ 2/93      1K
    QDATA                 1/ 2/93      1K
    SAVINGS               1/ 2/93      1K


                    ↑,↓ Select
    Esc-Cancel      F1-Help           ← Back Up
```

> **TIP:** For faster backups, press Ctrl-B at the Main menu to skip directly to the Select Backup Drive window. Then follow steps 5 through 8 of the preceding Quick Steps to back up your files. This lets you back up only the currently selected file.

> **TIP:** To back up the current account file when you exit Quicken, press Ctrl-E at the Main menu. Quicken displays the Select Backup Drive window. Type the letter of the floppy drive you want to use, and press Enter. When Quicken indicates the backup is complete, press Enter to exit Quicken and return to DOS.

Setting the Backup Reminder Frequency

Because backing up your data is so important, Quicken includes a feature that you can set to automatically remind you to back up your account files. You enter a Backup Reminder Frequency for each file. When the Backup Reminder Frequency is set, Quicken checks the date of the last backup every time you use the file. If the time period you've chosen for this file has expired and you make changes to the file, Quicken displays the message shown in Figure 3.13 when you try to leave the file or exit the program.

Figure 3.13
Quicken can remind you to back up your data.

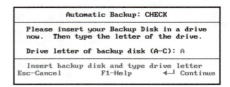

You can proceed with the backup at this point, or you can press Esc to cancel the reminder. Use the following Quick Steps to set the Backup Reminder Frequency.

Setting the Backup Reminder Frequency

1. Select the file you want Quicken to remind you to back up.

2. From the Main menu, select Set Preferences.

   Quicken pops up the Set Preferences menu.

3. Select File Activities.

   Quicken displays the File Activities menu.

4. Choose Set Backup Frequency.

   Quicken displays the Backup Reminder Frequency dialog box, as shown in Figure 3.14.

5. Enter the number corresponding to the frequency you want and press Enter or click on Continue.

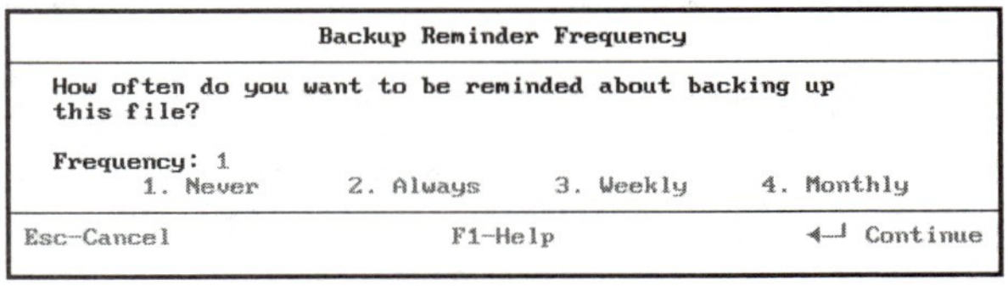

Figure 3.14
The Backup Reminder Frequency window.

Restoring Backed-Up Account Files

Backup disks are like brain surgeons: you're glad they're around but you hope you'll never have to use them. Unfortunately, hard disks crash and files can be accidentally deleted. When this happens, Quicken can restore your data from the backups. Use the following Quick Steps to restore your account files.

> Files restored from backups are only as up-to-date as the backed-up files. If you accidentally delete a file, try other methods to get it back first. If you have DOS 5.0, use UNDELETE, or use a utility program, such as PC Tools or The Norton Utilities. Use your backups as a last resort.

Restoring Backed-Up Account Files

1. Place the floppy disk that contains the backed-up files in the appropriate drive.

2. From the Main menu, select Set Preferences.

   Quicken pops up the Set Preferences menu.

3. Select File Activities.

   Quicken displays the File Activities menu.

continues

continued

4. Choose **Restore File**.	Quicken prompts you to enter the drive letter of the disk containing the backup files.
5. Enter the drive letter and press **↵Enter** or click on **Continue**.	The Select File to Restore window appears, as shown in Figure 3.15.
6. Select the file you want Quicken to restore and press **↵Enter** or click on **Restore**.	Quicken restores the file and displays a message when the operation is complete. If the file already exists, Quicken will ask you to press **↵Enter** to overwrite the file.
7. Press **↵Enter**.	Quicken returns you to the File Activities menu.

Figure 3.15
The Select File to Restore window.

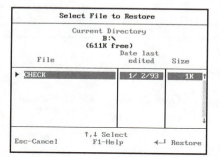

The Book Examples

Now that you are comfortable working with account files, it's time to get up to speed with the examples you will follow throughout this book. Earlier in this chapter, if you were following along with the text, you created two account files: one called HOME for the Johnson family finances and another called BOOKSHOP for Book City.

You must now set up accounts for each of these files. Tables 3.3 and 3.4 outline the various accounts that you need to create for each file. You will be working with these accounts throughout the remainder of the book. Select the appropriate account file and then enter the values listed in the tables to practice working with accounts.

Table 3.3
The HOME File Accounts

Account Type	Name	Balance	Date	Description
Bank Checking	Checking	$5,000	9/26/92	Last National
Bank Savings	Savings	$10,000	9/26/92	Last National
Credit Card VISA*	VISA	$0	9/26/92	Last National
Cash	Cash	$200	9/26/92	Spending cash
Other Assets	House	$150,000	9/26/92	
Other Assets	Belongings	$0	9/26/92	Jewelry, antiques
Other Liabilities	Mortgage	$125,000	9/26/92	
Other Liabilities	Car loan	$10,000	9/26/92	

*When you set up a credit card account, Quicken prompts you to enter an optional credit limit for the card. For this example, enter $2,500.

Table 3.4
The BOOKSHOP File Accounts

Account Type	Name	Balance	Date	Description
Bank	Checking	$50,000	9/26/92	Last National Checking
Cash	Petty cash	$200	9/26/92	
Other Assets	Inventory	$100,000	9/26/92	Books and so on
Other Assets	Receivables	$0	9/26/92	Owed from publishers
Other Liabilities	Payables	$0	9/26/92	Owed to publishers

In This Chapter

About Quicken Categories

Working with Categories

Adding Your Own Categories

Using Subcategories

Creating Classes

Creating Subclasses

Viewing a Category List

1. Activate the account file whose category list you want to view.
2. Choose the account whose category list you want to view.
3. Press Ctrl-C or choose Categorize/Transfer from the Shortcuts menu.

Adding a Category

1. Press Ctrl-C or choose Categorize/Transfer from the Shortcuts menu.
2. Select <New Category> at the top of the list and press Enter.
3. Type a name for the category, and press Enter.
4. Select the desired options for the new category, and press Enter or click on Setup.

Viewing a Class List

1. Select the account file whose class list you want to see.
2. Select the account you want to work with and press Enter or select Use Register from the Main menu.
3. Press Ctrl-L or choose Select/Set Up Class List from the Shortcuts menu.

Adding a Class

1. Display the Class List for the account you want to add classes to.
2. Highlight <New Class> and press Enter, or double-click on <New Class>.
3. Type a class name and press Enter.
4. Type a description of the class and press Enter or click on Setup.

Chapter 4

Using Categories and Classes

In Chapter 3, "Working with Quicken Accounts," you created your first account, and you saw how Quicken stored this account in a file called QDATA. If you followed the examples, you also created two other account files, HOME and BOOKSHOP, and you added several accounts to each file. At this point, you're almost ready to begin recording your transactions in Quicken. This chapter will cover the final bit of preparation that you need: setting up categories and classes for your transactions.

> **NOTE:** In Quicken, a *transaction* is a financial event, such as writing a check, withdrawing or depositing money into your account, making an ATM (automated teller machine) withdrawal or deposit, paying a bill electronically, or entering a bank charge.

About Categories

In Quicken, you use categories to sort your income and expenses into groups. For example, you could tell Quicken to group together all gas, water, and electricity bills under a category called Utilities. Then, whenever you pay one of these bills, you tell Quicken to record the payment under the Utilities category. At the end of the month or year, Quicken can generate a report that includes the total amount of money that went toward utilities. Table 4.1 shows the breakdown by expenses you can achieve using categories.

Table 4.1
Monthly Expenses by Category

Category	Amount
Rent	$ 500
Food	200
Clothing	150
Utilities	50
Transportation	100
Total Expenses	**$1,000**

You use categories by assigning them to specific transactions in the register or Write Checks screen. If you deposit your paycheck in your checking account, for example, you would enter the transaction in the check register and then assign the deposit to the Salary category. You'll learn how to do this in Chapter 5, "Working with the Register." But first, you must set up the categories you want to use.

Standard and Custom Categories

You may recall from Chapter 3 that for each account file you create, Quicken asks you to select a list of standard categories

Using Categories and Classes 67

(predefined categories supplied by Quicken). You were given a choice of Home or Business categories (or both).

However, Quicken doesn't force you to use only the categories on these lists. Using the techniques described later in this chapter, you're free to modify, delete, or add categories on the standard lists, and you can edit the categories at any time. Quicken will automatically update any transactions assigned to a category you have changed.

Viewing the Categories

Before you modify either of the category lists, you should familiarize yourself with each list. You may find that, for now, the standard categories are enough to satisfy your needs.

This section explains how to display and navigate the category listing. If you want to follow along, you should have Quicken up and running on your system, and you should select the HOME account file that you created in Chapter 3. (To activate the HOME account file, choose Set Preferences, File Activities, Select/Set Up File, highlight HOME, and press ⏎Enter.) The following Quick Steps describe how to view the category listing for the current account file.

Viewing the Category List

1. Highlight Checking in the Select Account window and press ⏎Enter, or (if the Checking account is already active) choose Use Register from the Main menu.

   Quicken displays the register for the checking account.

   continues

> *continued*
>
> **2.** Press Ctrl-C or select Categorize/Transfer from the Shortcuts menu.
>
> Quicken displays the Category and Transfer List, as shown in Figure 4.1.

Figure 4.1
The Category and Transfer List.

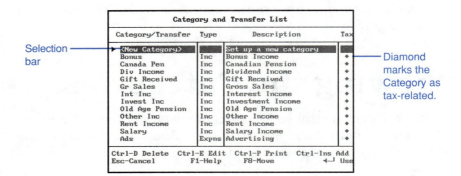

The Category and Transfer List is divided into four columns:

Category/Transfer Lists the category names. *Transfers* are the other accounts associated with this file, such as Savings, Cash, and so on (see Figure 4.2). If you move funds between accounts, you categorize the transaction as a transfer.

Type Classifies the category as either income (Inc), expense (Expns), or subcategory (Sub). Notice that the transfers shown in Figure 4.2 are classified by their account type.

Description Contains a brief description of the category. Descriptions are optional.

Tax Marks whether each category is tax-related (tax-related categories are shown with a diamond).

The categories are listed in alphabetical order, with the income categories grouped first, followed by the expense categories, and then the transfers.

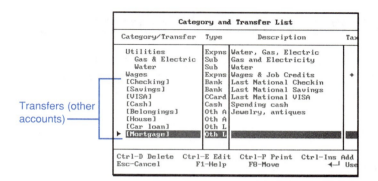

Figure 4.2
The Transfers for the HOME account file.

Navigating the Category List

Because the Category List is somewhat lengthy, Quicken provides some shortcut methods for moving through the list. For example, to go to the bottom of the list, press End; to return to the top of the list, press Home. Notice, too, that when you move through the list, Quicken highlights the current category with a *selection bar*. (The selection bar is a different color—reverse video if you have a monochrome monitor—line running across the Category List window.)

Table 4.2 summarizes the keys you can use to navigate the Category and Transfer list.

Key	Effect
↓	Moves down one line.
↑	Moves up one line.
PgDn	Moves down one screenful.
PgUp	Moves up one screenful.
End	Moves to the end of the list.
Home	Moves to the beginning of the list.
Any character	Moves to the first category that begins with that character.

Table 4.2
Keys Used with the Category and Transfer List

Working with Categories

As you gain experience with Quicken, you'll discover many new ways to look at your financial picture. In particular, as you grow comfortable working with categories, you'll find that you can modify them to focus on any aspect of your finances.

Editing Categories

You can edit the categories provided by Quicken (and those you create later by yourself) at any time. You might want to do this, for example, if you made a mistake when you created a category, or if you want to customize a standard category. For example, recall that Mrs. Johnson teaches desktop publishing courses at the local college. To track this income, she could change the standard income category Other Inc to Teaching.

When you edit a category, you can change the category name, its type, the description, and whether it is tax-related. The changes you make are automatically reflected in all the transactions associated with that category. To make changes to an existing category, use the following Quick Steps.

Editing a Category

1. Display the Category and Transfer List window as outlined earlier in this chapter.

2. Highlight the category you want to edit.
   The selection bar moves to the selected category.

3. Press Ctrl-E or click on Edit.
   Quicken displays the Edit Category window, as shown in Figure 4.3.

Using Categories and Classes

4. To change the category name, use `Del` to remove the original name, type in the name you want, and press `↵Enter`.

    The cursor moves to the Income, Expense or Subcategory field.

5. To change the category type, type **I** for income, **E** for expense, or **S** for subcategory, and then press `↵Enter` or click on the next field.

    The cursor moves to the Description field.

6. Type a new description for the category and press `↵Enter` or click on the next field.

    The cursor moves to the Tax-related field.

7. To change the Tax-related field, select **Y** if the category is tax-related or **N** if it is not.

8. To save your changes, press `↵Enter` or click on Setup.

    Quicken returns you to the Category and Transfer List. The changes you made are reflected in the list.

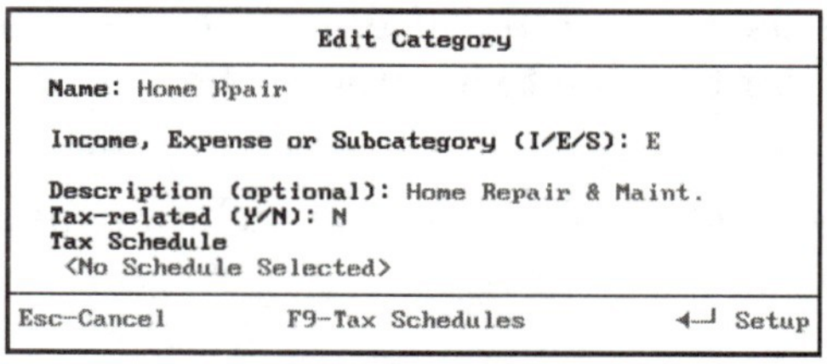

```
                    Edit Category
Name: Home Rpair

Income, Expense or Subcategory (I/E/S): E

Description (optional): Home Repair & Maint.
Tax-related (Y/N): N
Tax Schedule
   <No Schedule Selected>

Esc-Cancel        F9-Tax Schedules        ↵ Setup
```

Figure 4.3
The Edit Category window.

CAUTION When entering a category name, you can use any character except these four: [,], /, and :. If you try to use one of these characters in a category name, Quicken beeps and returns you to the Name field.

TIP: If you use a mouse, you can toggle fields such as Tax-related and Income, Expense or Subcategory by clicking anywhere on the field or field name. For example, click anywhere on `Tax-related` to toggle the field between `Y` and `N`.

Deleting a Category

If there are categories you think you will never use, you can delete them. Deleting categories makes it easier to traverse the Category List, and it cuts down on the amount of memory that Quicken uses. When you delete a category, Quicken removes the category reference from all associated transactions.

CAUTION If you delete the wrong category accidentally, the only way to restore the category references in the transactions is to re-enter them by hand. Be absolutely certain you want to delete a category before doing so.

The following Quick Steps show you how to delete a category.

Using Categories and Classes

Deleting a Category

1. Display the Category and Transfer List window as outlined earlier in this chapter.

2. Highlight the category you want to delete.

3. Press Ctrl-D or click on Delete. Quicken displays the warning screen.

4. Press Enter or click on Delete to confirm the deletion, or press Esc or click on Cancel to cancel the deletion. Quicken deletes the category, beeps, and returns you to the Category and Transfer List.

Printing the Category List

For easy reference, you can print the Category List, as described in the following Quick Steps.

Printing the Category List

1. Turn on your printer and make sure it is on-line.

2. Display the Category and Transfer List window as outlined earlier in this chapter.

continues

> *continued*
>
> 3. Press `Ctrl`-`P` or click on Print.
>
>   Quicken displays the Print Category and Transfer List window, as shown in Figure 4.4.
>
> 4. Press the appropriate number to select the print destination for the listing.
>
> 5. Press `Ctrl`-`↵Enter` or click on Print.
>
>   Quicken prints the list and returns you to the Category and Transfer List.

Figure 4.4
The Print Category and Transfer List window.

```
        Print Category and Transfer List

Print to: 1
    1. Rpt-<Other Dot-Matri    3. Chk-<Other Dot-Matri
    2. Alt-<Other Dot-Matri    4. Disk

Esc-Cancel                                  Ctrl↵ Print
```

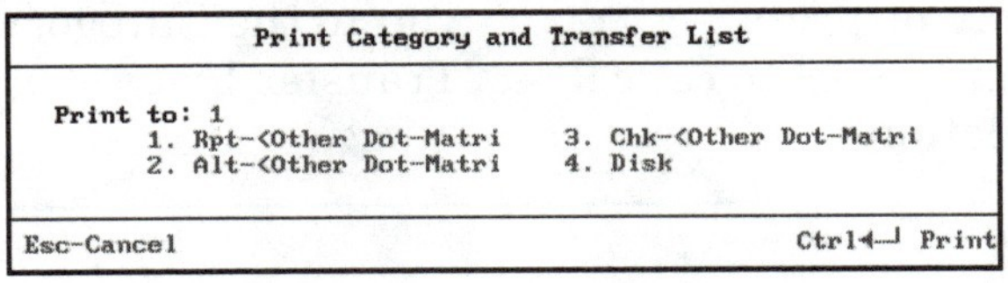

Adding Your Own Categories

While the predefined categories supplied by Quicken are extensive, for many Quicken users they are only a starting point. You can also add your own categories. When deciding what types of categories to add, ask yourself the following questions:

- *What am I using Quicken for?* For instance, if budgeting is high on your list, you'll need to set up categories to cover every item on your budget. If you want to compare actual photocopying expenses with a budget target, for example, you'll need to create a photocopying category.

Using Categories and Classes

- *What is important in my life financially?* For example, if you've moved recently, your moving expenses may warrant a category because these expenses are tax deductible. If, on the other hand, you use a dry cleaner a couple of times a year, you probably don't need a separate Dry Cleaning category.

- *What kind of reports do I need?* Quicken reports are often based on categories, so it's best to choose your categories in a way that makes your reports concise and meaningful. For instance, if you want Quicken to generate a tax summary, you should have a category for every line on the tax forms and schedules you use.

Avoid overlapping categories, such as Food and Groceries. Pick one category and delete the other.

The following Quick Steps lead you through the process of making a category. If you want to follow along, activate the HOME account file and add a category called Moving Expenses.

Adding a Category to the List

1. Display the Category and Transfer List window.

2. Highlight <New Category> at the top of the list and press ↵Enter, or double-click on <New Category>. Quicken displays the Set Up Category window, as shown in Figure 4.5.

continues

continued

3. Type a name for the category, up to 15 characters (do not use [,], /, or :) and press `Enter` or click on the next field.	The cursor moves to the Income, Expense or Subcategory field.
4. Type **I** for income, **E** for expense, or **S** for subcategory, and press `Enter` or click on the next field.	The cursor moves to the Description field.
5. (Optional) Type a brief description for the category, and press `Enter` or click on the next field.	The cursor moves to the Tax-related field.
6. Type **Y** if the category is tax-related and then press `F9` or click on Tax Schedules. Type **N** if it's not tax-related and skip to step 10.	For tax-related categories, Quicken displays the Tax Schedule window, as shown in Figure 4.6.
7. Select the appropriate tax schedule from the list and press `Enter`.	The Tax Line window appears.
8. Select the appropriate tax line and press `Enter` or click on Continue.	The Schedule Copy Number dialog box appears, prompting you to specify which copy of the tax form this category applies to.
9. Type a number and press `Enter`, or just press `Enter` to accept 1.	Quicken returns you to the Set Up Category window.
10. Press `Enter` or click on Setup.	Quicken creates the new category and returns you to the Category and Transfer List.

Using Categories and Classes

Figure 4.5
The Set Up Category window.

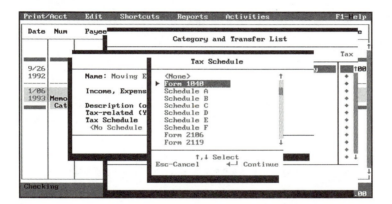

Figure 4.6
The Tax Schedule window.

Practicing with Category Suggestions

As an exercise, try entering the Home category suggestions outlined in Table 4.3. Use the HOME file for these additions.

Category Name	Type	Description	Tax
Teaching Inc	I	Teaching income	Y
DTP Inc	I	Desktop pub income	Y
Casualty & Theft	E	Casualty and theft	Y
Moving Exp	E	Moving expenses	Y
Cable	E	Monthly cable TV	N
Computer	E	Computer expenses	Y
Sports	E	Sports equipment, fees	N

Table 4.3
Suggested Category Additions for the HOME File

Several business categories for the Book City Bookshop are suggested in Table 4.4. Switch to the BOOKSHOP file and add the listed categories.

Table 4.4
Suggested Category Additions for the BOOKSHOP File

Category Name	Type	Description	Tax
Copying	E	Photocopying expense	Y
Bad Debt	E	Bad debt (write-off)	Y
Postage	E	Postage	Y
Supplies	E	Misc. supplies	Y
Pub Ret	I	Returns to publishers	Y
Pub Purch	E	Purchases from publishers	Y
Dues & Subs	E	Dues and subscriptions	Y

Using Subcategories

Subcategories let you create a more detailed financial picture. To see how this works, look under the Category/Transfer column in Figure 4.7. Notice that the Auto category has three subcategories: Fuel, Loan, and Service. By breaking down the automobile expenses in this way, you end up with a more detailed view of how you spend money on your car.

Figure 4.7
The automobile expenses subcategories.

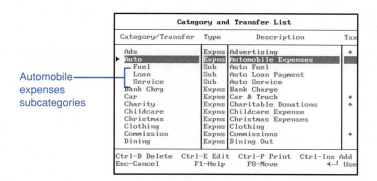

Why not just create a separate category for each automobile expense? You could do this, but you would lose some flexibility at report time. For example, look at the report shown in Figure 4.8. Notice that not only are the individual automotive expense subcategories shown, but their subtotal is as well. You could use the subtotal as a tax-form deduction and track the individual subcategories for your own purposes.

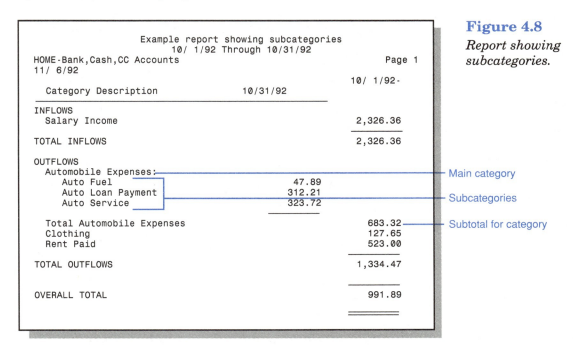

Figure 4.8
Report showing subcategories.

You can also create subcategories of subcategories. For example, you can add an Interest subcategory to the Auto:Loan subcategory to create Auto:Loan:Interest. (Note that Quicken uses the colon (:) to designate a subcategory; Auto:Loan means that Loan is a subcategory of Auto.) Although you can create even more subcategory levels, it is a good idea to stay within one or two levels. More than this will make your reports unnecessarily complex.

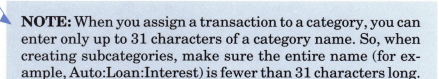

NOTE: When you assign a transaction to a category, you can enter only up to 31 characters of a category name. So, when creating subcategories, make sure the entire name (for example, Auto:Loan:Interest) is fewer than 31 characters long.

Adding, Editing, and Deleting Subcategories

Adding a subcategory to the Category and Transfer List is similar to adding a category. For example, you could add a Software subcategory to the Computer expense category. Follow these Quick Steps to add a subcategory to the list.

Adding a Subcategory

1. Display the Category and Transfer List window.

2. Highlight the category or subcategory to which you want to add a subcategory and press Ctrl-Ins. — Quicken displays the Set Up Category window.

3. Type a subcategory name, up to 15 characters (do not use [,], /, or :). Press Enter or click on the next field. — The cursor moves to the Income, Expense or Subcategory field. An S, denoting a subcategory, is already in the field.

4. Press Enter or click on the next field. — The cursor moves to the Description field.

5. Type a brief description for the subcategory, and press Enter or click on the next field. — The cursor moves to the Tax-related field.

Using Categories and Classes

6. Type **Y** if the category is tax-related and then press `F9` or click on Tax Schedules. Type **N** if it is not tax-related and skip to step 10.	Quicken displays the Tax Schedule window.
7. Highlight the appropriate tax schedule from the list and press `Enter` or click on Continue.	The Tax Line window appears.
8. Highlight the appropriate tax line and press `Enter` or click on Continue.	The Schedule Copy Number dialog box appears.
9. Type a number and press `Enter`, or just press `Enter` to accept 1.	Quicken returns you to the Set Up Category screen.
10. Press `Enter` or click on Continue.	Before creating the subcategory, Quicken displays a note asking you to read about subcategories before using them.
11. Press `Enter` or click on Setup.	Quicken returns you to the Category and Transfer List.

Quicken also allows you to edit and delete subcategories. Follow the same steps that you used to edit and delete categories.

When you delete a subcategory, the transactions associated with the subcategory become categorized with the next higher level category. For example, if you delete the Service subcategory from the Automotive Expense category, all transactions assigned to Service will be recategorized under the more general Auto category.

Practicing with Subcategory Suggestions

As an exercise, try adding the subcategories listed in Table 4.5 to the HOME account file.

Table 4.5
Suggested Subcategories for the HOME File

Category	Subcategory	Type	Description	Tax
Education	Books	S	School books	N
	Supplies	S	School supplies	N
Sports	Equipment	S	Sports equipment	N
	Fees	S	Club fees	N

Switch to the BOOKSHOP file and add the subcategories listed in Table 4.6.

Table 4.6
Suggested Subcategories for the BOOKSHOP File

Category	Subcategory	Type	Description	Tax
Postage	Out	S	To customers	Y
	In	S	From publishers	Y
Gr Sales	Reg Sales	S	Regular sales	Y
	Spec Ord	S	Special orders	Y

Using Classes

Another way to track your income and expenses is to use *classes*. For example, you can divide your expenses into two classes: business and personal. Quicken will then use these classes to keep your business and personal expenses separate.

To illustrate how classes work, return to the Johnson household. Whenever Mrs. Johnson purchases software for her business, she assigns it to the Computer:Software subcategory. But what happens when the Johnsons buy software that is not business-related (such as a game)? They could categorize this as a Miscellaneous expense or create a separate category for home software, but that could become confusing. By setting up separate classes for business and personal expenses, Mrs. Johnson can differentiate between her business software and the rest of the family's software.

One common business use of classes is to track sales by product type. In the case of Book City, it would be interesting to track sales by book type. For example, you could create a class for each section in the store: Cooking, Science Fiction, Computer Books, and so on. The information supplied by such classes could be invaluable when making strategic business decisions such as shelf space allotment, inventory management, and advertising budgeting.

Like categories, classes are assigned to individual transactions in the register or Write Checks screen. You can type the class name in the transaction's Category field or select one from the Class List (which is separate from the Category and Transfer List). You'll learn how to do this in the next chapter.

Using Classes

Here are a few more examples of ways you can use classes:

- If you are a property manager, set up a class name for each property. This allows you to track items such as rental income and maintenance expenses for each location.

- If you own a business with several salespeople, assign a class name to each person to monitor individual sales and expenses.

- If you are a consultant, set up a class for each client. This way you can track expenses client-by-client and bill them accordingly.

Adding Classes

Quicken does not come with any preset classes (unlike the Categories List) because classes tend to be specific to the user's financial situation. The examples in the previous section should serve to give you some ideas about how you might use classes, but the specific classes you create are up to you.

As a general guideline, you should ask yourself how you need to track your finances. If you cannot track your finances in such a way using categories, you probably need to create classes. This section explains the basic steps required to set up a class. As an example, perform the following two sets of Quick Steps to set up a Fiction class for Book City. To follow along, you should have the BOOKSHOP account file selected.

Displaying the Class List

1. Select the account file whose class list you want to see.

    If you just opened the file (such as BOOKSHOP), Quicken will prompt you to choose an account.

2. Select the account you want to work with and press ⏎Enter or select Use **R**egister from the Main menu.

    Quicken displays the register screen for the selected account.

3. Press Ctrl-L or select Select/Set Up Class from the **S**hortcuts menu.

    Quicken displays the Class List, as shown in Figure 4.9.

Using Categories and Classes

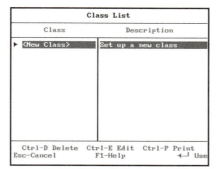

Figure 4.9
The Class List window.

Adding a Class to the Class List

1. Display the Class List for the account you want to add classes to.

2. Highlight <New Class> and press ⏎Enter, or double-click on <New Class>.

   The Set Up Class window appears, as shown in Figure 4.10.

3. Type the class name (using the same conventions you used for category names), and then press ⏎Enter or click on the next field.

   The cursor moves to the Description field.

4. Type a description of the class, if desired, and press ⏎Enter or click on Setup.

   Quicken creates the new class and returns you to the Class List.

Figure 4.10
The Set Up Class window.

Classes are sorted alphabetically by class name. Use the same techniques to navigate the Class List that you learned for the Category and Transfer List.

As an exercise, add two other classes to the BOOKSHOP file: Nonfiction and Stationery.

Modifying Classes

You can make changes to a class if, for example, you made a mistake entering a class or if you would prefer a more descriptive class name. When you rename a class, Quicken automatically updates the name in all associated transactions. The following Quick Steps describe how to edit a class.

Editing a Class

1. From the Class List, highlight the class you want to edit and press Ctrl-E or click on Edit.

   The Edit Class window appears, as shown in Figure 4.11.

2. Change the class name, if desired, and press Enter or click on the next field.

   The cursor moves to the Description field.

3. Edit the description of the class, if desired, and press Enter or click on Setup.

   Quicken returns you to the Class List.

Figure 4.11
The Edit Class window.

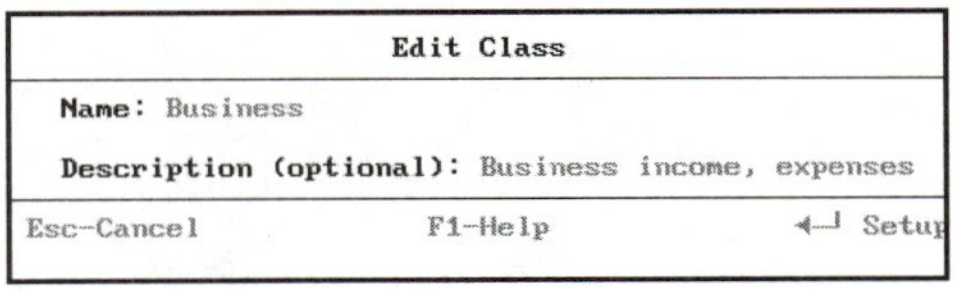

Deleting a Class

You can delete a class at any time. You might want to do this if, for example, you no longer need to track the information that the class provides. Or, your business might change, making a class name obsolete (such as if you sell a piece of property that has its own class).

When you delete a class, Quicken removes the classification from all associated transactions. Follow the next Quick Steps to delete a class.

> If you delete the wrong class accidentally, the only way to restore the class references in the transactions is to re-enter them individually. Be certain that you want to delete a class before doing so.

Deleting a Class

1. From the Class List, highlight the class you want to delete and press Ctrl-D or click on Delete.

   Quicken displays a message warning you that you are about to delete a class.

2. Press Enter or click on Delete to confirm the deletion, or press Esc or click on Cancel.

   Quicken deletes the class and returns you to the Class List.

Using Subclasses

To see how you might use subclasses, return to the Book City example. Earlier, you set up some classes according to book type. Another use for classes is to group income and expense transactions according to when they occurred.

Because Book City is a retail operation, it would be interesting to know what percentage of yearly sales occurs during the Christmas season. To do this, you would set up two subclasses: Christmas and Non-Christmas. All gross sales that occurred from October 1 to December 24 would be classified as Christmas. At the end of the year, you would generate a report that would break down each book class into two gross sales lines: one for sales during the Christmas period and one for all other times (see Figure 4.12). This will give you some idea of the types of books you need to stock next Christmas.

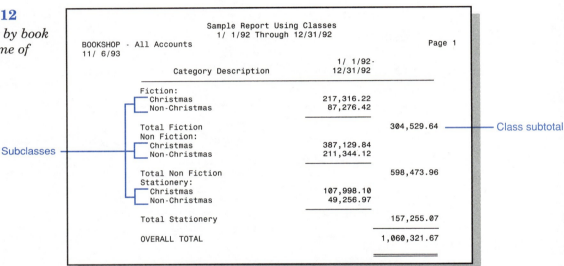

Figure 4.12
Gross sales by book type and time of year.

As mentioned earlier, classes are fluid; you can assign them to any category or any transaction that makes sense. Subclasses are also fluid because you can associate a subclass with any class. For example, Book City's Christmas subclass can be assigned to any of the book type classes such as Fiction, Nonfiction, and Stationery. This is unlike subcategories, which are fixed to a specific category.

When you add subclasses, they look just like any class in the Class List. How does Quicken know the difference? Simple: within each transaction you just tell the program that you're using a subclass. (If this is unclear to you now, don't worry. You'll be learning all about this and other transaction techniques in the coming chapters).

In This Chapter

Accessing the Register

Navigating the Register Screen

Entering Transactions in the Register

Editing and Deleting Existing Transactions

Transferring Funds Between Accounts

Printing the Register

Opening a Register

1. Activate the account whose register you want to use.
2. Choose Use Register from the Main menu.

Or

1. Choose Select Account from the Main menu.
2. Select the account whose register you want to use.

Entering a Transaction

1. Display the register and press Ctrl-I.
2. Enter the transaction date and press Enter.
3. Enter the check number, if necessary, and press Enter.
4. Enter the name of the person you are paying, if necessary, and press Enter.
5. Enter the debit amount in the Payment field or enter the credit amount in the Deposit field.
6. Enter a description of the transaction, if desired, and press Enter.
7. To select a category, press Ctrl-C, highlight the category, and press Enter.
8. To select a class, press Ctrl-L, highlight the class, and press Enter.
9. Press Ctrl-Enter.

Deleting a Transaction

1. Highlight the transaction you want to delete.
2. Press Ctrl-D.
3. Press Enter to confirm the deletion.

Chapter 5

Working with the Register

All the Quicken registers are similar—they all resemble a typical paper checkbook register. You can use this electronic register to record information for any transactions that you currently track on paper, for example:

- Checks written by hand, as opposed to those generated by Quicken. (For information on entering transactions using Quicken's Check Writing feature, see Chapter 6, "Writing and Printing Checks.")

- Deposits made at your bank, or stocks and bonds purchased from your broker.

- ATM (automated teller machine) deposits, withdrawals, and bill payments.

- Account transfers, including loan principal payments.

- Account interest, fees, and penalties.

- Electronic transactions (direct-deposit paychecks, bills paid using an electronic service such as CheckFree or IntelliCharge, and so on).

Although the paper and Quicken registers may appear to be the same, the Quicken register offers a number of major advantages:

- Quicken updates your balance automatically whenever you record a transaction. In a paper checkbook register, math errors are the most common cause of account discrepancies (and bounced checks).

- Quicken automatically sorts your entries by date and check number.

- You can assign categories and classes to your register transactions to help track them.

- Quicken offers a powerful reconciliation feature that can help you balance your checkbook.

In this chapter, you will learn the basics of working with the check register: getting around the screen; adding, editing, and deleting transactions; and printing the register. (Chapter 7 deals with the slightly more complex issues of splitting and memorizing transactions.) Although this chapter focuses on the checking-account register, you can use the techniques you learn in this chapter to work with the other Quicken registers as well. (See Chapter 9, "Your Finances with Other Quicken Accounts," for specific instructions.)

Using the Register Screen

Before you can work with a register, you must display it. The following Quick Steps describe the procedure. Before you begin, however, make sure the account file you want to work with is active. For example, to work with the sample HOME account file, choose Set Preferences, File Activities, Select/Set Up File, highlight HOME, and press ⏎Enter.

Working with the Register

Opening the Register

1. Press Ctrl-A.

   The Select Account window appears.

2. Highlight the account whose register you want to use and press Enter, or double-click on the account's name.

   The register screen appears. (See Figure 5.1.)

TIP: If the account you want to work with is already active, you can display the register by selecting Use Register from the Main menu. An even quicker way is to press Ctrl-R.

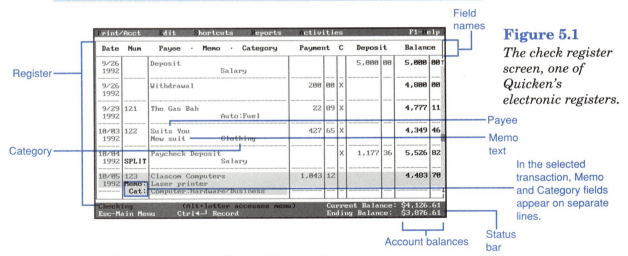

Figure 5.1
The check register screen, one of Quicken's electronic registers.

Navigating the Register Screen

In Chapter 2, you learned several mouse and keyboard techniques for getting around in Quicken. Take a moment to experiment with the mouse or arrow keys to move around the register screen. As you press the arrow keys, notice that Quicken uses two types of cursors to tell you where you are on the screen:

- A screen-wide, transaction highlight bar shows which transaction you're currently working on.
- A blinking cursor shows where you are in the selected transaction.

While it's easy to see that you can just point and click with the mouse to move around the register screen, keyboard shortcuts are less obvious. Table 5.1 summarizes the keys available in the register screen.

Table 5.1
The Register Keys

Key	Effect
↑	Moves up one line or transaction.
↓	Moves down one line or transaction.
→	Moves right one character or column.
←	Moves left one character or column.
Ctrl-→	Moves right one word.
Ctrl-←	Moves left one word.
Tab or ↵Enter	Moves to next column.
⇧Shift-Tab	Moves to previous column.
PgDn	Moves down one screenful.
PgUp	Moves up one screenful.
Ctrl-PgUp	Moves to start of current month.
Ctrl-PgDn	Moves to start of next month.
Home	Moves to the beginning of the current entry or to the date of the current transaction.
End	Moves to the end of the current entry or to the category of the current transaction.
Ctrl-Home	Moves to first register entry.
Ctrl-End	Moves to last register entry.

The Register Fields

The check register is divided into seven columns containing nine fields for your transaction information: Date, Num (Check Number), Payee, Memo, Category, Payment, C (Cleared), Deposit, and Balance. (A *field* is a screen area where you can enter information.) Most of these fields (except Memo and Category) will be familiar to you from your paper checkbook register. Other Quicken accounts use similar fields.

The Date Field

The Date field is for the date of the transaction, which is set in the month/day/year format. Quicken uses the current date (from your computer's internal clock), but you can type in the date or you can use the shortcuts listed in Table 5.2 to change the date.

Table 5.2
Date Shortcut Keys

Key	Effect
+	Moves forward one day.
-	Moves back one day.
T	Moves to today's date.
M	Moves to first day of the month.
H	Moves to last day of the month.
Y	Moves to first day of the year.
R	Moves to last day of the year.

> **Tip:** Here's an easy way to remember some of these shortcut keys: **MontH** and **YeaR**. The first and last letters of the word *MontH* enter the first and last days of the month. Likewise, the first and last letters of the word *YeaR* enter the first and last dates of the year.

You can always change a date you've entered. Remember, however, that Quicken organizes your register entries by date. If you change the date of a transaction, the position of the transaction in the register will likely change.

You can enter *postdated transactions,* which are transactions that have a date *after* the current date. These entries are separated from other transactions by a double line (see Figure 5.2). On a color monitor, postdated entries are shown in a different color. After you record a postdated transaction, the status bar shows both the current balance (the balance not including the postdated entries) and the ending balance (the balance including postdated items).

Figure 5.2
Postdated entries are separated by a double line.

Double line separates post-dated transactions.

Date	Num	Payee · Memo · Category	Payment	C	Deposit	Balance
9/26 1992		Withdrawal	200 00	X		4,800 00
9/29 1992	121	The Gas Bah Auto:Fuel	22 89	X		4,777 11
10/03 1992	122	Suits You New suit Clothing	427 65	X		4,349 46
10/04 1992	SPLIT	Paycheck Deposit Salary		X	1,177 36	5,526 82
10/05 1992	123	Clascom Computers Laser printer Computer:Hardw→	1,043 12			4,483 70
11/04 1992	Memo: Cat:	Globe Travel Trip down pymnt Travel	250 00			4,233 70

Checking   (Alt+letter accesses menu)   Current Balance: $4,483.70
Esc-Main Menu   Ctrl↵ Record   Ending Balance: $4,233.70

Current balance does not include post-dated transactions.

Ending balance includes post-dated transactions.

VERSION 6

Quicken 6 now offers a pop-up calendar to help you see the month at a glance. To use the calendar, press Ctrl-K. The calendar appears, as shown in Figure 5.3. You can then perform the following actions:

- To insert a date from the calendar into the Date field of your transaction, highlight the date in the calendar and press F9.

- To go to the first transaction on a selected date, highlight the date in the calendar and press ↵Enter.

- To go to a past or future month, press PgUp or PgDn.

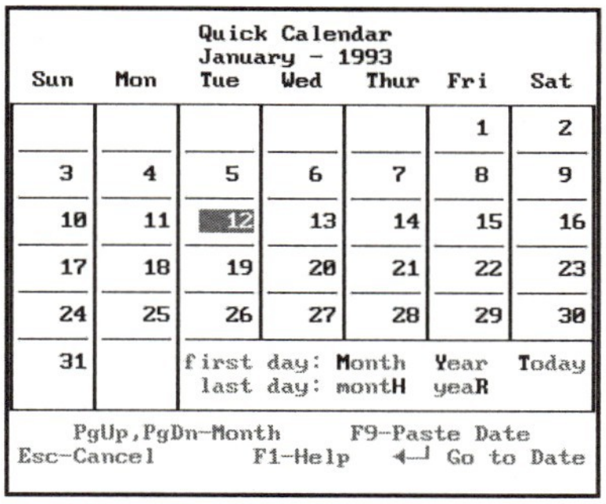

Working with the Register

Figure 5.3
Quicken's new pop-up calendar.

The Check Number Field

The Num (check number) field is just to the right of the date. If you write your checks by hand, enter the number printed on the check. If you use Quicken to write your checks, the program inserts the number automatically. Do not enter anything in the Num field if the transaction is not a check.

> **TIP:** Use [+] (plus) and [-] (minus) to enter a check number quickly. When the cursor is anywhere in the Num field of the current transaction and you press [+], Quicken looks up the number of the last check in the register, adds one to it, and inserts the new number in the Num field. Press [-] to decrease the number.

You can have Quicken warn you if you try to enter a duplicate check number by performing the following steps:

1. From the Main menu, select Set Preferences.
2. Select Checks & Reports Settings.
3. Tab to option 5. Warn if a check number is re-used, and press [Y].
4. Press [Ctrl]-[↵Enter].

The Payee Field

In the Payee field, you insert the name of the person or company that you make a check out to (up to 31 characters). For any other transaction, such as a deposit or a bank fee, enter an appropriate description, as shown in Figure 5.4.

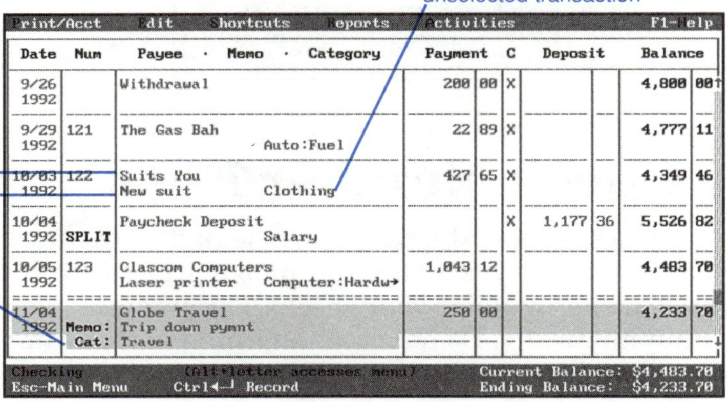

Figure 5.4
Some Payee field examples.

The Memo Field

In the Memo field, you can enter an optional message to provide additional information about the transaction. Memos are generally restricted to 31 characters.

The Category Field

The Category field contains the category and/or class designation assigned to the transaction. (See Chapter 4 for a complete discussion of the contents of this field.) If the transaction is a transfer to or from another account, the name of the account appears in this field.

Quicken uses the forward slash (/) to distinguish between categories and classes. For example, Supplies/Business means that the transaction is *categorized* as Supplies and *classified* as Business.

Quicken uses the colon (:) to separate subcategories from categories and subclasses from classes. For example, `Auto:Service` assigns the transaction to the Service subcategory of the automotive expenses. Similarly, `/Fiction:Christmas` tells Quicken that, for this transaction at least, Christmas is a *subclass* of Fiction.

The Payment Field

You enter all *debit* transactions in the Payment field. Examples of debits are checks, bank service charges, withdrawals, and transfers to another account.

Enter the amount using numbers only (Quicken doesn't accept a dollar sign, and commas are added automatically) and separate the cents with a period. For example, to enter the amount $1,347.62, you would type `1347.62` and press `Tab`. Quicken formats the entry with commas (if needed) and places the cents in the cents column.

The Cleared Field

One of the biggest advantages of using the Quicken register is that you can use Quicken's sophisticated reconciliation feature to help balance your account. When you complete a reconciliation, Quicken displays an X in the C (cleared) field for the transactions that have cleared your bank. Leave this field blank when you enter transactions.

The Deposit Field

You enter all *credits* in the Deposit field. Examples of credits are paycheck deposits, interest, and transfers from another account. The Deposit field is set up the same as the Payment field, and you enter amounts using the same conventions.

The Balance Field

The running balance in your account is found in the Balance field. Quicken updates this field automatically whenever you record, edit, or delete a transaction.

Adding a Transaction to the Register

Adding a transaction in the Quicken register is very similar to adding an entry in a paper checkbook register. For example, the following transaction can be recorded in the register for the HOME checking account:

Date	10/10/1992
Number	126
Payee	Brimson's Furniture
Payment	$357.09
Memo	New desk
Category	Office/Business

If you want to follow this example, you need to set up a Business class using the steps outlined in Chapter 4. The following Quick Steps describe how to enter a transaction.

Adding a Transaction to the Register

1. Select Use Register from the Main menu or press Ctrl-R.

   Quicken displays the register.

2. Press Ctrl-End.	The transaction highlight bar moves to the end of the register, as shown in Figure 5.5.
3. Enter the transaction date and press Enter.	The cursor moves to the Num field.
4. Enter the check number, if necessary, and press Enter.	The cursor moves to the Payee field.
5. Enter the name of the person the check is made out to, if necessary, and press Enter.	The cursor moves to the Payment field.
6. If the transaction is a credit, press Enter twice and go to step 7. Otherwise, enter the debit amount, press Enter three times, and skip to step 8.	Quicken formats the amount and moves to the Memo field.
7. Enter the credit amount and press Enter.	Quicken formats the amount and moves to the Memo field.
8. Enter a description of the transaction, if desired, and press Enter.	The cursor moves to the Category field.
9. To select a category, pull down the **Shortcuts** menu and select **Categorize/Transfer**, or press Ctrl-C.	Quicken displays the Category and Transfer List.

continues

continued

10. Highlight a category and press `Enter`, or double-click on a category.	Quicken returns you to the register.
11. To select a class, pull down the Shortcuts menu and choose Select/Set Up Class, or press `Ctrl`-`L`.	Quicken displays the Class List.
12. Highlight a class and press `Enter`, or double-click on a class.	Quicken returns you to the register.
13. To record the transaction, pull down the Edit menu and select Record Transaction or press `Ctrl`-`Enter`.	Quicken briefly flashes a RECORDING message in the lower left corner of the screen and then beeps when the transaction has been recorded. (See Figure 5.6.)

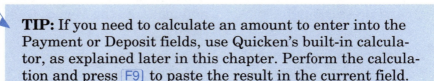

TIP: If you need to calculate an amount to enter into the Payment or Deposit fields, use Quicken's built-in calculator, as explained later in this chapter. Perform the calculation and press `F9` to paste the result in the current field.

Keep Your Paper Checkbook Register

While you're learning Quicken, keep your paper checkbook register and duplicate the entries you make in the Quicken register. Although Quicken is easy to learn and use, mistakes can happen. By keeping a second set of books for a while, you'll be better able to recover from a mishap.

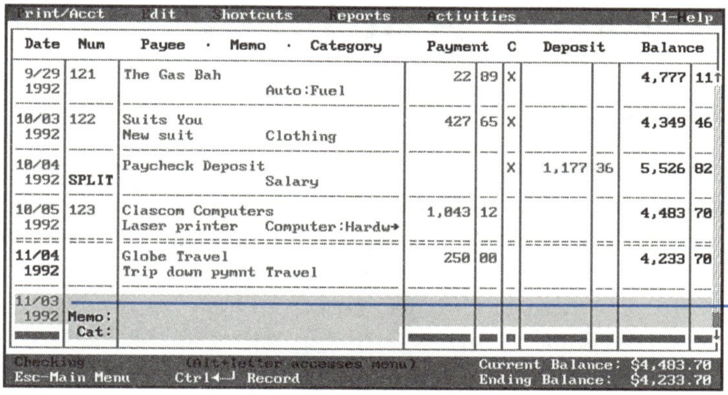

Working with the Register

Figure 5.5
The last entry of the check register.

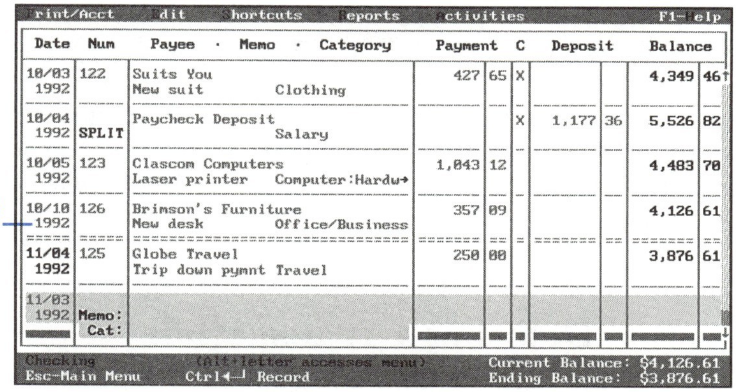

— A blank transaction

Figure 5.6
The completed transaction.

A completed transaction

> **TIP:** You can enter a category quickly by typing the first few letters of the category name in the Category field. As you type, Quicken fills in the rest of the name for you. Keep typing until Quicken displays the name of the category you want to use.

You can insert new transactions anywhere in the register so you don't have to go all the way to the bottom to record a transaction. Press Ctrl-I, and Quicken inserts a blank entry above the currently selected transaction.

Editing a Register Transaction

If you make a mistake when entering a transaction, don't worry. Quicken allows you to edit your transactions at any time. You can make changes to any field except the account balance. Simply highlight the transaction you want to change, use `Tab` to move to the field you want to change, and then type your correction. To record the transaction, press `Ctrl`-`Enter` or select **Record Transaction** from the **Edit** menu.

Deleting a Transaction

You may find it necessary to delete an entire transaction. This would happen if you entered a transaction into the wrong account or duplicated an existing entry. Use the following Quick Steps to delete a transaction.

Deleting a Transaction from the Register

1. Highlight the transaction you want to delete.

2. Select **Delete Transaction** from the **Edit** menu or press `Ctrl`-`D`.

   A message box appears asking you to confirm that you want to delete the transaction.

3. Press `Enter` to delete the transaction or `Esc` to cancel the deletion.

   If you delete the entry, Quicken recalculates the balance and then returns you to the register.

Copying a Transaction

In the next chapter, you will learn how to memorize transactions so you can enter the same transaction by selecting it from a list. However, you can also enter a transaction by copying it from one place in the register and pasting it into a different location, or from one register to another (you cannot copy and paste between investment and noninvestment registers). To copy a transaction, perform the following Quick Steps.

> **CAUTION**
>
> If you copy a transaction over an existing transaction, the copy will replace the existing entry. To turn on a warning that will help prevent you from doing this accidentally, choose Set Preferences from the Main menu, select Transaction Settings, tab down to the Confirm when overwriting field, type Y, and press ↵Enter.

Copying and Pasting a Transaction

1. Highlight the transaction you want to copy.

2. Choose Copy Transaction from the Shortcuts menu, or press Ctrl-Ins.   The transaction is copied to your computer's memory.

3. Press Ctrl-I to enter a new transaction or press End to move to the bottom of the register.

continues

continued

4. Choose **Paste Transaction** from the **Shortcuts** menu, or press ⇧Shift-Ins. If you are pasting the copy over an existing transaction, a warning appears.

5. If a warning appears, press Y to confirm the replacement or press Esc to cancel.

TIP: Once you've copied a transaction, you can paste it repeatedly until you copy a different transaction or edit the register.

Voiding a Transaction

There are times when it's better to void a transaction than to delete it:

- You stop payment on a check.
- You make an error on a check and discard it.
- You lose a check.
- A check is returned to you uncashed.

By voiding the check in these cases, you maintain a complete record of all your numbered checks. You can void any type of transaction, but the best practice is to void only checks and delete all other erroneous entries. Follow the next Quick Steps to void a transaction.

CAUTION Once you've voided a transaction, there's no way to restore it. Be sure you want to void a transaction before doing so.

Voiding a Register Transaction

1. Highlight the transaction you want to void.

   A message box appears asking you to confirm that you want to void the transaction.

2. Select **Void Transaction** from the **Edit** menu or press `Ctrl`-`V`.

3. Press `↵Enter` to void the transaction or `Esc` to cancel.

   If you void the entry, Quicken appends VOID: to the Payee name, removes the amount, and marks the transaction as cleared.

4. To record the void, pull down the **Edit** menu and select **Record Transaction**, or press `Ctrl`-`↵Enter`.

   Quicken flashes a RECORDING message in the lower left corner of the screen, recalculates the balance, and then beeps.

Transferring Funds Between Accounts

During a *transfer,* money is taken from one Quicken account and is deposited into another. For example, you could move funds from your savings account to your checking account to cover a check, or you could take a cash advance from your credit card. In each case, a transfer involves two transactions: a *debit* from the source account (which appears in the Payment field of the source account register), and a *credit* to the destination account (which appears in the Deposit field of the destination account register).

The beauty of Quicken transfers is that you enter only one side of the transfer. Quicken automatically records the offsetting transaction in the other account. If, like most people, you use more than one Quicken account, you'll find that this feature saves you time and ensures that transfers between accounts are recorded accurately.

To create a transfer, you enter the other account's name in the Category field. You may have noticed that the Category and Transfer List contains the names of all your accounts in brackets. Just as with categories, these bracketed names can be entered manually into the Category field or selected from this list. To record the transfer, follow these Quick Steps.

Transferring Funds Between Accounts

1. Activate the account *from which* you want to transfer money.

2. Begin the transaction as you normally would, entering the date, payee name, and amount of the transfer in the Payment field.

3. Tab to or click on the Category field.

4. Press Ctrl-C to display the Category and Transfer List and select the account *to which* you want to transfer the funds.

   Quicken returns you to the register and inserts the account's name in the Category field.

5. Press Ctrl-Enter or F10, or click on Record.

   Quicken records the transfer (see Figure 5.7) and enters the offsetting transaction in the other account.

Working with the Register

TIP: To enter an account name in the Category field quickly, type a left bracket ([) and enough letters to identify the account uniquely. Press ⏎Enter to use the account name.

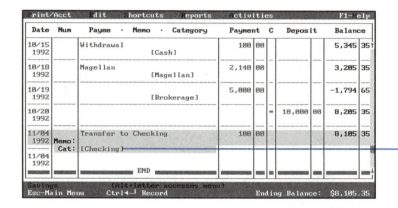

Figure 5.7
The transfer in the source account (savings).

Funds transferred to this account

Editing Transfers

When you create a transfer, Quicken maintains a link between the two transactions. This way, if you make changes to one of the transactions, the other transaction is changed automatically. For example, if you delete one of the transactions in a transfer, the offsetting entry in the other account is also deleted. Similarly, changes to the date, amount, or even the account name result in a change in the corresponding information in the other account.

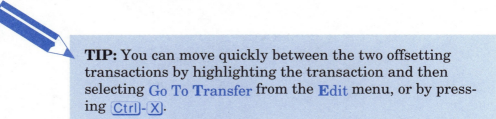

TIP: You can move quickly between the two offsetting transactions by highlighting the transaction and then selecting Go To Transfer from the Edit menu, or by pressing Ctrl-X.

Printing the Register

If you like to work with a paper copy of your register, or if you need a copy for your records, you can print the register or any part of it. The following steps explain how to print the register.

1. Display the register you want to print.

2. Select Print Register from the Print/Acct menu or press Ctrl-P. The Print Register window appears, as shown in Figure 5.8.

3. Enter the range of transaction dates you want printed and press Enter to move to the Print to field.

4. Select the print destination and press Enter to move to the Title field.

5. Type a title for the register, if you want, and press Enter to move to the Print one transaction per line field.

6. Press Y if you want an abbreviated version of the check register, and then press Enter to move to the Print transaction splits field.

7. Press Y to print split transactions and then press Enter to move to the Sort by check number field.

8. Press Y to list the checks by check number rather than by date.

9. Press Ctrl-Enter or click on Print. Quicken prints the register.

Working with the Register

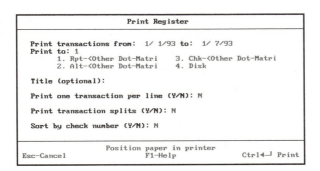

Figure 5.8
The Print Register window.

Using Quicken's Basic Math Calculator

When you work in the register, you'll often find that you need to make calculations, such as determining sales tax for a purchase. A convenient way to perform these calculations is to use Quicken's basic math calculator, shown in Figure 5.9. This calculator is available in any Quicken screen that has an Activities menu. To use it, select **Calculator** from the **Activities** menu or use the Quick Key combination, Ctrl-O.

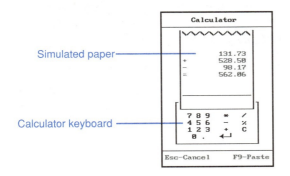

Figure 5.9
The basic math calculator.

You use the on-line calculator the same way you use a regular calculator. Enter numbers using your keyboard's numeric keypad (or the number keys at the top of the keyboard) and use the following special keys to perform the mathematical operations:

Key	Operation
+	Addition
-	Subtraction
*	Multiplication
/	Division
%	Percentage
.	Decimal point (you can use up to eight decimal places)
Enter or =	Displays the result of the calculation
C	Clears the calculator

You can also use your mouse by clicking on the appropriate calculator keys.

> **TIP:** You can use the calculator results as field entries. For example, suppose you want to calculate a sum and write a check for the result. Place the cursor in the amount field of the check, and press Ctrl-O to call up the calculator. Perform the calculation and then press F9 to paste the result in the amount field.

When you finish using the calculator, press Esc to remove it from the screen.

Working with the Register

In This Chapter

Using Quicken Checks

Accessing the Write Checks Screen

Writing Checks

Editing Checks

Printing Checks

Writing a Check

1. Display the Write Checks screen.
2. Type the name of the person or company that the check is to be made out to and press `Enter`.
3. Type the check amount without the dollar sign and press `Enter`.
4. Type the payee's address and press `Enter`.
5. Type a memo to appear on the check and press `Enter`.
6. Type or select a category or class for the check.
7. Pull down the **Edit** menu and select **Record Transaction**.

Editing a Check

1. Display the Write Checks screen.
2. Select the check you want to edit.
3. Move to the field you want to edit and make your changes.
4. Pull down the **Edit** menu and select **Record Transaction**.

Printing a Check

1. From the Write Checks screen, press `Ctrl`-`P`.
2. Select the printer you want to use and press `Enter`.
3. Enter the necessary printing instructions.
4. Press `Ctrl`-`Enter`.
5. If you chose to print only selected checks, use the `Space bar` to tag the checks you want to print.
6. Press `Enter`.
7. Type the check number of the first check to be printed and press `Enter`.

Chapter

6

Writing and Printing Checks

In the previous chapter, you learned how to enter transactions in the check register, including manually written checks. With Quicken's check-writing and check-printing feature, you can write checks electronically, have them posted automatically to the register, and print them.

Using Quicken Checks

To write checks from within Quicken, you need special preprinted checks from Intuit, the publisher of Quicken. All the information required by financial institutions is printed on each check, including your name, address, bank name, account number, and check number. Intuit guarantees that these checks will be accepted by any bank, credit union, or savings and loan in the United States and Canada. You can order any of the three following types of Quicken checks:

Standard checks These are 3 ½ inches by 8 ½ inches. Figure 6.1 shows a sample standard check that comes with Quicken.

Voucher checks These are standard-sized checks with an extra 3 ½-inch-high voucher stub below the check. The voucher stub is useful for showing payroll deductions or a description of the invoices for which the check was issued.

Wallet checks These are 2 ⅚ inches by 6 inches with a 2 ½-inch-wide register stub to the left of the check. The register stub gives you a record of the check showing the check number, date, payee, amount, and any memo or category associated with the check.

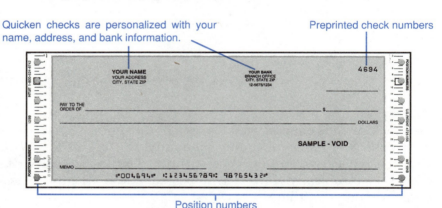

Figure 6.1
A sample standard Quicken check.

You can order your checks in one of two forms: *continuous* (for dot-matrix and daisywheel printers) and *single-sheet* (for inkjet or laser printers). To order your Quicken checks, see the catalog that came with the program. If you don't have a catalog, perform the following steps to print out an order form, or call Intuit at (800) 624-8742 for more information:

1. Press Ctrl-R or, from the Main menu, select Use Register to display the check register screen.

2. Pull down the Activities menu and select Order Supplies. Quicken displays the Product Order window, as shown in Figure 6.2.

3. Press ↓ to display the Intuit Catalogue menu, and select the product you want to order.

4. Work through the series of submenus that appear to specify precisely what you want.

5. Press F7 and enter the address you want the merchandise shipped to.

6. Press F8 and enter the billing information.

7. Press Ctrl-⏎Enter when the order is complete. Quicken prints the order form.

8. Mail your completed order form and payment to

   Intuit
   P.O. Box 3024
   Menlo Park, CA 94026-9917

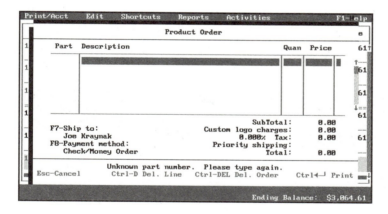

Figure 6.2
The Product Order window.

NOTE: If you use Quicken checks and you also write checks using your checkbook, you can keep track of both sets of checks. For Quicken checks, use the Write Checks screen. For your checkbook checks, record your transactions in the checking account register. Just be careful not to use the same check number twice.

The Write Checks Screen

This section will teach you some of the features of the Write Checks screen. To display the Write Checks screen, shown in Figure 6.3, select the bank account you want to use and do one of the following:

- Select **Write/Print Checks** from the Main menu.
- Press Ctrl-W from most Quicken screens.
- At the register screen, select **Write Checks** from the **Activities** pull-down menu.

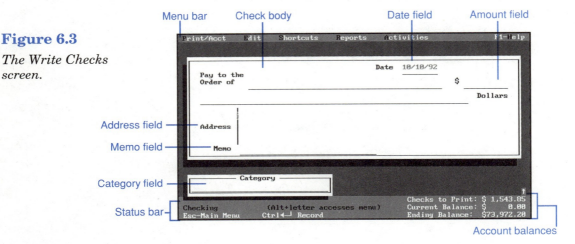

Figure 6.3
The Write Checks screen.

The Check Fields

Most of the fields in the Write Checks screen are similar to those found in the check register. The following sections explain the various fields.

The Date Field

When you write a Quicken check, you'll generally use the current date in this field (Quicken enters the current system date automatically). However, you can change the date if you want to postdate a check. If you postdate checks, Quicken displays three account balances in the lower right corner of the screen, as shown in Figure 6.3:

Checks to Print   The total of all checks written but not yet printed.

Current Balance   The account balance of all transactions through the current date only (does not include postdated checks). This line is displayed only if you have postdated checks.

Ending Balance   The account balance based on all transactions, including postdated checks. Quicken updates this line every time you record a check.

By keeping an eye on all three balances, you'll know how much money you need to pay your bills and whether there is enough in your account to cover the checks when they come due.

Quicken gives you the option of spelling out the month on the check. For example, 10/10/91 would appear as 10 Oct 91; 1/2/92 would be written 2 Jan 92. To activate this option, follow these steps:

1. From the Main menu, select Set Preferences.
2. Select Checks & Reports Settings.
3. Move the cursor to Option 3, Print months as Jan, Feb... on checks, and type Y.
4. Press Ctrl-Enter to activate the option.

The Amount Field

The amount field ($) is equivalent to the Payment field found in the check register. Notice that the check actually has two fields for the amount: one field for a numeric entry (for example, 32.15) and one field for a text entry (for example, Thirty-Two and 15/100). Type only the numeric entry. When you press Enter, Quicken fills in the text amount.

The Address Field

You can enter up to five lines of the payee's address in the Address field. You can copy the payee's name from the Pay to the Order of field into the Address field by pressing ["].

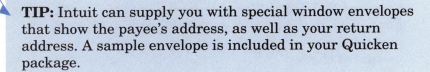

> **TIP:** Intuit can supply you with special window envelopes that show the payee's address, as well as your return address. A sample envelope is included in your Quicken package.

The Memo Field

Use the Memo field to include information that the payee may require, such as an account number for a bill payment. If you use Intuit window envelopes, the contents of the Memo field will appear in the window, so do not put any sensitive information (such as a credit card number) in the Memo field. Instead, you can tell Quicken to print an extra message line on the check (see Figure 6.4) by following these steps:

1. From the Main menu, select Set Preferences.
2. Select Checks & Reports Settings.
3. With the cursor on Option 1, Extra message line on check, type Y.
4. Press [Ctrl]-[↵Enter] to activate the option.

The Check Number Field

The Write Checks screen doesn't include a place to enter a check number because Quicken checks are prenumbered, as required by most banks. Quicken actually waits until the check is printed before adding the number to the check register. Until that time, the Check Number field in the register displays five asterisks (*****).

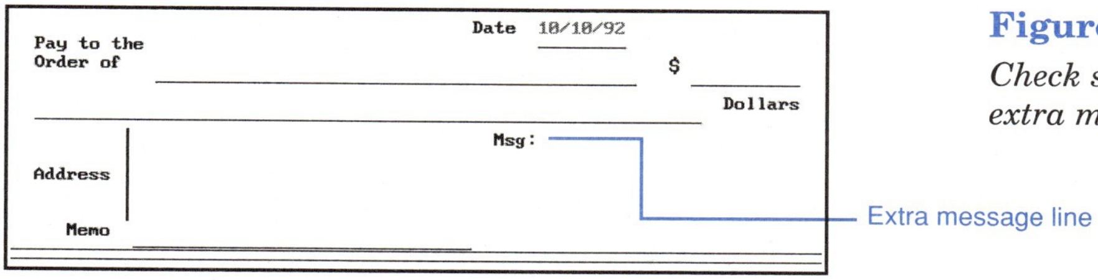

Figure 6.4
Check showing extra message line.

Writing a Check

Writing a check in Quicken is as simple as filling in the fields. As an example, select the BOOKSHOP account file and enter the following transaction information in the checking account using the Quick Steps that follow:

Date	Today
Amount	$2,120.10
Payee	Bestsellers Publishing
Address	123 5th Avenue New York, N.Y. 10019
Memo	Acct. # 12-3456
Category	Pub Purch

Quick Steps

Writing a Check

1. Display the Write Checks screen. The Write Checks screen appears with the current date displayed.

continues

continued

2. To change the date, press Shift-Tab or click on the Date field, type the date you want, and press Enter or click on the Pay to the Order of field.

3. Type the name of the person or company that the check is to be made out to. Press Enter or click on the $ field.

    The cursor moves to the $ field.

4. Type the check amount without the dollar sign. Press Enter or click on the Address field.

    Quicken writes out the amount in the Dollars field and moves the cursor to the Address field.

5. (Optional) Type the payee's address, and then press Enter or click on the next line.

    When you press Enter on the last address line, the cursor moves to the Memo field.

6. (Optional) Type a memo to appear on the check, and then press Enter or click on the Category field.

    The cursor moves to the Category field.

7. Type or select a category or class for the check, but do not press Enter.

    Figure 6.5 shows the completed check before it has been recorded.

8. Pull down the Edit menu and select Record Transaction, or press Ctrl-Enter.

    Quicken enters the check in the check register and displays a blank check. The Checks to Print information is updated.

9. Repeat steps 2 through 8 to write another check.

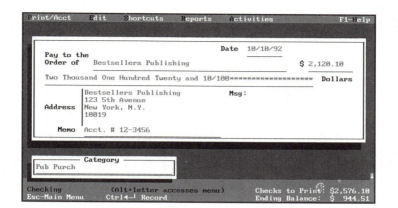

Figure 6.5

The completed check before it is recorded.

If you followed the sample transaction, press Ctrl-R to display the check register. Notice how the check appears in the register with all the information you entered (see Figure 6.6). Press Ctrl-W to return to the Write Checks screen.

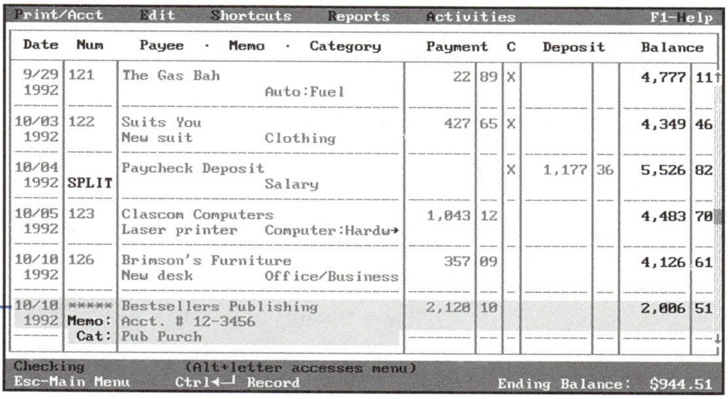

Figure 6.6

Quicken records the check in the register automatically.

Completed check transaction

TIP: With Quicken's QuickFill feature, you can enter a category by typing the first few letters of the category name in the Category field. For more about QuickFill, see Chapter 7.

Reviewing Your Checks

Quicken keeps all the checks that are waiting to be printed in a *stack* that you can browse through. The stack is sorted by check date, and there is always a blank check at the top of the stack. Table 6.1 lists the keys you can use to review these checks.

Table 6.1
Special Keys Used in the Write Checks Screen

Key	Effect
PgUp	Moves to the preceding check.
PgDn	Moves to the next check.
Ctrl-Home	Moves to the first check.
Ctrl-Esc	Moves to the last check.

Editing Checks

Until you print a check, you're free to change any of the entries in the Write Checks screen. Table 6.2 lists keys you can use to move around on the check and edit it.

Table 6.2
The Write Checks Screen Editing Keys

Key	Effect
Ctrl-→	Moves to the right one word.
Ctrl-←	Moves to the left one word.
Home	Moves to the first character in the field.
Esc	Moves to the right of the last character in the field.
Ctrl-Backspace	Erases the field.
Home, Home	Moves to the Date field.
Esc, Esc	Moves to the Category field.

The following Quick Steps show you how to edit a check.

Editing a Check

1. Display the Write Checks screen.

2. Select the check you want to edit.

3. Move to the field you want to edit and make your changes.

4. To record your changes, pull down the Edit menu and select Record Transaction, or press Ctrl-↵Enter.

Quicken changes the entry in the check register and displays the next check in the stack. If you change the amount, the Checks to Print information is updated.

Deleting a Check

You may find it necessary to delete a check that you haven't printed yet. (Unprinted checks have no number assigned to them, so they can be deleted. If you have printed the check, you should *void* it instead; see the next section, "Voiding a Check.") The following Quick Steps describe how to delete a check.

Once you've deleted a check, there's no way to restore it. Be sure you want to delete a check before doing so.

Deleting a Check

1. Display the Write Checks screen.

2. Select the check you want to delete.

3. Select **Delete Transaction** from the **Edit** menu, or press `Ctrl`-`D`.

   Quicken displays a message box asking you to confirm that you want to delete the check.

4. Press `Enter` to delete the check or press `Esc` to cancel the deletion.

   Quicken removes the check from the register, beeps, and displays the next check in the stack.

Voiding a Check

After you have printed a check, it is better to void it than delete it. There are several cases where you'll need to void a check:

- You stop payment on a check.
- You make an error on a check and discard it.
- You lose a check.
- A check is returned to you uncashed.

By voiding the check in these cases, you maintain a complete record of all your numbered checks. The following Quick Steps describe how to void a check.

> **CAUTION**
> Once you've voided a check, there's no way to restore it. Be sure you want to void a check before doing so.

Writing and Printing Checks **127**

> ## QUICK STEPS
>
> **Voiding a Check**
>
> 1. Display the check register or Write Checks screen.
>
> 2. Select the check you want to void.
>
> 3. Select **V**oid Transaction from the **E**dit menu or press `Ctrl`-`V`.
>
>   Quicken switches to the Register screen and displays a message box asking you to confirm that you want to void the check.
>
> 4. Press `↵Enter` to void the transaction or press `Esc` to cancel.
>
>   If you void the entry, Quicken appends VOID: to the payee name, removes the amount, and then marks the transaction as cleared.
>
> 5. To record the void, pull down the **E**dit menu and select **R**ecord Transaction, or press `Ctrl`-`↵Enter`.
>
>   Quicken flashes a RECORDING message in the lower left corner of the screen, recalculates the balance, and then beeps.

Setting Up Your Printer

This section will teach you how to set up your printer to use it with Quicken and how to position checks properly in the printer. You'll have to order your checks from Intuit, but for now you can use the sample checks that came with the program or use regular paper.

When you installed Quicken, the installation program asked you to select a printer. The specific printer settings, such as the printer port and the character style, were set to default values. You may want to change some of these settings (or even the printer itself) for printing checks. Most of the time, the settings assigned by Quicken are fine. If you want to check or change the settings, follow these steps:

1. From the Write Checks screen, pull down the Print/Acct menu and select Change Printer Styles. Or, from the Main menu, select Set Preferences and choose Printer Settings.

2. Select Settings for Printing Checks. Quicken displays a list of available styles for your printer (see Figure 6.7).

3. To select a different printer, press Esc, choose a printer from the list, and press Enter. If you don't see your printer listed, try using one of the generic printers such as <Other Dot-Matrix>.

4. Highlight the style you want and press Enter. Quicken displays the Check Printer Settings window, as shown in Figure 6.8.

5. If necessary, make any changes to the printer settings. When you finish, press Ctrl-Enter.

TIP: For more information about any of the settings listed, tab to the setting and press F1.

Getting Ready to Print

Before you can print any actual Quicken checks, you should print some samples to make sure the text aligns properly on the check. If you haven't done so already, create a few dummy checks in the Write Checks screen for testing purposes.

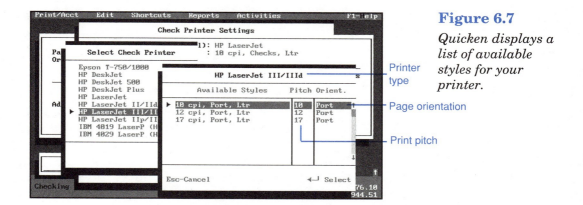

Figure 6.7
Quicken displays a list of available styles for your printer.

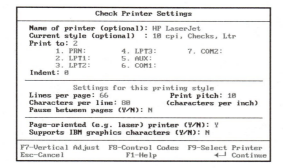

Figure 6.8
The Check Printer Settings window.

Setting Vertical Alignment on a Daisywheel or Dot-Matrix Printer

To understand how Quicken sets the alignment of your checks, take a look at one of the checks that came with the Quicken package. Notice the numbers printed on the tear-away strips on either side of the check. Now look at the sample check in Figure 6.9. Look at the pointer line that Quicken prints. On a perfectly aligned check, the pointer line will point to number 26. When you print the sample check, if the pointer line points to a different number, just tell Quicken the number and it adjusts the alignment automatically.

Figure 6.9

A sample check showing the pointer line.

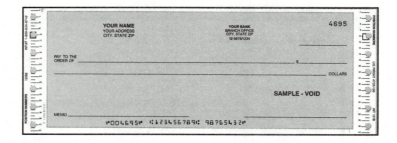

To begin, load the checks in your printer the same way you would any continuous-form paper. Make sure your printer is turned on and that it is on-line. To print the sample check, follow these steps:

1. From the Write Checks screen, select **Print Checks** from the **Print/Acct** menu or press Ctrl-P. The Print Checks window appears.

2. Press F9. Quicken displays a message telling you that you're about to print a sample check.

3. Press Enter. Quicken prints the check and displays the Type Position Number window, as shown in Figure 6.10.

4. Without moving the check, look for the pointer line printed on the check and note the number that it points to (this is called the *position number*).

5. If the position number is 26, your checks are aligned properly and you can press Enter to return to the Print Checks window. Otherwise, type the position number in the window and press Enter.

6. Quicken prints another check and redisplays the Type Position Number window. The position number should be closer to 26 this time. If it's right on 26, press Enter. Otherwise, repeat the process until the alignment is correct.

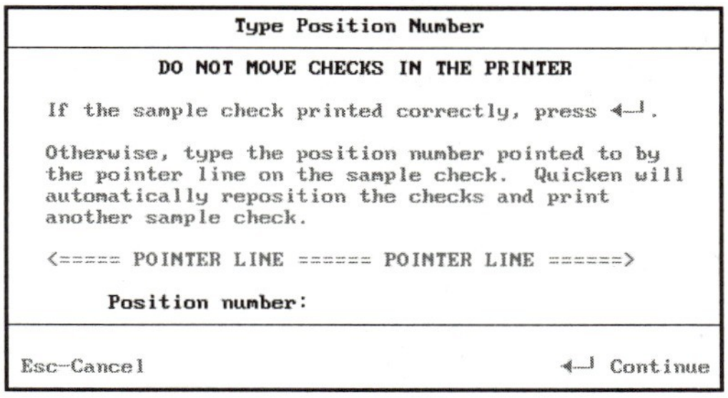

Figure 6.10
The Type Position Number window.

Setting Vertical Alignment on a Laser Printer

If you use a laser printer, Quicken automatically aligns your checks. After printing the checks, however, Quicken lets you fine-tune the vertical alignment of text on the check. To use this feature, print the checks as explained later in this chapter. When Quicken is done printing the checks, it displays the Did Checks Print OK? window. Wait until the checks are done coming out of the printer, and then examine the text to see if it is properly aligned on the page. If the text is too high or too low, perform the following steps:

> **NOTE:** If the vertical alignment of your laser-printed checks is off by a little, but not enough to warrant reprinting the checks, don't adjust vertical alignment now. Wait until you print your next batch of checks, then, when Quicken prompts you to enter a check number to start with, press F7 and enter your adjustment, as shown in Figure 6.11.

1. Once the checks are done printing, press `F7` to display the Vertical Check Alignment window, shown in Figure 6.11.

2. Enter the number of half lines up or down that the text needs to be adjusted. For example, if the text is one line too high, enter `2` to have the text moved one full line. Enter the adjustment in the Partial Page Adj field, if you printed a partial page of checks or in the Full Page Adj if you printed a full page.

3. Type `H` or `L` in the Higher/Lower field to specify the direction of the adjustment.

4. Press `Enter` to save your settings. Quicken returns you to the Did Checks Print OK? screen.

5. Type the number of the first incorrectly printed check, and press `Enter`. You are returned to the Print Checks screen.

6. To reprint the checks, press `Enter`.

7. Type the check number you want to start with.

8. If you have unprinted checks on the page, press `F9`, specify the number of unprinted checks on the page, and press `Ctrl`-`Enter`.

9. Press `Enter` to start printing.

Figure 6.11

The Vertical Check Adjustment window lets you adjust the vertical alignment for a laser printer.

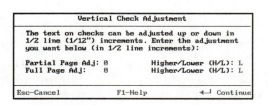

TIP: To prevent the sample checks from jamming, put at least 25 sheets of regular paper underneath the checks in the paper tray. This provides a cushion for the slippery check stock. Also, try to flatten out the creases as much as possible before using the sample checks.

Setting Horizontal Alignment

If you print a sample check, and the text appears too far to the left or right on the check, you can fix the problem by changing the Indent setting in the Check Printer Settings window. See "Setting Up Your Printer" earlier in this chapter for instructions on how to display this window. With the Check Printer Settings window displayed, tab to the Indent field, type the number of spaces you want to indent, and press Ctrl-Enter.

If the setting is 0 and the text is indented too far, you may have to move the feed mechanism on your printer to reduce the indent.

Printing Checks

You're now ready to start printing real checks. Quicken gives you a choice of printing all of the checks you've written or only selected ones. The following is a summary of the options you can set when printing checks:

Print to The printer to use when printing checks. The default is set to the Check Printer.

Print All/Selected checks The number of checks to print.

Print checks dated through The last date you want to print. This field appears only if you have postdated checks.

Type of checks to print on   The check format (standard, wallet, or voucher; continuous or laser).

Number of additional copies   The number of copies to print on a laser printer.

Forms Leader   Tells Quicken if you're using a Forms Leader to help print partial pages of checks on an inkjet printer.

For an example, print the Book City check for Bestsellers Publishing recorded earlier in this chapter. Follow these Quick Steps to print a check.

Printing a Check

1. From the Write Checks screen, pull down the **Print/Acct** menu and select **Print Checks**, or press Ctrl-P.

   Quicken displays the Print Checks window, as shown in Figure 6.12.

2. Select the printer you want to use and press Enter field.

   The cursor moves to the Print All/Selected checks

3. Type A to print all the available checks or type S to select specific checks to print. Press Enter.

   If you have postdated checks, the cursor moves to the Print checks dated through field.

4. If you have postdated checks, type the last date you want printed and press Enter.

   The cursor moves to the Type of checks to print on field.

5. Type the number corresponding to the type of checks you use and press Enter.

   The cursor moves to the Number of additional copies field.

6. If you use a laser printer, type the number of extra copies you want. Press `Enter`.

   The cursor moves to the Forms Leader field.

7. Type **Y** if you're using a Forms Leader with your inkjet printer.

8. Press `Ctrl`-`Enter`.

   If you choose to print selected checks, Quicken displays the Select Checks to Print window (see Figure 6.13).

9. Use the `Space bar` to tag the checks you want to print. To select all the checks, press `F9`.

   For each tagged check, Quicken displays the word `Print` in the right column.

10. When you're ready to continue, press `Enter`.

    Quicken displays the Enter Check Number window.

11. Type the check number of the first check to be printed and press `Enter`.

    Quicken prints the checks. Figure 6.14 shows the check for Bestsellers Publishing.

```
                    Print Checks
              There is 1 check to print.
Print to: 3
    1. Rpt-<Other Dot-Matri     3. Chk-Epson LQ
    2. Alt-<Other Dot-Matri

Print All/Selected checks (A/S): A
Type of checks to print on: 1
    1. Standard                 4. Laser Standard
    2. Wallet                   5. Laser Voucher
    3. Voucher                  6. Laser Wallet
Number of additional copies (Laser only): 0
Forms Leader (Inkjets only) (Y/N): N

To print a sample check to help with alignment, press F9.
              F9-Print Sample
Esc-Cancel    F1-Help                    Ctrl⏎ Print
```

Figure 6.12
The Print Checks window.

Figure 6.13
The Select Checks to Print window.

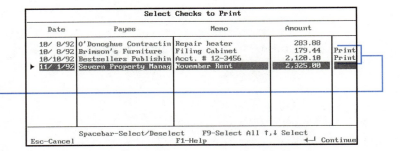

Checks tagged for printing

Figure 6.14
The printed check.

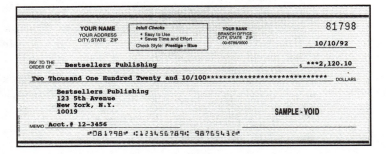

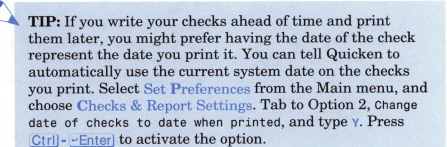

TIP: If you write your checks ahead of time and print them later, you might prefer having the date of the check represent the date you print it. You can tell Quicken to automatically use the current system date on the checks you print. Select Set Preferences from the Main menu, and choose Checks & Report Settings. Tab to Option 2, Change date of checks to date when printed, and type Y. Press Ctrl-↵Enter to activate the option.

Fixing Printing Problems

When Quicken finishes printing your checks, it asks you if your checks printed properly (see Figure 6.15). Take a moment to look at your printed checks. If you don't see any problems, press ↵Enter. Otherwise, type the number of the first check that printed incorrectly and press ⏎Enter. Quicken returns you to the Print Checks window. Make any required adjustments and then repeat the steps outlined in the preceding section to reprint the check.

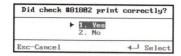

Figure 6.15
Quicken asks if your check printed properly.

Earlier in this chapter, you learned how to set the vertical alignment of your checks. You may also need to adjust the horizontal alignment, the print pitch, or other printing parameters. Table 6.3 lists a few of the most common problems and solutions.

Symptom	Remedy
Printer doesn't print	Check the printer connection. Make sure the printer is on-line.
Check is blank	Check the printer ribbon or cartridge.
Prints too far to the left	For a continuous-form printer, slide the checks to the left. For a laser printer, increase the indent setting.
Prints too far to the right	For a continuous-form printer, slide the checks to the right. For a laser printer, decrease the indent setting.
Prints over the right or left sides	Reduce print pitch setting.
Prints properly on the left, but doesn't reach the right side setting.	Increase print pitch

Table 6.3
Common Printing Problems and Solutions

In This Chapter

Splitting Transactions

Saving Time with Memorized Transactions

Automating Entries with QuickFill

Splitting a Transaction

1. Highlight the transaction you want to split (or start with a blank transaction).
2. Select Split Transaction from the Edit menu.
3. Type a category name in the first Category field, and press ↵Enter.
4. Type a description of the item, if desired, and press ↵Enter.
5. Type the amount for this item, and press ↵Enter.
6. Repeat steps 3 through 5 to enter more categories (up to 30) until the entire check amount is accounted for.
7. Press Ctrl-↵Enter.

Memorizing a Transaction

1. Enter the transaction information that you want to memorize.
2. Select Memorize Transaction from the Shortcuts menu.
3. Check to make sure the highlighted information is correct and then press ↵Enter.
4. Complete and record the transaction as you normally would.

Recalling a Memorized Transaction

1. Move to a blank transaction in the register.
2. Select Recall transaction from the Shortcuts menu.
3. Highlight the transaction you want to recall and press ↵Enter.
4. Fill in the rest of the fields as needed and record the transaction.

Using QuickFill

1. Tab to the Payee or Category field.
2. Start typing the name of the payee or category until Quicken inserts the name you want to use.
3. Press Tab⇥ or ↵Enter.

Chapter 7

Splitting, Memorizing, and Automating Transactions

In the last two chapters, you learned the basics of entering transactions using both the account registers and the Write Checks screen. In this chapter, you will expand your understanding of transactions to include some of the more advanced features, which are designed to give you even more control over your finances and to make working with Quicken faster and easier.

Chapter 7

Splitting Transactions

Sometimes a single category cannot cover all the aspects of a transaction. For example, say you write a check to a department store that covers clothes, automotive supplies, and home furnishings. You don't want to assign the entire amount of the check to a single category.

To handle such transactions, Quicken lets you split a single transaction among up to 30 different categories (or classes). In effect, you define a list of categories to apply to the transaction, each of which is assigned a dollar amount from the total. This total still appears in the register, but the categories exist behind the scenes. Follow these Quick Steps to split a transaction.

Splitting a Transaction

1. Highlight the transaction you want to split (or start with a blank transaction).

2. Select **Split Transaction** from the **Edit** menu or press Ctrl-S.

   Quicken displays the Split Transaction window, as shown in Figure 7.1.

3. Type a category name in the first Category field, and then press Enter.

   The cursor moves to the Memo field.

4. Type a description of the item, if desired, and press Enter.

   The cursor moves to the Amount field.

5. Type the amount for this item, and press Enter.

   The cursor moves to the next line, and the remaining amount that has not been assigned to a category appears on this line (see Figure 7.1).

Splitting, Memorizing, and Automating Transactions   141

> 6. Repeat steps 3 through 5 to enter more categories (up to 30) until the entire check amount is accounted.
>
>   Each time you press `Tab` after entering an amount Quicken updates the Amount field.
>
> 7. Press `Ctrl`-`↵Enter`.
>
>   Quicken returns you to the register or Write Checks screen.

```
                    Split Transaction
         Category               Memo              Amount
1:Computer:Software         Computer game          42.75
2:Computer:Hardware/Business Disks                 75.95
3:                                                -125.05
4:
5:
6:
```
                                    ↑
              Amount not yet split into a category

Figure 7.1
The Split Transaction window.

Although in most cases you'll want to enter a dollar amount for each transaction split, there are times when allocating a split using a percentage makes sense. For example, say you want to set aside 5% of your earnings to purchase IRAs. To use percentages, enter a percent, rather than a dollar amount, in the Amount field, for example, type **5%**.

When you return to the Write Checks screen, Quicken fills the Category field with the first category in the split and displays the word SPLIT to let you know that there are other categories associated with the transaction (see Figure 7.2).

> **TIP:** When entering transaction splits, you can copy some or all of the information from the previous split. Position the cursor on the field you want to copy the information into and press `"`. In the Category field, press `"` once to copy the main category, twice for the first subcategory, and so on. You can copy classes, subclasses, and memos in the same way.

Figure 7.2
The split transaction.

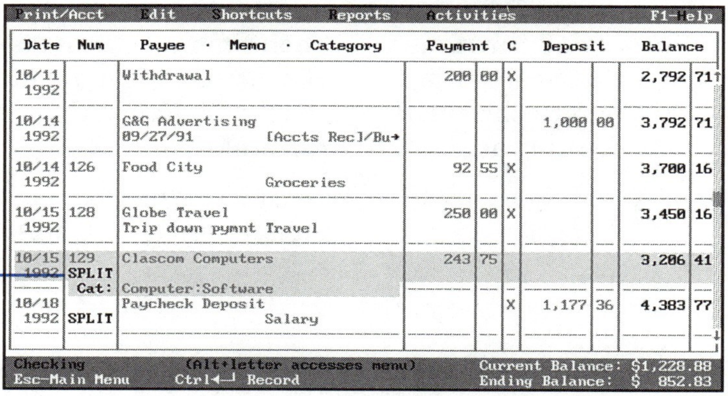

SPLIT indicates split transaction.

Date	Num	Payee · Memo · Category	Payment	C	Deposit	Balance
10/11 1992		Withdrawal	200 00	X		2,792 71
10/14 1992		G&G Advertising 09/27/91 [Accts Rec]/Bu→			1,000 00	3,792 71
10/14 1992	126	Food City Groceries	92 55	X		3,700 16
10/15 1992	128	Globe Travel Trip down pymnt Travel	250 00	X		3,450 16
10/15 1992 SPLIT Cat:	129	Clascom Computers Computer:Software	243 75			3,206 41
10/18 1992 SPLIT		Paycheck Deposit Salary		X	1,177 36	4,383 77

Checking (Alt+letter accesses menu) Current Balance: $1,228.88
Esc-Main Menu Ctrl↵ Record Ending Balance: $ 852.83

Getting a Jump on Taxes

If you don't want to wait for your W-2 forms to find out how much you actually paid in taxes, keep your own records by splitting your salary deposit, as shown in Figure 7.3. Enter the gross salary followed by the taxes and other deductions (notice that deductions are entered with a minus sign). When you are ready to do your taxes, generate a tax report, as explained in Chapter 13, to have Quicken determine the total state, federal, and local income taxes you've paid. This also provides a way for you to double-check the figures on your W-2's.

FYI IDEAS

Figure 7.3
An income transaction showing deduction splits.

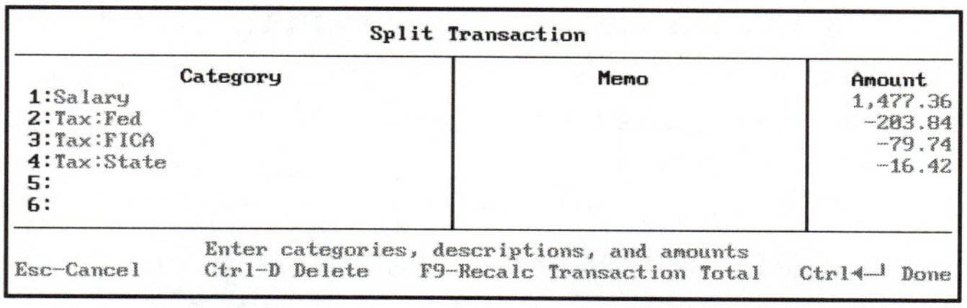

	Split Transaction		
	Category	Memo	Amount
1:	Salary		1,477.36
2:	Tax:Fed		−203.84
3:	Tax:FICA		−79.74
4:	Tax:State		−16.42
5:			
6:			

Enter categories, descriptions, and amounts
Esc-Cancel Ctrl-D Delete F9-Recalc Transaction Total Ctrl↵ Done

NOTE: You can use either minus key on your keyboard, and you can enter the minus before or after entering the number for expense items that reduce a deposit.

Editing a Split Transaction

If you make a mistake recording a split transaction, or if your categories change and you want to split a transaction further, you can easily edit the split. Follow these steps to edit a split transaction:

1. Highlight the transaction you want to edit.
2. Press Ctrl-S to display the Split Transaction window.
3. Make your changes to the Split Transaction fields.
4. Press Ctrl-Enter to save the split.

Deleting Transaction Splits

If you no longer want to track some or all of the splits in a transaction, you can delete them. Follow these steps to delete splits from a transaction:

1. Highlight the transaction whose splits you want to delete.
2. Press Ctrl-S to display the Split Transaction window.
3. Place the cursor on the line you want to delete and press Ctrl-D or click on Delete. Quicken removes the line from the window.
4. Press Ctrl-Enter to save the change and return to the register.

Memorizing Transactions

One of the first things most people notice when they start working with Quicken is how repetitive many of the entries are. You record your paychecks every couple of weeks, and the utility, phone, and car loan payments come up like clockwork every month. When you start using categories, classes, and split transactions extensively, these repetitive entries become time-consuming as well.

Quicken provides you with a shortcut to reduce the time you spend recording these kinds of entries: *memorized transactions*. With memorized transactions, Quicken stores some or all of the details of the transaction (for example, the payee, the category, and the amount—but not the date). You can recall these transactions with just a few keystrokes.

Bills are the most common candidates for memorization because many bills are the same from month to month. Other items you should consider memorizing are mortgage payments, car loan payments, account withdrawals, salaries, and credit card installments. You can memorize transactions from any account register and from the Write Checks screen.

Memorizing a Transaction

Quicken can memorize all or part of a transaction from any account register or Write Checks screen. A check to pay a utility bill, where the amount changes every month, is a good example of a transaction you'd memorize only part of. To see how this works, memorize the following utility payment:

Payee	Port Hope Hydro
Address	P.O. Box 1234\
	Port Hope, N.Y. 10001
Memo	Account # 1234567-89
Category	Utilities:Gas & Electric

Follow these Quick Steps to memorize the transaction.

Splitting, Memorizing, and Automating Transactions — 145

QUICK STEPS

Memorizing a Transaction

1. Enter the transaction information that you want to memorize.

2. Select **M**emorize Transaction from the **S**hortcuts menu or press `Ctrl`-`M`.

   Quicken highlights the filled-in fields (except the date) and displays a message, as shown in Figure 7.4.

3. Check to make sure the highlighted information is correct and then press `↵Enter` or click on Memorize.

   Quicken memorizes the transaction and returns you to the register or Write Checks screen.

4. Finish the check and record the transaction as you normally would.

Quicken stores all memorized transactions together, regardless of the account you're using. This lets you share memorized transactions between accounts—you can share a memorize transaction between your checking account and your credit card account, for example.

You don't need to be in the process of entering a transaction to memorize one. You can memorize transactions that have already been recorded simply by highlighting the transaction in the register and pressing `Ctrl`-`M`. Of course, all the transaction information will be memorized because the transaction is complete.

Figure 7.4
The highlighted information is about to be memorized.

Transaction information about to be memorized

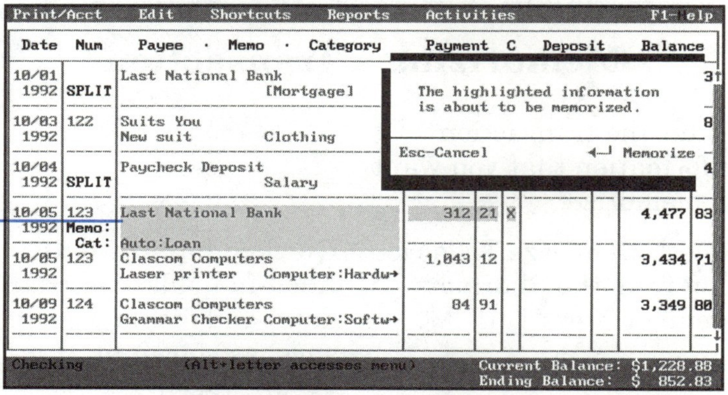

> **TIP:** You can create memorized transactions without entering an actual transaction. To do so, press Ctrl-T, select <New Transaction> and enter the necessary information in the Edit/Set Up Memorized Transaction window.

Recalling Memorized Transactions

Once you've memorized a transaction, you're free to recall it at any time. Follow these Quick Steps to recall a memorized transaction.

Recalling a Memorized Transaction

1. Move to a blank transaction in the register.

2. Select **R**ecall transaction from the **S**hortcuts menu or press Ctrl-T.

   Quicken displays the Memorized Transaction List, as shown in Figure 7.5.

3. Highlight the transaction you want to recall and press `Enter` or click on Use. Quicken returns to the register and enters the memorized data.

4. Fill in the rest of the fields as needed and record the transaction.

Memorizing Split Transactions

When you memorize a split transaction, Quicken gives you the option of memorizing the split amounts or percentages. If you memorize the split amounts, you use the transaction like any other memorized item. However, if you elect to memorize the percentages, the way you recall the transaction is different. Follow these steps to recall a memorized transaction with percentage splits:

1. Select **Recall Transaction** from the **Shortcuts** menu or press `Ctrl`-`T`. Quicken displays the Memorized Transaction List. Percentage split transactions show a percentage in the Amount field.

2. Highlight the transaction you want to recall and press `Enter` or click on Use. Quicken displays the Recall Split Percentage window, as shown in Figure 7.6.

3. Enter the transaction amount that you want divided among the splits and press `Enter`. Quicken returns to the register and enters the memorized data.

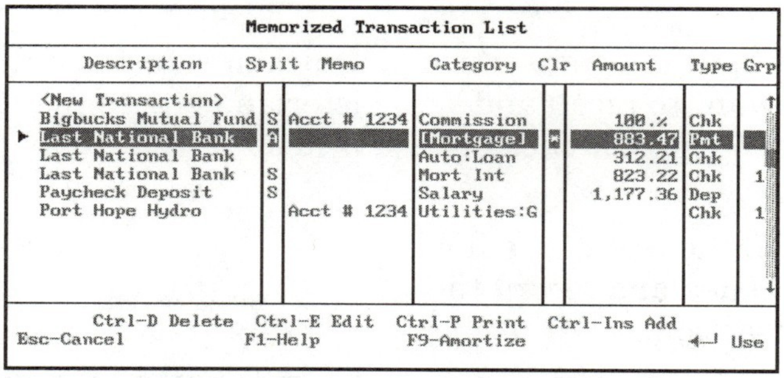

Figure 7.5
The Memorized Transaction List.

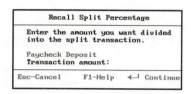

Figure 7.6
The Recall Split Percentage window.

Editing Memorized Transactions

You can edit your memorized transactions by following these Quick Steps.

Editing a Memorized Transaction

1. Select **R**ecall Transaction from the **S**hortcuts menu or press Ctrl-T.

   Quicken displays the Memorized Transaction List.

2. Highlight the transaction you want to edit and press press Ctrl-Esc or click on Edit.

   The Edit/Setup Memorized Transaction window appears, as shown in Figure 7.7.

3. Make your changes to the appropriate fields.

Splitting, Memorizing, and Automating Transactions

4. (Optional) To split the memorized transaction, press Ctrl-S and enter the splits in the Split Transaction window. Press Ctrl-Enter or click on Done when you finish.

5. (Optional) Press F8 or click on Address to edit the address and message of a check. Press Ctrl-Enter or click on Continue when you finish.

   When you press F8, the Memorized Transaction Address window appears.

6. (Optional) To change the payment type, press F9 or click on Type. Select the type and press Enter or click on Continue.

   When you press F9, Quicken displays the Select Memorized Payment Type window.

7. When you finish, press Ctrl-Enter or click on Continue.

   If you edit a split transaction, Quicken asks if you want to memorize the split amounts or percentages. Make your choice and press Enter. Quicken records the changes and returns you to the Memorized Transaction List.

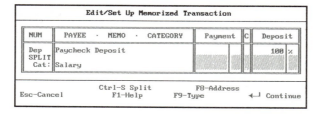

Figure 7.7

The Edit/Setup Memorized Transaction window.

Deleting Memorized Transactions

You can delete from the Memorized Transaction List those items you no longer need. Quicken stores memorized transactions in memory, so the more you have, the less memory Quicken has to work with. Follow these steps to delete a memorized transaction:

1. Select **R**ecall Transaction from the **S**hortcuts menu or press [Ctrl]-[T]. Quicken displays the Memorized Transaction List.

2. Highlight the transaction you want to delete and press [Ctrl]-[D] or click on Delete. A message appears warning you that you're about to delete a memorized transaction.

3. Press [↵Enter] or click on Delete to delete the transaction. To cancel the deletion, press [Esc] or click on Cancel.

Using QuickFill to Automate Your Work

VERSION 6

New to Quicken 6 is a feature called QuickFill, which allows you to insert a field entry by typing only a few characters of the entry. For example, if you move to the category field and type **s**, Quicken automatically inserts Salary in the field. If you then type **u**, Quicken inserts the category that starts with Su: Subscriptions. You can also use [Ctrl]-[+] and [Ctrl]-[-] to insert the next or previous category into the field.

Table 7.1 shows the fields in which you can use the QuickFill feature and what information QuickFill inserts in each field.

Table 7.1
Fields in Which You Can Use QuickFill

Field name	Information that QuickFill Inserts
Payee	Payee names from memorized transactions and from the last three months in the register.
Category	Category and class names from the Category List and Class list.
Security	Items from the security list for investment accounts.
Action	Items from the action list for investment accounts.

Before you use QuickFill, make sure the feature is turned on. From the main menu, choose Set Preferences and then Transaction Settings. Make sure the Activate QuickFill Feature (option 8) is set to Y, and then press Ctrl-↵Enter.

Once the QuickFill feature is activated, using the feature is easy, as explained in the following Quick Steps.

Recalling a Transaction with QuickFill

1. Press Ctrl-I in the register window, or display a new check in the Write Checks window.

2. Tab to the Payee field and start typing the name of the person or company the transaction is for.

   As you type, Quicken searches the Memorized Transaction List and the last three months of the register and inserts the first Payee name that matches your entry.

3. Continue typing or press Ctrl-+ or Ctrl-- until the Payee name you are looking for appears.

continues

> *continued*
>
> **4.** Press `Tab` or `Enter`.   Quicken inserts the entire memorized transaction or the previous transaction that was entered for the specified Payee.
>
> **5.** Press `Ctrl`-`Enter` or `F10` to record the transaction.

The procedure for recalling category and class names is basically the same: you start typing the name of the category or class, and Quicken inserts the first name that matches your entry. However, keep in mind that you may have to specify a category and a subcategory or a category and a class. In such cases, perform the following steps:

1. Tab to the Category field.

2. Start typing the name of the category.

3. Keep typing until the desired category name is displayed, or use `Ctrl`-`+` or `Ctrl`-`-` to display the category name.

4. Press `End` to move to the end of the category name.

5. Type a colon (`:`) to separate a subcategory from a category, or type a forward slash (`/`) to separate a class from a category.

6. Start typing the name of the subcategory or class you want to insert.

7. Keep typing until the desired subcategory or class name is displayed, or use `Ctrl`-`+` or `Ctrl`-`-` to display the name.

8. Repeat steps 4 through 7 until you have entered all the necessary information in the Category field.

9. Press `Ctrl`-`Enter` to record the transaction.

Splitting, Memorizing, and Automating Transactions

In This Chapter

The Reconciliation Process

How Quicken Reconciles Accounts

Starting the Reconciliation

Marking Cleared Transactions

Looking for Errors

Adjusting for Unresolved Differences

Starting the Reconciliation Process

1. From the account register, pull down the Activities menu and select Reconcile.
2. Make sure the amount shown in the Bank Statement Opening Balance field matches the amount on the bank statement.
3. Enter the ending balance from the statement and press Enter.
4. If necessary, change the opening date for the bank statement and press Enter.
5. If necessary, change the ending date for the bank statement and press Enter.
6. If the bank statement includes a service charge, enter the amount in the Service Charge field.
7. If the bank statement shows that some interest was paid to your account, enter the amount in the Interest Earned field.
8. Press Ctrl-Enter or click on Continue when finished.

Marking a Cleared Transaction

1. Highlight an uncleared transaction that is listed on your bank statement.
2. If the uncleared transaction and bank statement amounts match, press the Space bar to mark it as cleared.

Completing the Reconciliation Process

1. From the Reconciliation Summary window, press Ctrl-F10 or click on Done.
2. Type Y and press Enter or click on Continue if you want to print out the reconciliation report.
3. To print the report, select the print destination, enter an optional title, and indicate whether you want the full or summary report.
4. Press Ctrl-Enter or click on Print.

Chapter 8

Reconciling Your Accounts

If you're like most people, balancing your checkbook is a task you perform reluctantly. It's a tedious job at best, but it's necessary if you want to protect your money and keep your financial affairs in order. Now that you have Quicken, however, you may find the task less tedious and less time-consuming. In this chapter, you will learn how to use Quicken's reconciliation feature to balance your checkbook and catch and correct any reconciliation errors.

The Reconciliation Process

When you reconcile an account, you're comparing your records of what happened in the account with what the bank thinks. Your version is supported by the account register where you record your transactions, while the bank's version is shown in the account statement that you receive at the end of every month.

The problem is that, by the time you get your bank statement, it is slightly out of date. You may have written some checks and made some deposits while the statement was in the mail. And the statement may include some information you haven't recorded, such as service charges and account interest. Reconciling involves taking these differences into account and looking for other discrepancies. The entire process can be broken down into five steps:

1. Look at your bank statement for any unusual entries such as check numbers that aren't part of your sequence or returned checks that aren't yours.

2. Mark all the items in your register that have a corresponding line in the bank statement. These are the *cleared* transactions. Note any discrepancies in the amounts of the transactions.

3. Subtract any service charges from your register and add in any interest the account earned.

4. Calculate the net dollar amount of the transactions that haven't cleared the bank. You must include the uncleared checks and deposits.

5. If the difference between the balance showing in your register and the balance on your bank statement equals the amount calculated in step 4, your account is reconciled. Otherwise, you have to repeat steps 1 through 4 to try to find the error.

Reconciling Your Account with Quicken

When you reconcile your accounts with Quicken, the whole process is faster and easier because Quicken automates each step. You can use the HOME checking account (created in Chapter 3) to practice reconciliation in the following sections.

Starting the Reconciliation

To complete the first stage of the reconciliation, have the following information handy:

Bank statement opening balance This is the amount Quicken thinks should be the opening balance on the bank statement. If this amount differs from the actual opening balance on your statement, use the statement's opening balance.

Bank statement ending balance The ending balance from your bank statement.

Statement opening date The beginning date from your bank statement.

Statement ending date The ending date from your bank statement.

Service charge Any service charges incurred during the month and the date they were charged.

Interest earned Any interest earned during the month and the date it was deposited to your account.

The following Quick Steps describe how to begin reconciling your account.

Starting the Account Reconciliation

1. From the account register, pull down the **Activities** menu and select **Reconcile**. Quicken displays the Reconcile Register with Bank Statement window, as shown in Figure 8.1. If a help screen appears, read it and press F10.

continues

continued

2. Check the amount shown in the Bank Statement Opening Balance field.

3. If the opening balance shown on your statement is the same, skip to step 4. Otherwise, press ⇧Shift-Tab⇆ or click on the Opening Balance field, enter the statement value, and press ↵Enter.

   The cursor moves to the Bank Statement Ending Balance field.

4. Enter the ending balance from the statement. Press ↵Enter or click on the Statement opening date field.

   The cursor moves to the Statement opening date field.

5. If necessary, change the opening date for the bank statement and press ↵Enter or click on the Statement ending date field.

   The cursor moves to the Statement ending date field.

6. If necessary, change the ending date for the bank statement and press ↵Enter or click on the Service Charge field.

   The cursor moves to the Service Charge field.

7. If the bank statement includes a service charge, enter the amount in the Service Charge field. (You can assign a category to the charge and change the date, if needed.)

   Press ↵Enter from the Date field to move the cursor to the Interest Earned field.

Reconciling Your Accounts   159

8. If the bank statement shows that some interest was paid to your account, enter the amount in the Interest Earned field.

9. Press Ctrl-Enter or click on Continue when finished. Quicken enters the service charge and interest earned (if any) in your register and displays the Reconciliation Summary screen, as shown in Figure 8.2.

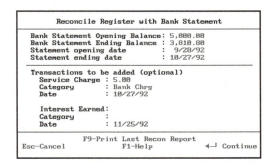

Figure 8.1
The Reconcile Register with Bank Statement window.

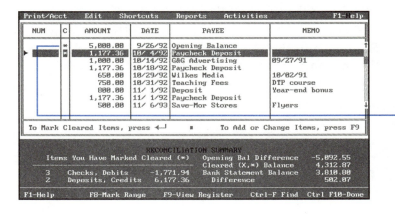

Figure 8.2
The Reconciliation Summary screen.

Marked items display an asterisk in this field.

Marking Cleared Transactions

You will use the Reconciliation Summary screen, shown in Figure 8.2, to mark all the transactions in the account register that have cleared the bank. The top half of the window displays, in check number order, a list of all the uncleared transactions in your register. The bottom half shows the progress of the clearing process. In particular, you should keep an eye on the following fields:

Opening Bal Difference If you *changed* the Bank Statement Opening Balance field in the Reconcile Register with Bank Statement window in the last section, the difference appears here. Otherwise, this field is not shown.

Cleared (X,*) Balance Shows the balance of cleared items in the register. The value you see when the Reconciliation Summary first appears includes the register balance as of the last cleared transaction and the service charge and interest earned (if any) that you entered in the last section. (Quicken enters these items as cleared.)

Bank Statement Balance The amount you entered in the Bank Statement Ending Balance field of the Reconcile Register with Bank Statement window.

Difference A comparison between the Cleared (X,*) Balance and the Bank Statement Balance. When you finish clearing transactions, this field should be zero.

The following Quick Steps describe how to mark the cleared transactions.

Marking Cleared Transactions

1. Highlight an uncleared transaction that is listed on your bank statement.

2. If the uncleared transaction and bank statement amounts match, press the [Space bar] or double-click on the transaction to mark it as cleared. If they don't match, see the section "Changing Uncleared Transactions."

   Quicken displays an asterisk (*) in the C (Cleared) field for the transactions you mark. To unmark a transaction, press [↵Enter] again.

3. Repeat steps 1 and 2 for all the transactions that appear on the bank statement.

   Each time you clear a transaction, Quicken updates the Reconciliation Summary.

TIP: Keep a pencil handy when reconciling, and each time you clear a transaction, place a check mark beside the item on the bank statement. This way you're less likely to miss any transactions. It also helps you identify items that appear on the statement but are missing from your register.

Marking a Range of Uncleared Transactions

If your bank statement contains an uninterrupted series of check numbers, you can mark the whole range as cleared by following these steps:

1. At the Reconciliation Summary window, press [F8] or click on Mark Range. The Mark Range of Check Numbers as Cleared window appears, as shown in Figure 8.3.

2. Enter the beginning and ending check numbers and press [↵Enter] or click on Continue. Quicken clears each check in the range you specify.

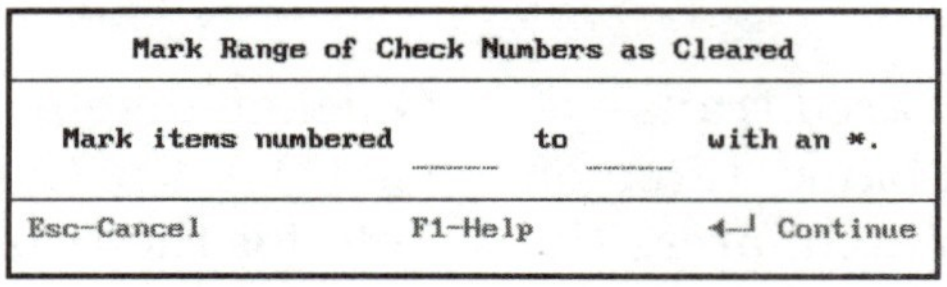

Figure 8.3

You can mark a range of check numbers.

Searching for Uncleared Transactions

If you have many uncleared transactions, Quicken can perform a transaction search by date, dollar amount, or check number. To search for a specific date, you must include the slashes (for example, `10/29/91`) so that Quicken knows you're using a date search. To search for a specific dollar amount, you must include the decimal point (for example, `123.45`). Follow these steps to search for an uncleared transaction:

1. At the Reconciliation Summary window, press Ctrl-F. Quicken displays the Find Item window, as shown in Figure 8.4.

2. Enter either a date, a dollar amount, or a check number.

3. Press Enter or click on Continue to begin the search. If you want to specify a direction, press Ctrl-N or click on Search Next to search forward in the list, or you can press Ctrl-B or click on Search Backward to search backwards.

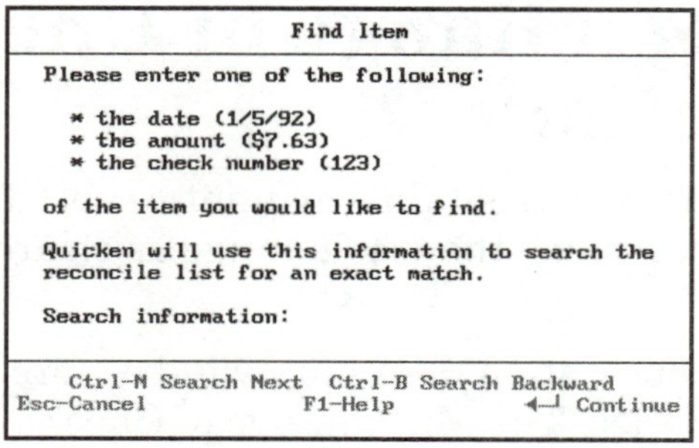

Figure 8.4

Use the Find Item window to search for transactions.

NOTE: When you enter the Reconciliation Summary, transactions are shown as a list. To display transactions in register format, press F9 or click on View Register. To return to the list format, press F9 again or click on View as List.

When Your Account Balances

Once you've marked all the items that have cleared the bank, the Difference field in the Reconciliation Summary should be zero. If it's not, you need to determine where the discrepancy comes from. (See the section "When Your Account Doesn't Balance" later in this chapter.) Otherwise, you've reconciled your account!

If your account balanced, you can exit the reconciliation screen and print a reconciliation report. This report is a summary of the cleared transactions and a listing of the remaining uncleared transactions in your register. You can print either a full report that shows all the transactions or a summary report that shows only the uncleared transactions. The following Quick Steps describe how to complete the reconciliation when your account balances.

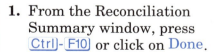

Completing a Reconciliation

1. From the Reconciliation Summary window, press Ctrl-F10 or click on Done. Quicken marks each of the cleared transactions with an X in the C (Cleared) field of the register. A window appears congratulating you on balancing your account (see Figure 8.5).

continues

continued

2. Type Y and press Enter or click on Continue if you want to print out the reconciliation report. Otherwise, just press Enter.

   If you choose to print the report, Quicken displays the Print Reconciliation Report window, as shown in Figure 8.6.

3. To print the report, select the print destination, enter an optional title, and indicate whether you want the full or summary report.

4. Press Ctrl-Enter or click on Print when you're done.

   Quicken prints the report.

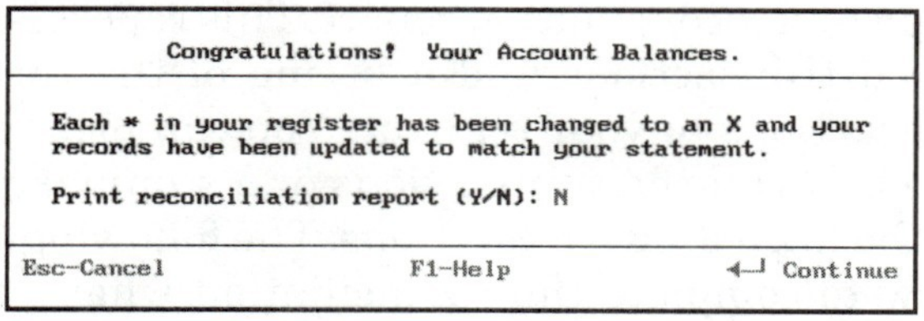

Figure 8.5
Quicken congratulates you when you balance your account.

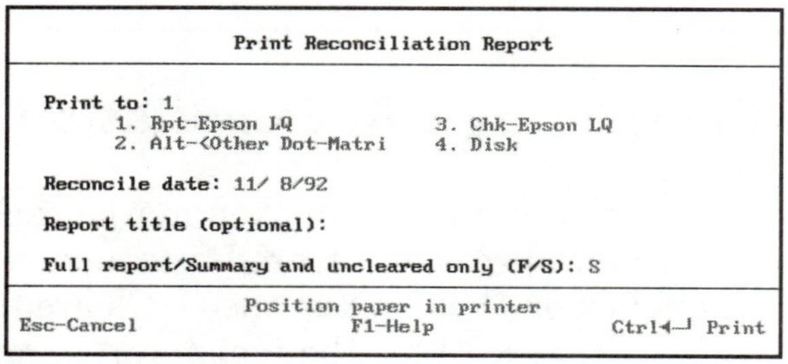

```
         Congratulations!  Your Account Balances.

  Each * in your register has been changed to an X and your
  records have been updated to match your statement.

  Print reconciliation report (Y/N): N

  Esc-Cancel              F1-Help              ↵ Continue
```

Figure 8.6
The Print Reconciliation Report window.

```
                   Print Reconciliation Report

  Print to: 1
        1. Rpt-Epson LQ              3. Chk-Epson LQ
        2. Alt-<Other Dot-Matri      4. Disk

  Reconcile date: 11/ 8/92

  Report title (optional):

  Full report/Summary and uncleared only (F/S): S

                   Position paper in printer
  Esc-Cancel              F1-Help              Ctrl↵ Print
```

When Your Account Doesn't Balance

If you're like most people, you may have an occasional problem balancing your account. You may have forgotten to record a transaction, or you may have entered a payment as a deposit. When you reconcile your account by hand, finding these errors is often an exercise in frustration. Now, with Quicken, you can use the Reconciliation Summary window to make things easier.

Ultimately, if your account doesn't balance, there are only two possible suspects:

- The total number of cleared transactions is wrong.
- The dollar amount of at least one cleared transaction is wrong.

The following steps outline a systematic approach to finding balancing errors using the Reconciliation Summary window.

> **NOTE:** In the following steps, *debit* items include payments, checks, withdrawals, service charges, and transfers from the account. *Credits* include deposits, interest earned, and transfers to the account.

1. Compare the number of debit items listed on your bank statement with the number of cleared items listed as `Checks, Debits` in the Reconciliation Summary (see Figure 8.7). If these numbers don't agree, try the following:

   If you have too many checks/debits on-screen, look for a debit that you mistakenly marked as cleared.

   If you have too few checks/debits on-screen, look for a debit that you missed marking as cleared or a debit that is listed on the bank statement but is missing from the register. If you find a missing transaction, see the section "Entering Missing Transactions."

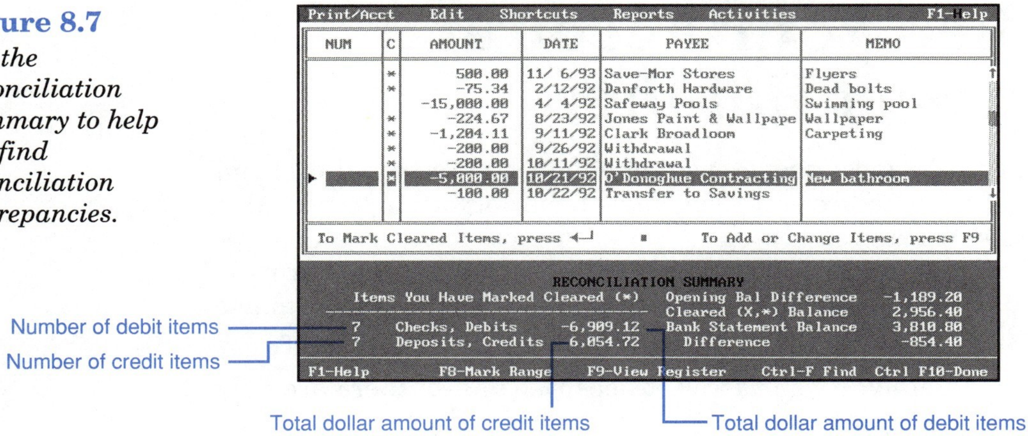

Figure 8.7
Use the Reconciliation Summary to help you find reconciliation discrepancies.

[Screenshot of reconciliation screen with callouts: "Number of debit items", "Number of credit items", "Total dollar amount of credit items", "Total dollar amount of debit items"]

2. Compare the number of credit items listed on your bank statement with the number of cleared items listed as Deposits, Credits in the Reconciliation Summary. If these numbers don't agree, try the following:

   If you have too few checks/debits on-screen, look for a credit that you missed marking as cleared or a credit that is listed on the bank statement but is missing from the register. If you find a missing credit, see the section "Entering Missing Transactions."

   If you have too many checks/debits on-screen, look for a credit that you mistakenly marked as cleared.

3. Compare the total dollar amount of the debit items listed on your bank statement with the total dollar amount of the cleared items listed as Checks, Debits in the Reconciliation Summary. If these don't agree, look for the following discrepancies and, if you find any, skip to the section "Changing Uncleared Transactions."

   If you have too much in debits on-screen, look for debits that are too large.

   If you have too little in debits on-screen, look for debits that are too small.

4. Compare the total dollar amount of the credit items listed on your bank statement with the total dollar amount of the cleared items listed as `Deposits, Credits` in the Reconciliation Summary. If these don't agree, look for the following discrepancies and, if you find any, skip to the section "Changing Uncleared Transactions."

If you have too little in credits on-screen, look for credits that are too small.

If you have too much in credits on-screen, look for credits that are too large.

> **TIP:** If the Reconciliation difference is a multiple of 9, you may have transposed two digits. For example, if you wrote a check for $86.50 and you entered it in the register as $68.50, you will have a reconciliation difference of $18.00, which is a multiple of 9.

When you get your difference down to zero, return to the section "When Your Account Balances" earlier in the chapter to complete the reconciliation. If you have a small difference that you just can't seem to find, go to the "Adjusting for Unresolved Differences" section later in this chapter.

Changing Uncleared Transactions

You might find a discrepancy in the amount of a transaction between your register and the bank statement. If you're sure the bank is wrong, contact your branch to have the error corrected, and adjust your register as discussed in the section "Adjusting for Unresolved Differences" later in this chapter. Most of the time, though, your register is wrong. To correct an uncleared transaction, follow these steps:

1. From the Reconciliation Summary window, press `F9` or click on View Register. Quicken switches to the register.

2. Make the correction to the transaction.

3. Press `Ctrl`-`Enter` or click on Record to record the transaction.

4. Press `F9` or click on View as List to return to the Reconciliation Summary screen.

Entering Missing Transactions

Occasionally, a transaction appears on your bank statement for which you have no record in your register. If you're sure the transaction is yours, you can enter it into the register by following these steps:

1. From the Reconciliation Summary window, press `F9` or click on View Register. Quicken switches to the register.

2. Press `Ctrl`-`I` to create an empty transaction.

3. Enter the missing transaction. Be sure to enter an asterisk (*) in the C (Cleared) field.

4. Press `Ctrl`-`Enter` or click on Done to record the transaction. The transaction is placed in the register according to the date you entered.

5. Press `F9` or click on View as List to return to the Reconciliation Summary screen. The new transaction appears on the list as cleared.

Adjusting for Unresolved Differences

Sometimes, despite all your efforts, a small difference remains between your register and the bank statement. You can choose to ignore this discrepancy by having Quicken enter an offsetting transaction in the register. This adjustment will bring your account into balance.

Reconciling Your Accounts 169

> **CAUTION**
>
> You should use Quicken's adjustment feature only as a last resort. If your account doesn't balance, it doesn't balance for a good reason: an error exists somewhere in the register. Making an adjustment only serves to add another error to your account (because the adjustment isn't an actual transaction).

Follow these steps to process an adjustment for an unresolved difference:

1. From the Reconciliation Summary screen, press Ctrl-F10 or click on Done. A window appears telling you about the problem and showing the difference amount (see Figure 8.8).

2. Press Enter or click on Continue to proceed with the adjustment. Quicken displays the Adding Balance Adjustment Entry window, as shown in Figure 8.9.

3. To record the adjustment, enter Y in the Add Balance Adjustment to register field and press Enter or click on the Category field.

4. Enter a category (optional) for the adjusting transaction and press Enter or click on Continue. A window appears telling that your register has been adjusted to agree with the bank statement.

5. To print a reconciliation report, type Y or click on the Print reconciliation report field until a Y appears, and press Enter. Otherwise, press Enter or click on Continue to return to the register.

Figure 8.8
Quicken summarizes the problem and the difference amount.

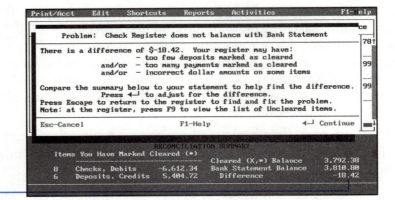

Difference amount

Figure 8.9
The Adding Balance Adjustment Entry window.

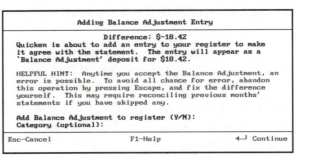

In This Chapter

Tracking Cash with a Cash Account

Maintaining a Credit Card Account

Monitoring Assets and Liabilities

Amortizing Loan Payments

Updating a Cash Balance

1. At the cash register, pull down the Activities menu and select Update Account Balance.
2. In the Update this account's balance to field, enter how much cash you currently have on hand, and press Enter.
3. Enter a category for the adjustment transaction, and press Enter.
4. Enter the date for the adjustment.
5. Press Ctrl-Enter or click on Continue to record the transaction.

Reconciling a Credit Card Account

1. At the credit card register, pull down the Activities menu and select Reconcile/Pay Credit Card.
2. Enter the requested information, and then press Ctrl-Enter or click on Continue.
3. Mark all cleared transactions.
4. Press Ctrl-F10 or click on Done.
5. Press Ctrl-C, and select the name of the account you want Quicken to use to pay the bill.
6. Press Tab or click on the Hand-written check field.
7. Type Y to have Quicken write a check for you or N to write your own check, and then press Enter.

Chapter 9

Your Finances with Other Quicken Accounts

Up to this point, we have been looking at the two most common Quicken accounts: savings and checking accounts. In this chapter, we take a look at some other common account types, including cash, credit card, other asset, and other liability. You will learn how to set up each of these accounts and what kinds of transactions you can enter into them. For general information about setting up accounts, see Chapter 3.

Recording Cash Transactions

In this age of credit cards, direct deposit paychecks, and electronic banking, cash transactions are easily forgotten. But cash isn't obsolete . . . yet. There are still plenty of people who use cash for major purchases or for such items as groceries. Depending on how you spend your cash and the level of detail you need, Quicken can track your cash transactions in two ways:

- Within a cash account.
- As transactions in another account.

In either case, Quicken helps you get a handle on where your cash is flowing.

Using a Cash Account

If you use cash for most of your transactions, or if you have a business and want to track petty cash expenditures, you should set up a cash account. The cash account enables you to assign categories and keep detailed records of your cash transactions.

To set up a cash account, follow the basic steps outlined in Chapter 3. When you enter the opening balance, use the amount of cash you have with you now.

To use your new cash account, select it from the Select Account to Use window. This register, shown in Figure 9.1, is almost identical to the check register, except for some of the column names.

You record cash transactions the same way you record checking account transactions. You can split and memorize your cash transactions, and you can transfer funds to and from other accounts.

Updating Your Cash Balance

Unless you're particularly thorough when entering your cash transactions, you probably won't record expenditures for such small items as newspapers, gum, and chocolate bars. You will find, however, that these small purchases add up, and after a while, your cash balance will be off by a few dollars. Every couple of weeks, you should have Quicken enter an adjustment to your account to update the balance. The following Quick Steps describe how to update your cash balance.

Your Finances with Other Quicken Accounts 175

Figure 9.1
The cash register.

Updating Your Cash Balance

1. At the cash register, pull down the **Activities** menu and select **Update Account Balance**.

   Quicken displays the Update Account Balance window, as shown in Figure 9.2.

2. In the Update this account's balance to field, enter how much cash you currently have on hand. Press ⏎Enter or click on the **Category for adjustment** field.

   The cursor moves to the Category for adjustment field.

3. (Optional) Enter a category for the adjustment transaction. Press ⏎Enter or click on the **Adjustment date** field.

   The cursor moves to the Adjustment date field.

4. Enter the date for the adjustment.

continues

continued

5. Press Ctrl-Enter or click on Continue to record the transaction.

The adjustment appears in the cash register, with Balance Adjustment in the Payee field. If necessary, you can split the transaction among several categories. (See Chapter 7 for instructions on how to split transactions.)

Figure 9.2
The Update Account Balance window.

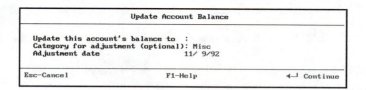

Accumulate small transactions

Some expenditures are small but occur regularly. A newspaper, for example, may cost you only 25 cents a day during the week and 50 cents on Saturday. If you need to monitor such an expense but can't be bothered to make daily entries, create a memorized transaction for a week's worth of papers. This way, you can recall the entry only once a week.

Tracking Cash in a Bank Account

If you don't have many cash transactions, track the cash from within your bank accounts. Set up a category called Misc. Cash and assign withdrawals and cash advances to this category. Then, whenever you have an important cash purchase, you can split the cash transaction and categorize the expenditure. You can also use this category when you deposit a check but keep some cash, as shown in Figure 9.3.

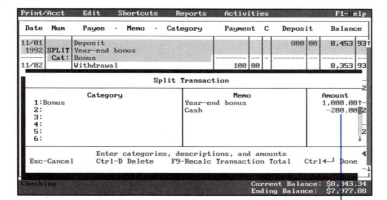

Figure 9.3

Recording a deposit, minus cash.

Cash taken is subtracted from deposit.

Recording Credit Card Transactions

Quicken helps you track your credit card expenditures. Not only can you properly categorize your credit card transactions, but you can monitor credit card interest charges and service fees. This way you can see how much you are *really* paying for the convenience of putting it on plastic.

Should You Create a Separate Credit Card Account?

Tracking your credit card expenditures with Quicken doesn't necessarily mean setting up a separate credit card account. In some cases, you might be better off using your checking account.

The method you use depends on such things as your bill-paying habits, the level of detail you want in your record keeping, and the number of cards you have.

You should set up a credit card account if

- You pay your balance over time.
- You want detailed records of credit card transactions.
- You want to track your current credit card balance.
- You have a Quicken IntelliCharge electronic charge account.

You should not set up a credit card account if

- You pay your balance in full each month.
- You don't use your credit card very often.

Setting Up a Credit Card Account

Setting up a credit card account is similar to setting up other accounts, except that you should enter your card's credit limit in each credit card account you set up. Follow these steps to enter a credit limit for your credit card:

1. Follow the instructions outlined in Chapter 3 for setting up an account. When entering an opening balance, use the balance owed from your last monthly statement. If you have an IntelliCharge account, be sure to specify this in the Starting Balance and Description window. When you finish, Quicken displays the Specify Credit Limit window.

2. Enter your card's credit limit (optional) and press ⏎Enter or click on Continue. The new account appears on the Select Account to Use window.

To use the new account, choose it from the Select Account to Use window. This register, shown in Figure 9.4, is almost identical to the check register, except for some of the column names.

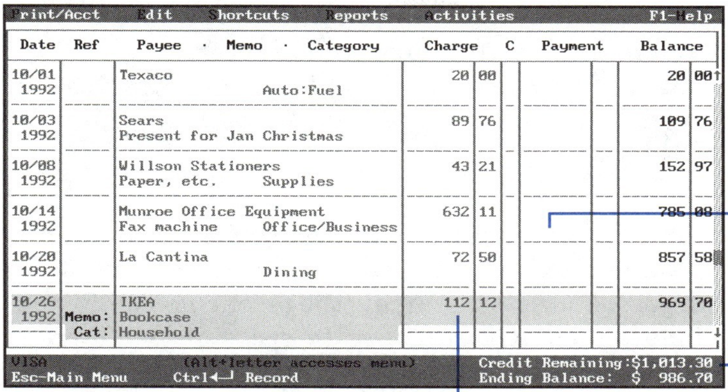

Figure 9.4
The credit card register.

Payments and credits are entered in this column.

If you entered your credit card limit, Quicken shows the credit remaining.

Charges and interest are entered in this column.

You work with the credit card register the same way you work with the check register. Credit card transactions can be split and memorized in the usual way. You can also transfer funds to and from other Quicken accounts. You can either enter your credit card transactions as you incur them or wait until you receive your monthly statement.

Reconciling Your Credit Card Accounts

As with your checking account, you should reconcile your credit card account every time you get your monthly statement. Credit card numbers are stolen all the time, so make sure your records agree with those of the credit card company. This is the best way to guard against fraud.

To make the reconciliation process easy, Quicken provides the following features:

- Automatically records any interest charges you incur.
- Creates an adjusting entry to account for the small purchases you choose to ignore.
- Writes a check to pay some or all of your bills.

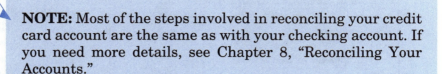

NOTE: Most of the steps involved in reconciling your credit card account are the same as with your checking account. If you need more details, see Chapter 8, "Reconciling Your Accounts."

If you record your credit card charges as they occur, you are ready to reconcile. If you use your monthly statement to record your charges, do so before starting the reconciliation. When you're ready, follow these Quick Steps to reconcile your credit card accounts.

Reconciling a Credit Card Account

1. At the credit card register, pull down the Activities menu and select Reconcile /Pay Credit Card.

   Quicken displays the Credit Card Statement Information window, as shown in Figure 9.5.

2. Use the information from your credit card statement to fill in the fields, and then press Ctrl-↵Enter or click on Continue.

   Quicken displays the Reconciliation Summary window, showing a list of uncleared transactions.

3. To mark a transaction as cleared, highlight it and press the Space bar, or double-click on the transaction.

   An asterisk appears in the C (Cleared) column for each item marked as cleared.

4. To add or edit a transaction, press F9 or click on View Register, make your changes, and press F9 or click on View as List.

5. Press Ctrl-F10 or click on Done. — If your account isn't balanced, Quicken displays the Adjusting Register to Agree with Statement window (see Figure 9.6). Otherwise, the Make Credit Card Payment window appears, and you can skip to step 7.

6. Categorize each of the entries, if desired, and then press Ctrl-Enter or click on Continue. — Quicken records the adjustments and displays the Make Credit Card Payment window.

7. Press Ctrl-C, and select the name of the account you want Quicken to use to pay the bill.

8. Press Tab or click on the Hand-written check field. — The cursor moves to the Hand-written check field.

9. Type **Y** to have Quicken write a check for you or type **N** to write your own check, and then press Enter or click on Continue. (If you set up Quicken to make electronic payments using CheckFree, you have three options for making the payment: **C**omputer Check, **M**anual Check, or **E**lectronic Payment.) — Quicken records the payment and returns you to the register for the selected account or to the Write Checks screen.

10. Complete the transaction and press Ctrl-Enter or click on Record. — Quicken records the check.

Figure 9.5
The Credit Card Statement Information window.

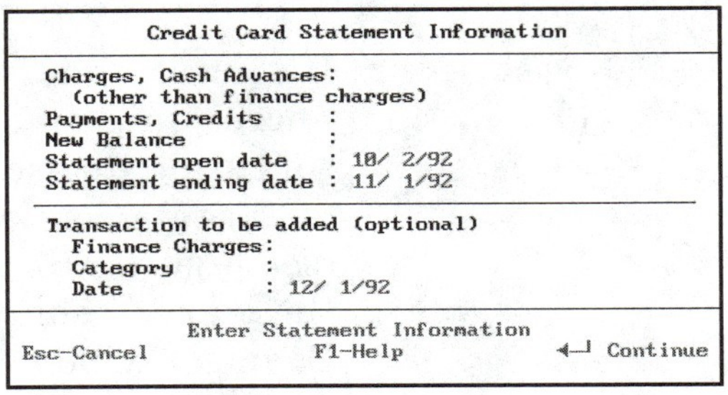

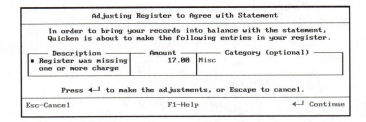

Figure 9.6
Quicken displays the adjusting entries needed to balance your account.

> **NOTE:** Quicken uses the full amount owed on your statement when it writes a check. To make a partial payment, simply adjust the check amount.

Tracking Credit Cards in a Checking Account

If you normally pay your credit card balance in full every month, or if you seldom use your card, enter your credit card transactions in the checking account. To do this, enter your payment in the checking account as you normally would. Then, with your statement in hand, split the payment among as many of the charges as you want to record. (The remainder can be categorized as Miscellaneous.)

Using IntelliCharge

Later releases of Quicken 5 and now Quicken 6 offer an electronic credit card feature, called IntelliCharge, that can help you automate your credit card transactions. To use the feature, you must apply for a Quicken credit card; the application form is included in the Quicken package.

Once you have your Quicken credit card, you can set up a special IntelliCharge credit card account. You set up the account just as you set up any credit card account, but you must specify that this is an IntelliCharge account in the Starting Balance and Description window.

When the account is set up, balancing it is simple. You receive your monthly statement on a disk or via modem through CompuServe. (CompuServe is an on-line information service that you can subscribe to.) With IntelliCharge, you no longer have to enter transactions manually. The data you get on disk or via modem automatically updates and balances your account. The following Quick Steps show how simple it is to update your account using the data on a disk.

Updating Your IntelliCharge Account

1. Activate your IntelliCharge account.

   The register for the IntelliCharge account appears on-screen.

2. Pull down the **Activities** window and select **Get IntelliCharge Data**.

   The Get IntelliCharge Statement window appears.

3. Insert the IntelliCharge data disk into floppy drive A or B.

continues

> *continued*
>
> 4. Type the letter of the drive that contains the disk into the Statement disk drive field, and press `⏎Enter`.
>
>   Quicken displays the Updating Account window, and displays each transaction as it is added to the register. Quicken then displays the Statement window.
>
> 5. Check the transactions to make sure they are accurate, and take note of any transactions that do not match your records.
>
> 6. Press `Ctrl`-`⏎Enter` to record the new transactions.

Recording Other Assets and Other Liabilities

So far, you've seen how to keep track of transactions in your bank accounts, a cash account, and your credit card accounts. For many people, this is enough to cover all of their day-to-day transactions, which is all they really need Quicken for. However, if you want to generate reports on such things as your *net worth* (the difference between what you have and what you owe), you need to learn about asset and liability accounts. In the simplest possible terms, an *asset* is something you own, and a *liability* is something you owe.

Setting Up Asset and Liability Accounts

Setting up asset and liability accounts is similar to setting up a bank or cash account. The only difference is that, depending on the type of account you're setting up, you need to give some thought to the opening balance. Here are some guidelines to follow when entering an opening balance:

- If the account is for a single asset, enter either the current value of the asset or its original cost.
- If the account is for a loan (a liability), enter the current loan balance.
- If the account is for a collection of assets or a collection of loans, enter **0**.

Entering Asset and Liability Transactions

You enter asset and liability transactions in much the same way you enter transactions for your bank accounts. Asset and liability transactions can be split and memorized, and you can transfer funds between accounts.

Figure 9.7 shows an example of a split transaction that would apply the principal paid to a mortgage account. A check to the Last National Bank is split between the interest expense (categorized as Mort Int) and the amount of principal paid (transferred to the mortgage account). You can do this with any kind of loan in a liability account.

> **TIP:** *Increase* and *decrease* have different meanings depending on whether you're talking about an asset or liability. An increase to an asset account means that you *have more* of something, while an increase to a liability account means that you *owe more* to someone.

Figure 9.7
You can split mortgage payments between principal and interest.

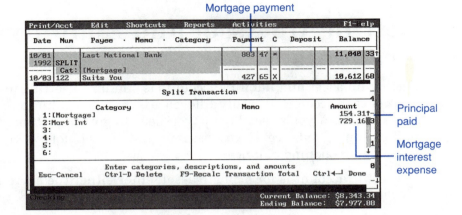

Updating Asset and Liability Values

When the value of an item changes, you can have Quicken record an adjustment in the register. If you have multiple assets or liabilities in the account, you must add up the current value for *each* item and enter the total as your adjustment. Follow these steps to adjust your asset and liability values:

1. At the asset or liability register, pull down the **Activities** menu and select **Update Account Balance**. Quicken displays the Update Account Balance window, as shown in Figure 9.8.

2. In the Update this accounts balance to field, enter the current value of the asset or liability. Press [Tab] or click on the **Category for adjustment** field.

3. (Optional) Enter a category for the adjustment transaction (Miscellaneous, for example). Press [Tab] or click on the **Adjustment date** field.

4. Enter the date for the adjustment. Press [Ctrl]-[↵Enter] or click on **Continue** to record the transaction.

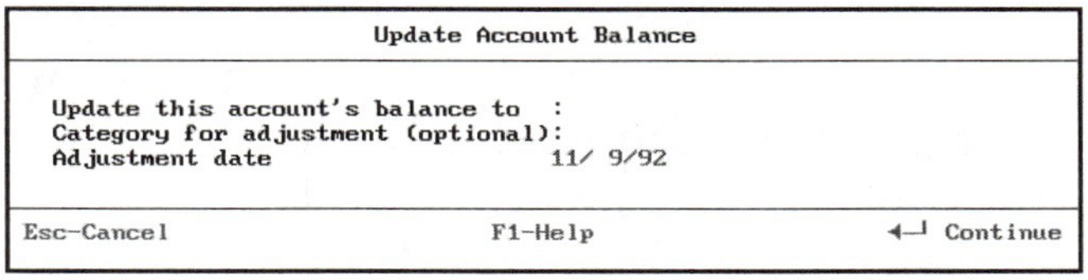

Figure 9.8
The Update Account Balance window.

The adjustment appears in the register, with `Balance Adjustment` in the Payee field. If the amount you entered was for several items and you assigned classes to these items, you can split the transaction between the appropriate classes.

> **NOTE:** The capital asset register includes a Depreciation transaction that decreases the value of the account. *Depreciation* is an allowance made for the decrease in value of an asset because of age and general wear and tear. Ask your accountant for more information about depreciation methods.

Marking Closed Assets and Liabilities

If you sell an asset or pay off a loan, *close* the item in the register. This involves two steps:

1. Enter the final transaction. For an asset sale, enter the money received in the Decrease column and transfer the funds to the account in which you deposited them. For a liability, enter the payment in the appropriate bank account and transfer it to the liability account.

2. Clear the item by entering an asterisk (*) in the C (Cleared) column of the register for *every* transaction associated with the asset or liability.

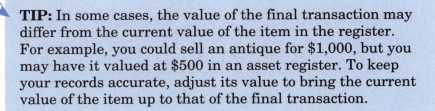

TIP: In some cases, the value of the final transaction may differ from the current value of the item in the register. For example, you could sell an antique for $1,000, but you may have it valued at $500 in an asset register. To keep your records accurate, adjust its value to bring the current value of the item up to that of the final transaction.

Amortizing Your Loan Payments

If you use a liability account to track a mortgage or loan, you'll probably memorize the monthly payments for convenience. The problem is that even though the amount of the check you send to the bank every month stays the same, the principal and interest you pay always changes. This is due to the *amortization* of the loan; the interest charges are high for the initial payments, but they steadily decrease.

If you tell Quicken the loan details (interest rate, payment, term, and so on), it will automatically calculate the interest charged and principal paid for each payment. The following Quick Steps assume that you have a liability account set up for tracking a loan payment.

Setting Up a Loan for Amortization

1. With the loan payment highlighted, press Ctrl-M to memorize the transaction, and press ↵Enter.
2. Press Ctrl-T.   The Memorized Transactions List appears.

3. Click on the transaction or use the arrow keys to highlight it, and then press `F9` or click on Amortize.

   Quicken displays the Set Amortization Information window, as shown in Figure 9.9.

4. Enter your regular payment, the interest rate, the term, and the number of payments you make per year.

   Quicken recalculates the loan amount each time you fill in a field.

5. Edit the Transaction Information if needed, and then tab to the Date of first payment field.

6. Type the date of the first payment for the loan, and then press `Tab` or click on the Payments made field.

   The cursor moves to the Payments made field.

7. Enter the number of payments you've made so far. If this is a new loan, enter **0**. Press `Enter` or click on Continue.

   Quicken records the amortization information and returns you to the Memorized Transactions List.

```
                Set Amortization Information
                        Loan Information
    Regular payment:       883.47
    Annual interest rate:  7%
    Total years:           25.00
    Periods per year:      12
    Loan amount:           124,999.43
    Current balance:       124,999.43
                      Transaction Information
    Payee:                 Last National Bank
    Memo:
    Principal category:    [Mortgage]
    Interest category:     Mort Int

    Date of first payment: 10/ 1/92    Payments made: 0

            F9-View Payment Schedule   Ctrl-D Unamortize
    Esc-Cancel              F1-Help                    ⏎ Continue
```

Figure 9.9

Enter the amortization information in the Set Amortization Information window.

You can then recall this transaction in the normal way. Quicken automatically adjusts the split amounts for the principal and interest.

VERSION 6 When you recall an amortized loan payment in Quicken 6, Quicken displays a Use Amortized Transaction window, like the one shown in Figure 9.10. You can use this window to enter any of the following information about your loan:

- *Current interest rate.* If you have a variable interest rate loan and the rate changes, enter the new interest rate in this field. Quicken will automatically recalculate the loan to show the effect of the new rate on your payment amount and the principal due.

- *Additional prepayment.* You can reduce your number of payments and the total amount a loan costs you by paying more than is required when a payment is due. Any additional money you pay reduces the principal of the loan and saves you money. Enter any additional payment here, and Quicken recalculates the loan and shortens the loan term.

- *Other regular charges.* If you have an escrow account to which part of your house payment is applied, and the amount changes, enter the new amount here.

Figure 9.10
Quicken 6 can handle variable interest rate loans and prepayments.

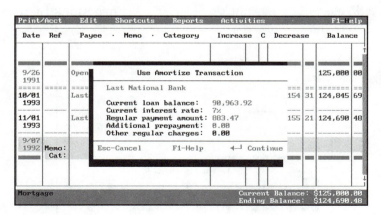

Recording Investment Transactions

Many people today use investments to try to stretch their hard-earned dollars. Millions of investors put their money into mutual funds, IRAs, and CDs. Quicken can help you keep track of these types of investments as well as stocks, bonds, annuities, unit trusts, and Keogh plans.

However, investment accounts require a full discussion of the various types of investments, which would be beyond the scope of this book. For more information, refer to the Quicken documentation or to a more advanced book about Quicken.

In This Chapter

An Overview of Quicken's Reports

Examples of Personal and Investment Reports

Creating and Printing Standard Reports

Customizing Reports

Creating a Basic Report

1. Open the Reports menu and select a report type.
2. Select the specific report you want to produce.
3. Type a report title, if desired, and press Tab⇥ or ↵Enter.
4. Type a range of dates you want the report to cover.
5. Press Ctrl-↵Enter or click on Continue.

Printing a Report

1. Make sure your printer is turned on and is on-line.
2. Pull down the File/Print menu and select Print Report.
3. Select the destination for the report.
4. Press ↵Enter or click on Print.

Chapter 10

Creating and Printing Reports

Up to this point, you have looked at using Quicken on a transaction-by-transaction basis. Although this is good for your daily transactions, you need an overall view of your fiscal situation as well. Quicken provides various views of your finances by allowing you to create financial reports. These reports extract and summarize the day-to-day financial information contained in your registers to give you an overall view of your fiscal situation. Whether you need to know your cash flow, net worth, or tax deductions, Quicken reports can do the job.

In this chapter, you'll learn about each type of report that Quicken offers, and how to customize and print reports.

The Reports Menu

Creating a Quicken report is virtually automatic. You select the type of report you want, and Quicken displays the necessary information on-screen in a predefined format. If you don't like the format, you can always make changes on the spot. Once you're satisfied with the layout, you can print the report to create a permanent record.

You select Quicken reports from the Reports menu (see Figure 10.1), which can be displayed in two ways:

- From the Main menu, use the arrow keys to highlight Create Reports and press ⏎Enter, or click on Create Reports.

- From any register or the Write Checks screen, press Alt-R or click on Reports in the menu bar.

Figure 10.1
The Reports menu.

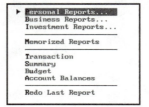

The Reports menu is divided into four sections. The top section contains the options that let you create the following predefined reports: personal, business, and investment. The next section contains the **M**emorized Reports option; once you create a report, you can have Quicken remember it for future use. The third section contains the four types of report layouts used to build custom reports: **T**ransaction, **S**ummary, **B**udget, and **A**ccount Balances. The last section contains an option that lets you re-create the last report you created.

Personal Reports

Select the Personal Reports option from the Reports menu to display a menu of seven personal reports, all predefined by

Quicken. As the name suggests, these reports are primarily designed for individuals, but you may also use these reports to track your business finances.

In the following sections, you will see examples of each of the seven personal reports predefined by Quicken.

> **TIP:** You should balance your checking and credit card accounts and update the balance in your cash, other asset, and other liability accounts before creating any reports. This way, you can be sure that the information contained in the reports is as accurate and up-to-date as possible.

Cash Flow Report

The cash flow report summarizes the Income and Expense categories from your bank, cash, and credit card accounts. A sample cash flow report is shown in Figure 10.2. Notice how the individual categories are grouped under two major headings: INFLOWS and OUTFLOWS. For purposes of this report, *inflows* are transactions assigned to income categories and transfers from other asset, other liability, and investment accounts. *Outflows* are transactions assigned to expense categories and transfers to asset, liability, and investment accounts. At the bottom of the report, Quicken calculates the OVERALL TOTAL—the difference between your inflows and your outflows.

Figure 10.2
A sample cash flow report.

```
                    Sample Cash Flow Report
                    10/ 1/92 Through 10/31/92
HOME-Bank,Cash,CC Accounts
Page 1
11/ 9/92
                                            10/ 1/92-
              Category Description          10/31/92

    INFLOWS
      Salary Income                          2,954.72
      Teaching Fees                            750.00

    TOTAL INFLOWS                            3,704.72

    OUTFLOWS
      Automobile Expenses:
        Auto Fuel                    45.00
        Auto Loan Payment           312.21

      Total Automobile Expenses                357.21
      Bank Charge                                5.00
      Christmas Expenses                        89.76
      Clothing                                 475.80
      Dining Out                               135.00
      Groceries                                254.99
      Household Misc. Exp                      112.12
      Miscellaneous                             30.24
      Mortgage Interest                        729.16
      Supplies                                  43.21
      Travel Expenses                          250.00
      Water, Gas, Electric:
        Gas and Electicity          33.45

      Total Water, Gas, Electric                33.45

    TOTAL OUTFLOWS                           2,515.94

    OVERALL TOTAL                            1,188.78
```

Unless you're wildly overspending, it's usually hard to tell on a day-to-day basis if you live beyond your means. Using the cash flow report on a regular basis to monitor the money coming in and going out of your accounts can help. Ideally, your inflows should exceed your outflows. If you find that this isn't the case most of the time, then you can use the report to figure out why.

Monthly Budget Report

The monthly budget report compares your income and expenses each month with your budgeted amount by category. Only transactions in your bank, cash, and credit card accounts are used. Before you can run this report, you need to set up monthly budget amounts for your income and expense categories. See Chapter 11, "Budgeting with Quicken," for details on the monthly budget report.

Itemized Categories Report

The itemized categories report lists all of the transactions from your accounts. An example of this report is shown in Figure 10.3. The transactions are listed in three sections:

Income/Expenses Lists individual income and expense transactions from your bank, cash, and credit card accounts. This is the detail behind the income and expense summaries in the cash flow report (without the transfers).

Transfers Lists all transfers between your bank, cash, and credit card accounts. This is the detail behind the transfer summaries in the cash flow report (not shown in Figure 10.3).

Balances Forward Lists any opening account balances that fall within the period of the report (not shown in Figure 10.3).

Chapter 10

Figure 10.3
A sample itemized categories report.

```
                    Sample Itemized Categories Report
                         10/ 1/92 Through 10/31/92
HOME-All Accounts                                                    Page 1
11/ 9/92

 Date    Acct      Num      Description    Memo        Category    Clr  Amount


         INCOME/EXPENSE
           INCOME
             Salary Income

 10/ 4 Checking          S Paycheck Deposit            Salary       X  1,477.36
 10/18 Checking          S Paycheck Deposit            Salary       X  1,477.36

              Total salary Income                                      2,954.72

             Teaching Fees

 10/31 Checking            Teaching Fees    DTP course Teaching/Busine    750.00

              Total Teaching Fees                                         750.00

          TOTAL INCOME                                                  3,704.72

          EXPENSES
            Automobile Expenses:

              Auto Fuel

 10/ 1 VISA                Texaco                      Auto:Fuel     *   -20.00
 10/ 1 Cash                Ed's Exxon                  Auto:Fuel         -25.00

              Total Auto Fuel                                            -45.00

              Auto Loan Payment

 10/ 5 Checking 123        Last National Ba            Auto:Loan     X  -312.21

              Total Auto Loan Payment                                   -312.00

            Total Automobile Expenses                                   -357.21

            Bank Charge

 10/27 Checking            Service Charge              Bank Chrg     X    -5.00

              Total Bank Charge                                           -5.00

            Dining Out

 10/31 Checking 132  S VISA            Acme Bar &   Dining               -40.00
 10/20 VISA                La Cantina               Dining           *   -72.00
 10/ 3 Cash                Sawasdee Thai Fo         Dining               -22.50

              Total Dining Out                                          -135.00

          TOTAL EXPENSES                                                -497.21


          TOTAL INCOME/EXPENSE                                         3,207.51
```

The itemized categories report shows *all* your transactions, so it can be pretty long if you use Quicken frequently or look at several months worth of data. If necessary, you can *filter out* some of the transactions. For example, you might want to include only certain categories or only amounts greater than $100. (See the section "Customizing Reports" later in this chapter for more information.)

Like the cash flow report, you can use the itemized categories report to monitor your inflows and outflows. If you spend too much money, use this report to examine your specific transactions and see where you can cut back.

Tax Summary Report

The tax summary report, shown in Figure 10.4, lists the transactions from all the accounts assigned to tax-related categories. The layout of this report is identical to the layout of the itemized categories report.

Use the tax summary report to prepare your taxes. The subtotals for each tax-related category are the amounts you enter as income and deductions on your federal and state income tax returns. (See Chapter 13, "Using Quicken at Tax Time," for details.)

Net Worth Report

If you add up everything you own and subtract from that everything you owe, you end up with your net worth. As Figure 10.5 shows, the net worth report does just that. The ASSETS section of the report lists the balances from your bank, cash, asset, and investment accounts. The LIABILITIES section lists the balances from your credit card and liability accounts. The bottom line (literally and figuratively) is the difference between these two, or the TOTAL NET WORTH.

Figure 10.4

A sample tax summary report.

```
                        Sample Tax Summary Report
                         10/ 1/92 Through 10/31/92
HOME-All Accounts                                                    Page 1
11/ 9/92

  Date   Acct        Num    Description      Memo       Category       Clr Amount

         INCOME/EXPENSE
           INCOME
             Salary Income
                                                                      ─────────
  10/ 4 Checking      S Paycheck Deposit                Salary         X  1,477.36
  10/18 Checking      S Paycheck Deposit                Salary         X  1,477.36
                                                                          ────────
                  Total Salary Income                                     2,954.72

             Teaching Fees
                                                                      ─────────
  10/31 Checking        Teaching Fees        DTP course  Teaching/Busine    750.00
                                                                          ────────
                  Total Teaching Fees                                       750.00
                                                                          ────────
              TOTAL INCOME                                                3,704.72

           EXPENSES
             Taxes:
                                                                      ─────────

             Federal Tax
                                                                      ─────────
  10/ 4 Checking      S Paycheck Deposit                Tax:Fed        X   -203.84
  10/18 Checking      S Paycheck Deposit                Tax:Fed        X   -203.84
                                                                          ────────
                  Total Federal Tax                                        -407.68

             Social Security Tax
                                                                      ─────────
  10/ 4 Checking      S Paycheck Deposit                Tax:FICA       X    -79.74
  10/18 Checking      S Paycheck Deposit                Tax:FICA       X    -79.74
                                                                          ────────
                  Total Social Security Tax                                -159.48

             State Tax
                                                                      ─────────
  10/ 4 Checking      S Paycheck Deposit                Tax:State      X    -16.42
  10/18 Checking      S Paycheck Deposit                Tax:State      X    -16.42
                                                                          ────────
                  Total State Tax                                           -32.84
                                                                          ────────
                  Total Taxes                                                 -600
                                                                          ────────
              TOTAL EXPENSES                                               -600.00
                                                                          ════════
              TOTAL INCOME/EXPENSE                                        3,104.72
                                                                          ════════
```

```
                    Sample Net Worth Report
                         As of 11/ 9/92
HOME-All Accounts                                                Page 1
11/ 9/92
                                              11/ 9/92
                       Acct                    Balance

          ASSETS
            Cash and Bank Accounts
              Cash                                 122.00
              Checking
                Ending Balance         8,343.34
                plus: Checks Payable     267.17
                                       _____
              Total Checking                     8,610.51
              Savings                            8,305.35
                                                _____
            Total Cash and Bank Accounts       17,037.86

            Other Assets
              Accts Rec                              0.00
              Belongings                        14,450.00
              Books                                  0.00
              Clothes                                0.00
              Computer Equip                         0.00
              House                            171,504.26
              Stereo                                66.14
                                                _____
            Total Other Assets                 187,020.26

            Investments
              Brokerage                         14,325.00
              Magellan                           4,149.25
                                                _____
            Total Investments                   18,474.25
                                                _____

          TOTAL ASSETS                         222,532.37

          LIABILITIES
            Checks Payable                         267.17
            Credit Cards
              VISA                                 986.70
                                                _____
            Total Credit Cards                     986.70

            Other Liabilities
              Mortgage                         124,690.48
                                                _____
            Total Other Liabilities            124,690.48
                                                _____
          TOTAL LIABILITIES                    125,944.35
                                                _____

          TOTAL NET WORTH                       96,588.02
                                                =========
```

Figure 10.5

A sample net worth report.

It's often convenient to know your net worth, such as when you apply for a loan. Also, some brokerages require a net worth statement before you can open certain types of accounts (for example, to trade futures and options).

Missing Check Report

The missing check report lists your checks in check number sequence (see Figure 10.6). The report tells you if a number is missing from the sequence or if a number is repeated. This information helps you track down account discrepancies. A missing check number could mean that you forgot to record the check or you entered the wrong number when you were printing the check. A duplicate check number could signify a bill entered twice in the register.

Tax Schedule Report

The tax schedule report lists the transactions from all of your accounts that were assigned categories and included tax schedule information (see Figure 10.7). The transactions are grouped according to the tax schedule and then by the tax form line description. You can use the tax form line subtotals to prepare your income tax return. You can also print this report to a file that can be read by certain tax preparation software. (See the section "Printing Reports" later in this chapter.)

Creating and Printing Reports

Figure 10.6
A sample missing check report.

```
Sample Missing Check Report
10/ 1/92 Through 10/31/92
HOME-Checking                                                        Page 1
11/ 9/92

  Date    Num    Description      Memo            Category      Clr  Amount
  ____    ___    _____      ____            _____           _____

          Checking

  10/ 3   122    Suits You        New Suit        Clothing       X   -427.65
  10/ 5   123    Clascom Computers Laser Printer  Computer:Hardware/  -1043.12

                 *** Duplicate Check 123   ***

  10/ 5   123    Last National Bank               Auto:Loan      X    312.21
  10/ 9   124    Clascom Computers Grammar Checke Computer:Software/  -84.91
  10/10   125    Brimson's Furniture New Desk     Office/Business    -357.09
  10/14   126    Food City                        Groceries      X    -92.55

                 *** Missing Check 127   ***

  10/15   128    Globe Travel     Trip down pymn  Travel         X   -250.00
  10/15   129  S Clascom Computers                —SPLIT—            -118.70
  10/21   130    World Wildlife Fund              Charity        X   -100.00
  10/21   131    Food City                        Groceries      X    -89.23
  10/22   132    Port Hope Hydro  Acct # 1234567  Utilities:Gas & El X -33.45

                 *** Duplicate Check 132   ***

  10/31   132  S VISA                             —SPLIT—            -221.10
  10/18        S Paycheck Deposit                 —SPLIT—        X   1,177.36
  10/14        S G&G Advertising  09/27/91        [Accts Rec]/Busine  1,000.00
  10/21          O'Donoghue Contract New Bathroom [House]            -5,000.00
  10/11          Withdrawal                                      X   -200.00
  10/ 4        S Paycheck Deposit                 —SPLIT—        X   1,177.36
  10/22          Transfer to Savings              [Savings]      X   -100.00
  10/27          Service Charge                   Bank Chrg      X     -5.00
  10/29          Wildes Media    10/02/91         [Accts Rec]/Busine   650.00
  10/31          Teaching Fees   DTP Course       Teaching/Business    750.00
  10/ 1        S Last National Bank               —SPLIT—        *   -883.47

          Total Checking                                            -4,563.76
```

Chapter 10

Figure 10.7
A sample tax schedule report.

```
                        Sample Tax Schedule Report
                         10/ 1/92 Through 10/31/92
HOME-Selected Accounts                                              Page 1
11/ 9/92

  Date   Acct        Num    Description      Memo       Category       Clr Amount

         Form 1040

         Other income-misc.

 10/31 Checking             Teaching Fees  DTP course Teaching/Busine      750.00

         Total Other income-misc.                                          750.00

         Fed. estimated tax

 10/31 Checking          S Paycheck Deposit             Tax:Fed        X  -203.84
 10/18 Checking          S Paycheck Deposit             Tax:Fed        X  -203.84

         Total Fed. estimated tax                                         -407.68

         Schedule A

         State and local taxes

 10/ 4 Checking          S Paycheck Deposit             Tax:State      X   -16.42
 10/18 Checking          S Paycheck Deposit             Tax:State      X   -16.42

         Total State and local taxes                                       -32.84

         Cash charity contributions

 10/21 Checking 130      World Wildlife F              Charity         X  -100.00
 10/31 Checking 132    S VISA             SPCA         Charity            -100.00

         Total Cash charity contributions                                 -200.00

         Home mortgage interest

 10/ 1 Checking        S Last National Ba               Mort Int       *  -729.16

         Total Home mortgage interest                                     -729.16

         Schedule C

         Other business expense

 10/ 5 Checking 123    Clascom Computer Laser print Computer:Hardwa    -1,043.12
 10/15 Checking 129  S Clascom Computer Disks       Computer:Hardwa       -75.95

         Total Other business expense                                  -1,119.07

         Office expense

 10/10 Checking 125    Brimson's Furnit New Desk   Office/Business       -357/09

         Total Office expense                                             -357.09

         Travel

 10/15 Checking 128    Globe Travel     Trip down p Travel             X  -250.00

         Total Travel                                                     -250.00

         W-2

         Salary

 10/ 4 Checking        S Paycheck Deposit             Salary           X  1,477.36
 10/18 Checking        S Paycheck Deposit             Salary           X  1,477.36

         Total Salary                                                    2,954.72

         FICA

 10/ 4 Checking        S Paycheck Deposit             Tax:FICA         X   -79.74
 10/18 Checking        S Paycheck Deposit             Tax:FICA         X   -79.74

         TOTAL FICA                                                       -159.48
```

Business Reports

Select Business Reports to display a menu of business report choices. There are eight business reports, all predefined by Quicken. The following list is a summary of these reports. For additional information about Quicken's business reports, refer to Chapter 14, "Setting Up a Business Accounting System."

P & L (profit and loss)   Summarizes your income and expenses by category. Quicken uses all accounts for this report.

Cash Flow   Shows the inflow of money to your accounts and the outflow of money from your accounts. Quicken uses only transactions from your bank, cash, and credit card accounts.

A/P (accounts payable) by Vendor   Lists your unprinted checks by payee.

A/R (accounts receivable) by Customer   Lists the outstanding balances for each of your customers by month. You'll need to tell Quicken to use only your A/R asset account.

Job/Project   Summarizes your income and expenses for each class. Quicken uses transactions from all accounts.

Payroll Report   Summarizes income and expenses for each employee. Quicken uses all accounts but only the transactions categorized as Payroll.

Balance Sheet   Shows the balances from all your accounts and compares your current assets and liabilities.

Missing Check   Identical to the personal missing check report.

Investment Reports

Select Investment Reports to display a menu of choices for investment reports. There are five investment reports predefined by Quicken:

Portfolio Value Shows the value of each of your securities on the date you specify. It shows the number of shares you have, the most recent price per share, the cost basis of the security, the unrealized (paper) gain or loss in dollars, and the market value on the date specified.

Investment Performance Shows the calculated average annual total return for each of your securities over a specified time. This includes not only increases and decreases in the market value of each security but also dividends and interest paid to you.

Capital Gains Report Details the realized short-term and long-term gains on securities sold during a specified time.

Investment Income Report Lists your income and expenses by category for each security in your investment accounts. The report shows dividends paid (both taxable and nontaxable), interest income (taxable and nontaxable), capital gains distributions, and margin interest expense during the specified time.

Investment Transactions Report Lists all of the transactions in your investment registers recorded over a specified time. For each transaction, the report shows the following information: transaction date, security, investment action, category (if any), price per share, number of shares, commission, available cash, current investment value, and the total of the cash plus the investment value.

Creating a Predefined Report

You can create most of the predefined Quicken reports by pressing just a few keystrokes. The following Quick Steps describe how to create a predefined report.

Creating and Printing Reports 207

Creating a Predefined Report

1. Open the **Reports** menu and select a report type.

   Quicken displays a menu of reports for the type you selected.

2. Select the specific report you want to produce.

   Quicken displays a setup window for the report, as shown in Figure 10.8.

3. Type a report title, if desired, and press `Tab` or `Enter`.

   The cursor moves to the first date range field.

4. Type a range of dates you want the report to cover in the Report on months from/through fields.

   The report will include only those transactions that were entered between the specified dates.

5. Press `Ctrl`-`Enter` or click on **Continue**.

   Quicken assembles the report and displays it on-screen. A sample cash flow report, as it appears on-screen, is shown in Figure 10.9.

Viewing the Report on the Screen

Before you print the report, examine it on-screen to make sure the information you want is included. Most of your reports will be too long or too wide to fit within the boundaries of your computer screen. Use the keys outlined in Table 10.1 to navigate the report.

If you have a mouse, you can use the scroll bars displayed on the bottom of the screen (for a wide report) or the right side of the screen (for a long report).

Chapter 10

TIP: If your report includes transactions, Quicken may cut the width of some of the columns to put as much of the report on-screen as possible. To view the report in its full width, select **Full Column Width** from the **Layout** pull-down menu.

Figure 10.8
A setup window for a report.

```
                    Cash Flow Report

  Report title (optional):

  Report on months from:  1/92 through: 11/92

  Esc-Cancel      F7-Layout  F8-Options  F9-Filter       ←┘ Continue
```

Table 10.1
Keys Used to Navigate an On-Screen Report

Key	Effect
Tab or →	Moves right one column.
Shift-Tab or ←	Moves left one column.
Ctrl-→	Moves right one screen.
Ctrl-←	Moves left one screen.
Home	Moves to the far left of the row.
End	Moves to the far right of the row.
↓	Moves down one row.
↑	Moves up one row.
PgDn	Moves down one screen.
PgUp	Moves up one screen.
Ctrl-End	Moves to the bottom of the report.
Ctrl-Home	Moves to the top of the report.

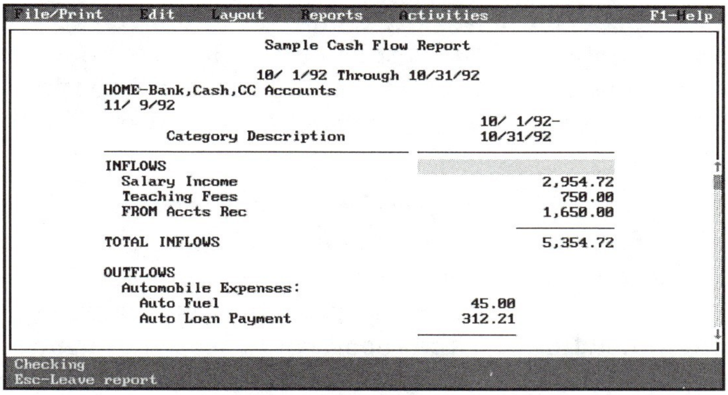

Figure 10.9
A sample cash flow report as it appears on-screen.

Customizing Reports

The predefined reports are convenient because you can display the information you want in just a few keystrokes. But there will be times when you won't want to see all the data that a predefined report provides, or you might want to see it in a different layout. For example, you might want a report that includes only business transactions.

Overall, there are three methods to customize your reports:

Select a custom report Choose one of the four custom report types (Transaction, Summary, Budget, or Account Balances) from the Reports menu.

Customize a predefined report in advance Select your customizing options from the setup window for the report. This method is discussed in a bit more detail later in this section.

Customize a displayed report Start with a predefined report and select your customizing options from pull-down menus on the report screen.

One of the easiest ways to create a customized report is to use the three options at the bottom of the report setup window—the window on which you type a report title and specify a date range. On most setup windows, you can select any of the following three options:

F7 Layout Press F7 or click on Layout to display the Create Summary Report window, shown in Figure 10.10. In addition to allowing you to change the report title and date range, this window lets you change the row and column headings for the report and choose to include transactions from all accounts or only from the current or selected accounts.

F8 Options Press F8 or click on Options to display the Report Options window. The options on this window will vary, depending on the type of report you are creating. Figure 10.11 shows the Report Options window for a cash flow report. This window lets you set the overall organization for the report and some options specifying the type of data and level of detail you want included on the report.

F9 Filter Press F9 or click on Filter to display the Filter Transactions window, shown in Figure 10.12. This window lets you select the types of information you want included in the report. For example, you can type a payee name in the first field to include transactions for only the specified payee. You can also choose to include or exclude some categories and classes from the report.

NOTE: Once a report appears on-screen, you can use the various options on the pull-down menus to customize the report. These menus contain the same options that are available in the windows shown in Figure 10.10 to 10.12.

Figure 10.10

The Create Summary Report window.

```
                    Create Summary Report

Report title (optional): Sample Cash Flow Report

Restrict to transactions from: 10/ 1/92 through: 10/31/92

Row headings (down the left side): 1
      1. Category           3. Payee
      2. Class              4. Account

Column headings (across the top): 1
      1. Don't Subtotal     5. Month           9. Category
      2. Week               6. Quarter        10. Class
      3. Two Weeks          7. Six Months     11. Payee
      4. Half Month         8. Year           12. Account

Use Current/All/Selected accounts (C/A/S): S

Esc-Cancel         F8-Options  F9-Filter              ← Continue
```

Figure 10.11

The Report Options window.

```
                        Report Options

Report organization: 2
      1. Income and expense      2. Cash flow basis

Transfers: 3
      1. Include all             3. External transfers only
      2. Exclude all

Include unrealized gains (Y/N): N

Show cents when displaying amounts (Y/N): Y
Normal/Suppressed/Reversed subcategory display (N/S/R): N

Esc-Cancel              Ctrl-D Reset                  ← Continue
```

Figure 10.12

The Filter Transactions window.

```
                      Filter Transactions

Restrict report to transactions matching these criteria
      Payee contains    :
      Memo contains     :
      Category contains:
      Class contains    :

Select categories to include...(Y/N): N
Select classes to include...   (Y/N): N

Tax-related categories only    (Y/N): N
Below/Equal/Above (B/E/A):     the amount:
Payments/Deposits/Unprinted checks/All (P/D/U/A) : A

Cleared status is
Blank ' ': Y   Cleared '*': Y   Reconciled 'X': Y

Esc-Cancel              Ctrl-D Reset                  ← Continue
```

Printing Reports

Once you're satisfied that the report you created is what you want, you can print it. The following Quick Steps describe how to print a report.

Printing a Report

1. Make sure your printer is turned on and is on-line.

2. Create the report as described in the previous section. — Quicken displays the report on your screen.

3. Pull down the **File/Print** menu and select **Print Report**, or press Ctrl-P. — Quicken displays the Print Report window, as shown in Figure 10.13.

4. Select the destination for the report. — For information on the Disk options, see the section "Printing to a Disk File" later in this chapter.

5. Press Enter or click on **Print**. — Quicken prints the report.

Figure 10.13
The Print Report window.

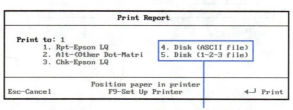

Print to disk options

Printing Wide Reports

If your report is too wide to fit on your screen but no wider than 132 characters, it's still possible to fit the report on an 8 ½-inch sheet of paper. All you need to do is change the settings on your dot-matrix or laser printer so that it prints in compressed mode (17 characters per inch). (If you have a wide-carriage printer, you can print the report on wide paper at the 10 character per inch setting.)

For even wider reports, if you have a laser printer that can print in landscape mode (sideways), you can print reports that are up to 176 characters wide (in compressed type).

If your printer can print in compressed mode or if you have a laser printer that can print in landscape mode, follow these steps to change the settings:

1. At the Print Report window, press F9 or click on Set Up Printer.

2. Select Settings for Printing Reports from the menu that appears. Quicken displays the available styles for your printer.

3. Select the style you want. Quicken displays the Report Printer Settings window.

4. Press Ctrl-↵Enter or click on Continue to return to the Print Report window.

Printing to a Disk File

The Print Report window gives you several options for printing your reports to disk files instead of to your printer:

ASCII file   Use this format to load the report into your word processor. When you select this option, Quicken prompts you for a DOS file name (you can add an extension and a path), the number of lines per page (enter 0 for continuous text), and the maximum character width.

1-2-3 file Select this format to use the report in Lotus 1-2-3. When you select this option, Quicken prompts you for a DOS file name (you can add a path), the number of lines per page (enter 0 for continuous), and the maximum width. Do not specify an extension when you enter the file name; Quicken uses a .PRN extension for these files. This format (called *Lotus import format*) can be read by most spreadsheet programs available today.

Tax file This option is available only when you print a tax schedule report. You use it to import the tax schedule information to a tax preparation program such as TurboTax and TaxCut. Enter a DOS file name (you can specify an extension and path), but you should leave the settings for lines per page and width at 0 and 80 respectively. (See the manual that comes with your tax software for instructions on how to import this file.)

In This Chapter

Establishing Budgeting Goals

Setting up Budget Amounts

Budgeting Shortcuts

Creating Budget Reports

Using Quicken's Financial Calculators

Setting Up a Budget

1. Pull down the Activities menu and select Set up Budgets.
2. Select the first cell in which you want to enter an amount.
3. Type your budget goal for the selected item in dollars.
4. Press [↵Enter] or click on the next cell.
5. Repeat steps 3 and 4 to enter all your budget amounts.

Creating a Budget Report

1. Pull down the Reports menu and select Personal Reports.
2. Select Monthly Budget.
3. Type a name for the report, if desired. Press [Tab⇆] or click on Report on months from.
4. Enter the months you want to see on the report, and then press [↵Enter] or click on Continue.

Using a Financial Calculator

1. Pull down the Activities menu and select Financial Planning.
2. Select the calculator you want to use.
3. Press [F8] to put a check mark next to the field that you want Quicken to calculate.
4. Fill in each of the unchecked fields with the appropriate amount. Press [Tab⇆] or [↵Enter] after each field.

Chapter 11

Budgeting and Financial Planning with Quicken

In Chapter 4, you learned how to create and use categories to keep track of your finances. Whenever you receive or spend money, you just tell Quicken to assign the transaction to one of the categories; Quicken automatically determines the totals for each category. In this chapter, you will put those categories to work to help you create and manage a budget. You will learn how to set budget goals for the various categories and how to generate budget reports that compare actual income and expenses to your goals. These reports will help you see where you are achieving your goals and where you are falling short.

You will also learn how to use Quicken's financial planning calculators to determine how much money you have to save or invest in order to achieve your financial goals.

Setting the Groundwork

Before you begin using Quicken to create and manage your budget, you must perform a few preliminary steps:

1. Make sure you've created the categories you think you will need and deleted any unnecessary categories.

2. Set a financial objective. For example, you may want to purchase a new car next year or get out of debt by the year 2000.

3. Estimate how much your goal is going to cost you. For example, you may need a down payment of $5000 for the new car.

4. Break down the total amount of money you need into a monthly amount. For example, if you need $5000 in one year's time, you will need to save about $400 a month. You can use Quicken's Financial Planning calculators to determine this amount, as explained later in this chapter.

Once you have your overall goal and the smaller subgoals, you can use Quicken's budgeting feature to track your income and expenses. What you are trying to do with your budget is to make sure, on a monthly basis, that your inflows exceed your outflows by the amount of money you are trying to save. For example, to save $400 a month, your inflows must exceed your outflows by at least that amount.

Setting Up a Quicken Budget

Creating a Quicken budget involves setting monthly budget amounts for some or all of the categories, subcategories, and transfers you set up in Chapter 4. You enter this information on the budget setup screen, as shown in Figure 11.1. To display this screen from any register, pull down the **Activities** menu and select **Set up Budgets**.

Budgeting and Financial Planning with Quicken

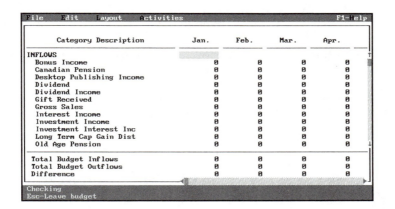

Figure 11.1
The budget setup screen.

At the top of the budget setup screen is the menu bar with four options: **F**ile, **E**dit, **L**ayout, and **A**ctivities. These menu options are discussed later in this chapter. Below the menu bar is an area where you enter your budget values. The left column shows the categories associated with the current account file. (There is a standard list that you can add to or delete from.) At the bottom of the screen are the inflow and outflow totals for each month. Quicken automatically calculates these totals and the difference between them.

Of course, there are many more categories and months than can fit on the screen. You can use the keys listed in Table 11.1 to navigate the budget setup screen.

Key	Effect
Tab	Moves to the right one month.
Shift-Tab	Moves to the left one month.
End	Moves to the far right (the TOTAL column).
Home	Moves to the Jan. (January) column.
↓	Moves down one category.
↑	Moves up one category.
PgDn	Moves down one screenful.
PgUp	Moves up one screenful.

Table 11.1
Keys for Navigating the Budget Setup Screen

You can also use the mouse: click on a cell to select it or use the vertical and horizontal scroll bars to move to other parts of the screen. (A cell is the rectangle formed by the intersection of a row and column.)

If you don't want to display all 12 months on-screen, you can change the layout of the budget setup screen in two ways:

- You could have four columns showing quarters; select **Quarter** from the **Layout** menu.
- You could have a single column showing the budget totals for the year; select **Year** from the **Layout** menu.

To return to the original layout, select **Month** from the **Layout** menu.

Setting Budget Amounts

To set budget goals for the categories, you must type a dollar amount for each category for all months you want included in the budget. Later in this chapter, we will look at some shortcuts for copying an entry across several months. Follow these steps to set budget amounts:

1. At the budget setup screen, select the first cell in which you want to enter an amount.

2. Type the amount. You can use whole dollar amounts; Quicken rounds off any cents you enter.

3. Press 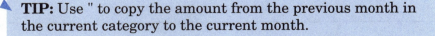 or click on the next cell. Quicken recalculates the totals at the bottom of the screen and moves the cursor down to the next category.

4. Repeat steps 1 through 3 to enter all your budget amounts for the first month. Figure 11.2 shows the completed Johnson budget for the month of January.

> **TIP:** Use " to copy the amount from the previous month in the current category to the current month.

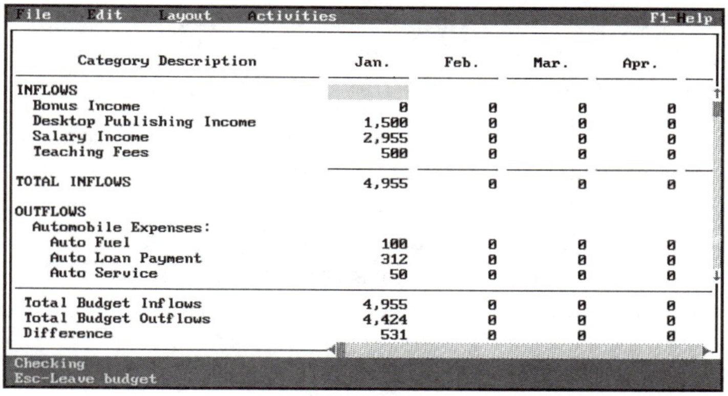

Figure 11.2
The Johnsons' budget with January completed.

Take a moment to look at the sample budget shown in Figure 11.2. The Johnsons have estimated their monthly income to be about $4,955. They want to save around $500 a month for a trip. This means that, barring any drastic changes to their income, they need to keep their total expense budget to around $4,400 per month, which is what they've done.

As you can imagine, entering a value into every month for even just a dozen or so categories would take a long time. Fortunately, Quicken provides you with several shortcut methods for entering budget amounts. These are summarized in the next few sections.

Copying Budget Amounts to Other Months

Once you've entered your budget amounts for a single month, Quicken can copy some or all of these amounts to future months. For example, if you have a bank loan, your monthly payment is constant, so you'd enter the payment in your first budget month and copy the same value to all future months. Quicken can perform two kinds of copying:

Fill Right This command copies the amount in the current cell to all the future months in the same category. To use this option, place the cursor on the cell you want to copy, pull down the Edit menu, and select Fill Right. Figure 11.3 shows the result when the Fill Right command is used on the Auto Loan Payment subcategory.

Fill Columns This command copies each of the budget amounts in the current month to all the future months. To use this option, place the cursor anywhere in the column you want to copy, pull down the Edit menu, and select Fill Columns. Figure 11.4 shows the result when the Fill Columns command is applied to the Johnsons' January budgets.

Figure 11.3
You can extend one budget amount to all future months.

Category Description	Jan.	Feb.	Mar.	Apr.
INFLOWS				
Bonus Income	0	0	0	0
Desktop Publishing Income	1,500	0	0	0
Salary Income	2,955	0	0	0
Teaching Fees	500	0	0	0
TOTAL INFLOWS	4,955	0	0	0
OUTFLOWS				
Automobile Expenses:				
Auto Fuel	100	0	0	0
Auto Loan Payment	312	312	312	312
Auto Service	50	0	0	0
Total Budget Inflows	4,955	0	0	0
Total Budget Outflows	4,424	312	312	312
Difference	531	-312	-312	-312

Figure 11.4
You can extend all budget amounts to all future months.

Category Description	Jan.	Feb.	Mar.	Apr.
INFLOWS				
Bonus Income	0	0	0	0
Desktop Publishing Income	1,500	1,500	1,500	1,500
Salary Income	2,955	2,955	2,955	2,955
Teaching Fees	500	500	500	500
TOTAL INFLOWS	4,955	4,955	4,955	4,955
OUTFLOWS				
Automobile Expenses:				
Auto Fuel	100	100	100	100
Auto Loan Payment	312	312	312	312
Auto Service	50	50	50	50
Total Budget Inflows	4,955	4,955	4,955	4,955
Total Budget Outflows	4,424	4,424	4,424	4,424
Difference	531	531	531	531

Budgeting Items that Recur Every Two Weeks

If you receive a paycheck every two weeks, you know that twice a year you are paid three times in a month (for example, on the 1st, the 15th, and the 29th). To take this into account, you'll have to enter a larger number in your salary category for those two months.

You could try figuring out which months those are and plan your budget accordingly, but you don't have to. Quicken can set up any of your categories as two-week budget items and then handle the chore of distributing your salary at the proper two-week intervals. You can do the same thing if you enter budget amounts for federal and state taxes. Follow these steps to set up two-week budget items:

1. At the budget setup screen, select the category you want to set up on a two-week budget.

2. Pull down the **Edit** menu and select **Two Week**. Quicken displays the Set Up 2 Week Budget window, as shown in Figure 11.5.

3. Enter the amount you want to budget at two-week intervals. For your salary, enter your approximate net pay if you're not tracking taxes. Otherwise, enter your gross salary. Press `Tab` or click on the **Every 2 weeks starting** field.

4. Enter the starting date for the item. For your salary, enter the date of an actual payday.

5. Press `Enter` or click on **Continue**. Quicken fills in the budget amounts.

Figure 11.6 shows the effect of setting up Mr. Johnson's gross salary of $1,477.36 on a two-week budget. Notice that the April budget for Salary Income is higher than the other months to reflect the extra paycheck Mr. Johnson receives that month.

Figure 11.5

The Set Up 2 Week Budget window.

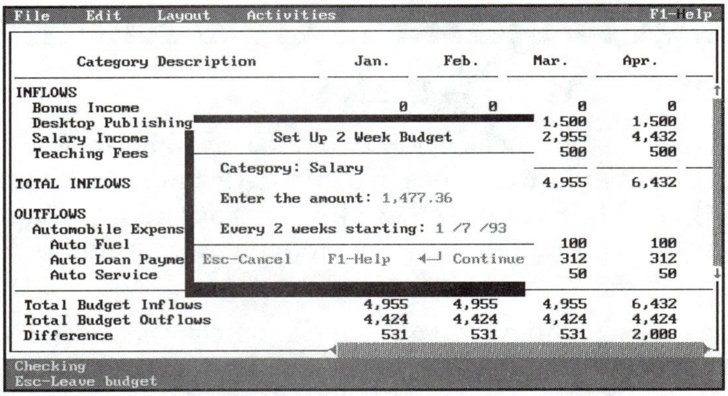

Figure 11.6

The salary category set up as a two-week budget.

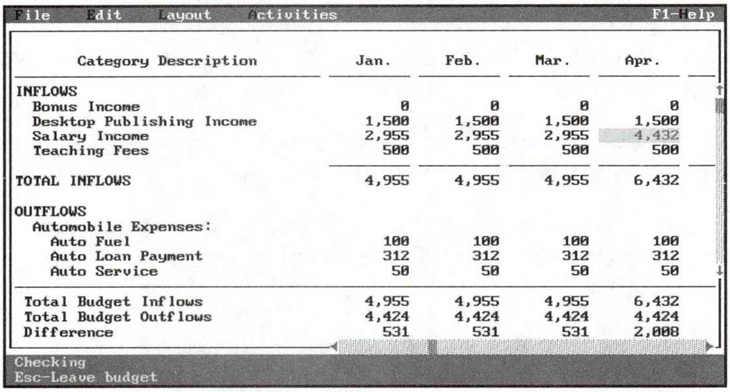

Using Historical Income and Expense Data

When estimating income and expenses for the year, many large companies use *zero-based budgeting*. Basically, zero-based budgeting means that you start all your budget items at zero and arrive at an amount based on the kinds of activities you're planning. Income and expenditures from the previous years are not taken into consideration.

For the home or small business, however, zero-based budgeting isn't really necessary. In most cases, you can get a more accurate estimate of your expenditures by taking previous data into account. Quicken's AutoCreate command can help you do this. There are two methods you can use:

Copy actual income and expense data AutoCreate copies the actual category and transfer information from any number of months (up to 12) into the same number of months in the budget. For example, you can take the historical data from May through August (four months) and copy it into the budget months January through April.

Copy average income and expense data AutoCreate calculates the average income, expense, and transfer amounts for any number of months (up to 12) and enters the averages in a single budget month. For example, you can take the computed average category and transfer amounts from September, October, and November and copy them into the February budget.

Follow these steps to use historical data in your budgets:

1. At the budget setup screen, pull down the Edit menu and select AutoCreate. Quicken displays the Automatically Create Budget window, as shown in Figure 11.7.

2. Enter the first month of actual data that you want to use. Press Tab or click on through.

3. Enter the last month of actual data that you want to use. Press Tab or click on Place budget starting in month.

4. Enter the month number of the first month that you want AutoCreate to copy the data to. For example, if you copy two months of data into January and February, enter 1 because January is the first month. If you copy averages, enter the month to which they should be copied. Press Tab or click on Round values to nearest.

5. Select the rounding option you prefer: $1, $10, or $100. Press Tab or click on Use average for period.

6. Type Y or click on the Use average for period field so a Y appears, to copy the average data to the month you selected in step 4.

7. Press Enter or click on Continue. AutoCreate gathers the data and copies it into the appropriate budget cells.

Figure 11.7

Quicken can automatically create a budget from your actual data.

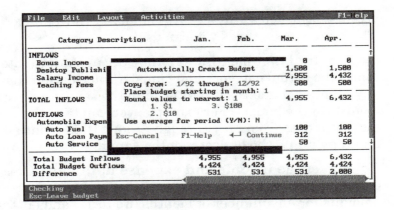

Budgeting Amounts for Transfers

When you first set up your budget, Quicken does not include transfers to other accounts on the budget setup screen. To have the budget setup screen display transfers, select the Budget Transfers option from the Edit menu. Quicken displays transfers out of your account in the OUTFLOWS section and transfers into your account in the INFLOWS section (see Figure 11.8). Enter budget amounts for your transfers as you did with your categories.

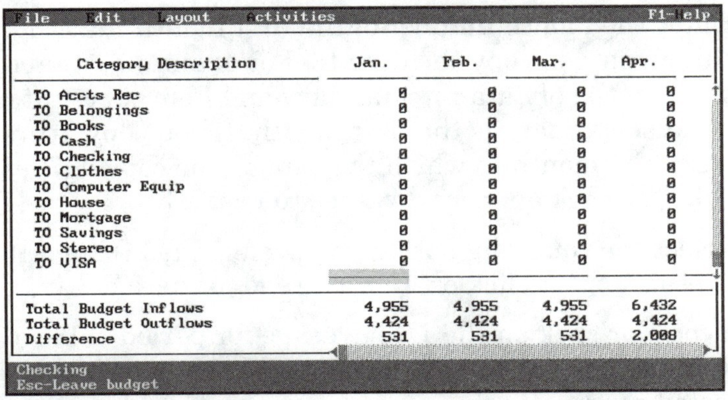

Figure 11.8

Transfers out of your account are displayed in the OUTFLOWS.

Producing Budget Reports

Entering your budget amounts is only the first stage of the budgeting process. You now have budget goals to which you can compare your actual income and expenses. To see how close you are to achieving your goals, you must generate a budget report. In this report, Quicken tallies how much you actually spent or received in each category and compares it to the goal for that category. Quicken can generate two kinds of reports:

> **The monthly budget report** A predefined report that compares your budget with what you actually spent on a monthly basis. It includes only bank, cash, and credit card accounts.
>
> **Custom budget reports** Reports that you create yourself. Like the monthly report, your custom budget reports compare actual income and expenses with your budgeted amounts. With a custom report, however, you can specify a number of options, such as how the report is organized and sorted and what transactions are used (filtering).

The Monthly Budget Report

At the end of each month, you should produce a monthly budget report to see how your budget estimates compared with your actual income and expenses. Follow these Quick Steps to produce a monthly budget report.

Producing a Monthly Budget Report

1. From the **Reports** menu, select **Personal Reports**.   Quicken displays the Personal Reports submenu.

continues

Chapter 11

> *continued*
>
> 2. Select Monthly Budget. — Quicken displays the Monthly Budget Report window, as shown in Figure 11.9.
>
> 3. Type a name for the report, if desired. Press [Tab⇥] or click on Report on months from. — The cursor moves to the Report on months from field.
>
> 4. Enter the months you want to see on the report, and then press [⤶Enter] or click on Continue. — Quicken assembles the report and displays it on the screen.

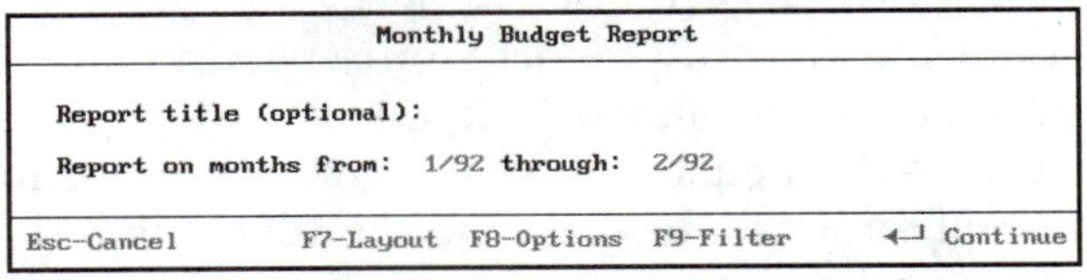

Figure 11.9
The Monthly Budget Report window.

```
                     Monthly Budget Report
 Report title (optional):
 Report on months from:  1/92  through:  2/92

 Esc-Cancel      F7-Layout  F8-Options  F9-Filter      ⤶ Continue
```

Figure 11.10 shows the January monthly budget report for the Johnsons. The most important line on the report is the bottom one: the TOTAL INCOME/EXPENSE. If the number is positive, you can pat yourself on the back for bettering your budget. If the TOTAL INCOME/EXPENSE is a negative number, then you didn't make your budget for that month. If you're only slightly under, don't worry about it; you can always make it up next month. If you're significantly under, look closely at your expenses to see where you can cut back.

```
                     January Monthly Budget Report
                        1/ 1/93 Through 1/31/93
HOME-All Accounts                                              Page 1
2/05/93
                                   1/ 1/93    -      1/31/92
        Category Description       Actual      Budget      Diff

   INCOME/EXPENSE
     INCOME
       Desktop Publishing Income   1,200.00    1,500.00    -300.00
       Salary Income               2,954.72    2,955.00      -0.38
       Teaching Fees                 750.00      500.00     250.00

     TOTAL INCOME                  4,904.72    4,955.00     -50.28

     EXPENSES
       Automobile Expenses:
         Auto Fuel                    22.89      100.00     -77.11
         Auto Loan Payment           312.21      312.00       0.21
         Auto Service                 75.31       50.00      25.31

       Total Automobile Expenses    410.41      462.00     -51.59
       Bank Charge                    5.00        5.00       0.00
       Charitable Donations         100.00       50.00      50.00
       Clothing                     427.65      300.00     127.65
       Computer expenses:
         Computer hardware          320.95      150.00     170.95
         Computer software          127.66      250.00    -122.34
         Computer expenses - Other    0.00       25.00     -25.00

       Total Computer expenses      448.61      425.00      23.61
       Dining Out                   123.75      200.00     -76.25
       Groceries                    251.24      350.00     -98.76
       Home Repair & Maint.         285.97      250.00      35.97
       Insurance                    175.00      200.00     -25.00
       Miscellaneous                 62.32      250.00    -187.68
       Mortgage Interest            729.16      729.00       0.16
       Office Expenses              357.09      200.00     157.09
       Supplies                      98.60      100.00      -1.40
       Taxes:
         Federal Tax                407.68      408.00      -0.32
         Social Security Tax        159.48      159.00       0.48
         State Tax                   32.84       33.00      -0.16
         Taxes - Other              177.20      250.00     -72.80

       Total Taxes                  777.20      850.00     -72.80
       Water, Gas, Electric
         Gas and Electricity         35.33       33.00       2.33
         Water                       24.75       20.00       4.75

       Total Water, Gas, Electric    60.08       53.00       7.08

     TOTAL EXPENSES                4,312.08    4,424.00    -111.92


   TOTAL INCOME/EXPENSE              592.64      531.00      61.64
```

Figure 11.10

The monthly budget report.

Custom Budget Reports

When you build your own custom report, you get the same kind of actual-versus-budget comparison as on a monthly budget report, but you have more control over the layout and the kinds of information contained in the report. When you first set up a budget report, you're asked to provide the following information:

Report title Provides an optional title for the report.

Restrict to transactions from Enters a range of dates for the budget comparison.

Column headings Determines the horizontal sort order of the report. For example, if you choose Week, the report will show a comparison of actual income and expenses to your budget for each week in your date range.

Use Current/All/Selected accounts Selects which accounts to use in the report.

In addition, you can select from various report options and transaction filters. Follow these steps to create a custom budget report:

1. Pull down the Report menu and select Budget. Quicken displays the Create Budget Report window, as shown in Figure 11.11.

2. Type a title in the Report title field, if you like. Press Tab or click on Restrict to transactions from.

3. Type the dates you want to use for the report. The default is the first of the year through to the current date. Press Tab or click on Use Current/All/Selected accounts.

4. Type your choice (C, A, or S) or click on the field name to cycle through the choices.

5. To set up the report options, press F8 or click on Options, and use the Report Options window to set your options.

6. To filter the transactions you use in the report, press F9 or click on Filter, and use the Filter Transactions window to specify which transactions you want to appear in the budget report.

7. When you finish, press ↵Enter or click on Continue. Quicken displays the report.

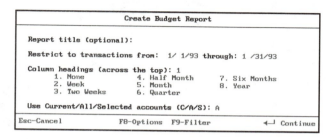

Figure 11.11
The Create Budget Report window.

Printing Your Budget Report

Once you're satisfied that the report you've created is what you want, you can print it out. Follow these steps to print your budget report:

1. Make sure your printer is turned on and is on-line.
2. Create the report as described in the previous section.
3. At the report screen, pull down the File/Print menu and select Print Report, or press Ctrl-P. Quicken displays the Print Report window, as shown in Figure 11.12.
4. Select the destination for the report.
5. Press ↵Enter or click on Print.

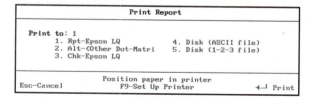

Figure 11.12
The Print Report window.

Using Quicken's Financial Planning Calculators

VERSION 6

Quicken 5 came with a loan calculator that automatically determined loan payments and created an amortization table for loans. Quicken 6 now offers five financial calculators to help you plan your finances and develop solid financial strategies:

- Loan Calculator
- Investment Calculator
- Retirement Calculator
- College Planning Calculator
- Refinance Calculator

The most useful feature of any of the financial calculators is that they allow you to play "what-if" with your finances. For example: What if the interest rate falls by 2%; will I save money by refinancing my house? What if I continue putting $100 in my retirement account each month; how much will I have saved when I reach the age of 65? What if I save a little more? With the financial calculators, you simply plug in various numbers and get immediate results.

These financial calculators are available in any of the registers or on the Write Checks screen. Use the following Quick Steps to access the calculators:

QUICK STEPS

Using a Financial Calculator

1. Pull down the Activities menu and select Financial Planning.

2. Select the calculator you want to use.

   Quicken displays the Calculator window for the selected calculator.

3. Press `F8` to put a check mark next to the field that you want Quicken to calculate.

   Quicken uses the data you enter in the other fields to calculate the selected field.

4. Fill in each of the unchecked fields with the appropriate amount. Press `Tab` or `Enter` after each field.

   When you press `Tab` or `Enter` after filling in the fields, Quicken calculates the checked field.

5. (Optional) Press `F9` or click on View Payment Schedule or Show Payments to view the payment schedule.

   Quicken displays the payment schedule. This will vary depending on the calculator you are using. Some calculators do not offer this option.

6. (Optional) Press `Ctrl`-`P` or click on Print to print out the payment schedule.

7. From the window that appears, select the appropriate printer and press `Ctrl`-`Enter` or click on Print.

The Loan Calculator

With the loan calculator, you enter the principal (the amount you borrowed), the annual interest rate, the term (the number of years you have to pay off the loan), and the number of periods per year. The calculator determines the amount of the monthly payment, as shown in Figure 11.13. You can press `F9` to view a payment schedule that shows how much of each payment goes for principal and interest.

Figure 11.13
The loan calculator.

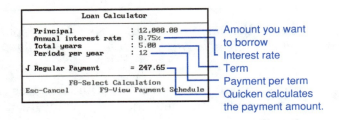

> ### 15- or 30-year Mortgage?
>
> Use the Loan Calculator to see how much money you would save by taking out a 15-year mortgage rather than a 30-year mortgage.
>
> Say you decide to take out a $70,000 loan at 10% to buy a house. You set up your loan for 30 years and see that you have monthly payments of $614. Take $614 and multiply it by 360 (the number of payments for a 30-year mortgage); the loan will cost $221,148.
>
> Change the term of the loan from 30 to 15, and you see that you would have monthly payments of $752. Take $752 times 180 (the number of payments for a 15-year mortgage); the loan will cost $135,399. In short, if you can afford $138 more per month, you will save $85,749.

The Investment Planning Calculator

The investment calculator, shown in Figure 11.14, can help you decide how much money you need to save in order to have a desired amount of money at the end of a specified time. The calculator can determine any of the following three variables, assuming you specify the other two variables:

- *Present Value.* You specify the future value of the investment (how much you want the investment to be worth after the specified number of years), the amount of any additional contributions, the number of years, and the annual yield. Quicken determines how much you have to invest initially to meet your goal. You can also have Quicken account for the inflation rate.

- *Additions each Year.* You specify the present value (the initial investment), the future value, the number of years, and the annual yield. Quicken determines how much you have to contribute each year to meet your goal.

- *Future Value.* You specify the present value, the additional contributions, the number of years, and the annual yield. Quicken determines how much the investment will be worth at the end of the specified number of years.

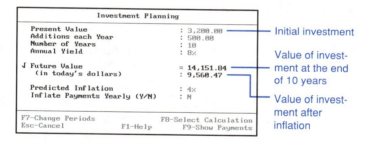

Figure 11.14

The investment calculator.

The Retirement Planning Calculator

How much money should you be sacking away for retirement? How much money will you have saved by the age of 65? How much can you expect to withdraw from your retirement account every year? And how much will those payments be worth when you are 65? The retirement calculator, shown in Figure 11.15 can tell you.

Figure 11.15

The retirement calculator.

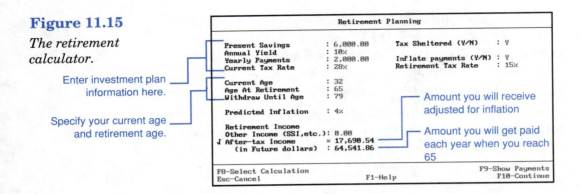

The College Planning Calculator

VERSION 6

In the good old days, you would worry about paying for college during the summer just before you enrolled. Not any more. Now you have to start saving while your child is still in the womb. To help you plan, Quicken offers the college planning calculator, shown in Figure 11.16.

Figure 11.16

The college planning calculator.

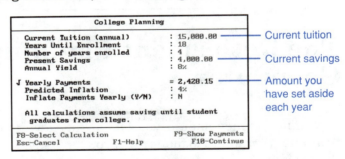

You plug in the current tuition, the number of years until enrollment, the amount you have currently saved, and the annual yield, and Quicken determines how much additional money you have to set aside each year. Or, you can supply the annual payments, and have Quicken determine how much tuition you can afford. The calculator also adjusts for inflation.

The Refinance Calculator

Whenever interest rates drop, home owners rush to banks and mortgage companies to refinance their homes. Many people spend lots of time only to find out that refinancing won't save them any money. Next time the interest rates drop, you can save yourself a trip to the bank by using Quicken's refinance calculator, as shown in Figure 11.17.

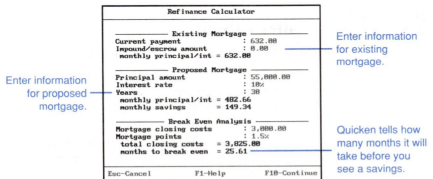

Figure 11.17
The refinance calculator.

You enter the requested information about your current mortgage and the proposed mortgage. Enter the amount of money you'll need for closing costs and the points you'll have to pay. Quicken determines the total closing costs and lets you know how many months it will take before you break even. If you plan on staying in the house beyond that amount of time, refinancing may be a good idea.

In This Chapter

Graphing Your Finances

Types of Quicken Graphs

Creating a Graph

Changing the Graphics Display Options

Filtering Data to be Graphed

Types of Quicken Graphs

- Income and Expense
- Net Worth
- Budget and Actual
- Investment

Creating a Graph

1. From the Main menu, choose View Graphs.
2. Choose the type of graph you want to create.
3. In the Graph months from field, type the first month you want graphed, and press Enter.
4. In the through field, type the last month you want included in the graph, and press Enter.

Filtering the Data to Be Graphed

1. From the Main menu, select View Graphs.
2. Select the type of graph you want to create.
3. Type the range of dates, and then press F9.
4. Complete the fields as desired to specify the data that you want included in the graph.
5. Press Ctrl-Enter or click on Continue.
6. Press Enter or click on Graph.

Chapter

12

Graphing with Quicken

VERSION 6

With Quicken 6, Intuit has introduced a new feature that allows you to graph your finances and view the graphs on-screen. (Although Quicken does not include a command for printing graphs, you'll learn a technique for printing graphs later in this chapter.)

Why graph? Because graphs give you a clearer picture of your finances than you get from reports. For example, a report may tell you that you are spending nearly $600 per month on clothing, while a pie graph will show that the amount you spend on clothing is almost as much as your house payment. Such comparisons become obvious with graphs.

To decide whether or not you need to graph your finances, use the following two criteria:

- If you want detailed information, create a report.
- If you want the big picture, create a graph.

Types of Graphs

Quicken uses four types of graphs to display your data. The following list explains the various types. Figures 12.1 to 12.4 show how the various graphs can be applied to the same data: income and expenses.

Double bar graphs show two bars side-by-side for each category being compared. For example, Quicken uses the double bar graph to display a comparison between income and expenses for each month, as shown in Figure 12.1.

Line graphs show a series of net values over time. For example, you can have Quicken display a graph that shows your income less expenses for each month of the year, as shown in Figure 12.2. This gives you a clear idea of how your net income varies from month to month.

Pie graphs show the portion that various items contribute to the composition of the whole pie. For example, the pie graph shown in Figure 12.3 represents the total expenses and the amount that each category contributes to the total.

Stacked bar graphs function as a combination of a line graph and a pie graph. As a line graph, the bars show an overall trend over time. As a pie graph, each bar is broken down to show the contribution of each item to the whole. The expense trend graph, shown in Figure 12.4, for example, indicates the change in expenses over time and the amount contributed by each expense category.

The View Graphs Menu

To create any graph, you must use the View Graphs menu, shown in Figure 12.5. To display this menu, select View Graphs from the Main menu. The View Graphs menu contains four options, each of which opens a submenu. The following sections describe each option and the types of graphs you can create.

Graphing with Quicken   241

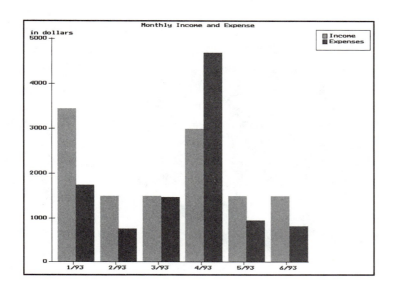

Figure 12.1
A double bar graph compares two sets of data at one point in time.

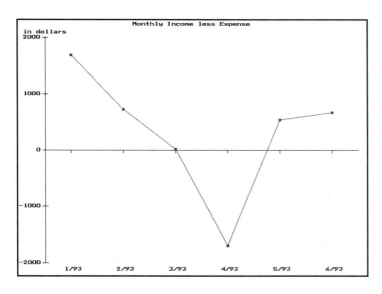

Figure 12.2
A line graph shows net values over time.

Figure 12.3

A pie graph shows each item's contribution to the whole.

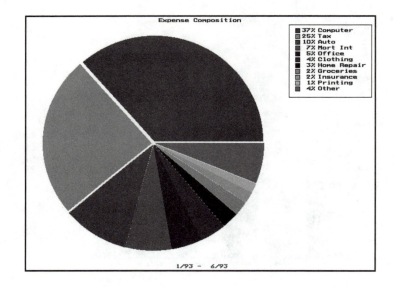

Figure 12.4

A stacked bar graph shows how values change over time, as well as how much each item contributes over time.

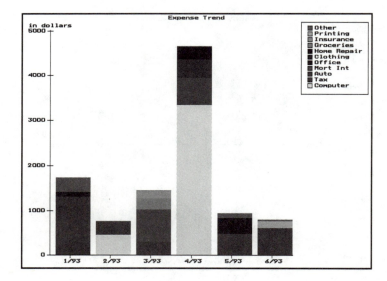

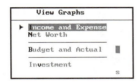

Figure 12.5
The View Graphs submenu.

Income and Expenses

The Income and Expense graphs provide some useful guidance concerning cash flow. You get to see how much money is coming in, how much is going out, and how much is left at the end of each month. These graphs also let you see whether your cash flow is improving or getting worse from month to month.

If you choose Income and Expense from the View Graphs menu, Quicken displays the submenu shown in Figure 12.6. This menu offers the following options:

Monthly Income and Expense Choose this option to create a side-by-side bar graph. Quicken displays pairs of bars, each pair consisting of one bar that represents income and one that represents expenses.

Monthly Income Less Expense Choose this option to view your net income (income less expenses) over time. Quicken creates a line graph showing how your net income varies from month to month.

Income Composition Choosing this option displays a pie graph that shows how much each income item contributes to your total income.

Income Trend Choosing this option displays a stacked bar graph that shows how your total income varies over time and how the contribution of each income item to the total changes.

Expense Composition Choose this option to display a pie graph that shows how each expense item contributes to your total expenses.

Expense Trend   Choose this option to display a stacked bar graph that shows how your total expenses vary over time and how the contribution of each expense item to the total changes.

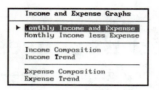

Figure 12.6
The Income and Expense submenu lets you graph income and expenses in various ways.

Net Worth

The net worth graphs are useful for examining the balances of various accounts and for determining whether your net worth is increasing or decreasing. With net worth graphs, you get a clear picture of whether you actually own more than you owe.

To create a net worth graph, select View Graphs from the Main menu, and then select Net Worth. Quicken displays the Net Worth submenu, shown in Figure 12.7. This menu offers the following options:

Monthly Assets and Liabilities   Choose this option to create a side-by-side bar graph that compares total assets to total liabilities for each month.

Monthly Assets Less Liabilities   Choose this option to create a line graph that shows how your net assets (assets less liabilities) vary from month to month.

Asset Composition   Choose this option to create a pie graph that shows the contribution of each of your assets to your total assets.

Asset Trend   Choose this option to create a stacked bar graph that shows how your total assets vary over time and how each asset's contribution to the whole varies over time.

Liability Composition   Choose this option to create a pie graph that shows the contribution of each liability to your total liabilities.

Liability Trend   Choose this option to create a stacked bar graph that shows your total liabilities over time and how each liability's contribution to the whole changes over time.

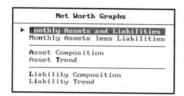

Figure 12.7
The Net Worth submenu lets you create graphs to see if you own more than you owe.

Budget and Actual

Most of us, at one time or another, wonder where all the money is going. With the budget graphs, you will see where all your money is going and whether your actual spending is anywhere near the budgeted amounts.

To create a budget graph, select View Graphs from the Main menu, and then select Budget and Actual. Quicken displays the Budget and Actual submenu, shown in Figure 12.8. This menu offers the following options:

Monthly Budget and Actual   Choose this option to create a side-by-side bar graph that compares your actual income and expenses to your budgeted income and expenses.

Monthly Actual Less Budget   Choose this option to create a line graph showing how close you are to meeting your budget. This graph will show whether you need to tighten your belt or whether you can loosen up and spend more.

Categories Over Budget   Choose this option to view a double-bar graph that shows categories for which you have overspent. This will tell you where you need to cut back.

Categories Under Budget Choose this option to view a double-bar graph that shows categories for which you have underspent.

Budget Composition Choose this option to create a pie graph that shows each budget item's contribution to the total budget.

Budget Trend Choose this option to create a stacked bar graph that shows how the total budget varies from month to month and how each budgeted item's contribution varies from month to month.

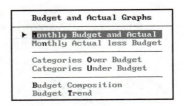

Figure 12.8
The Budget and Actual submenu lets you create graphs to determine if you are underearning or overspending.

Investment

The Investment graphs provide you with a view of how much money you have invested in each security and how those investments have done over time.

To create an investment graph, select View Graphs from the Main menu, and then select Investment. Quicken displays the Investment submenu, shown in Figure 12.9. This menu offers the following options:

Portfolio Composition Choose this option to view a pie graph showing how much each security is contributing to the total value of your investments.

Portfolio Value Trend Choose this option to display a stacked bar graph that shows how the value of your investment portfolio varies over time and how each security's contribution to the whole varies over time.

Price History Choose this option to display a line graph that shows how the price of each of your securities varies over time. This graph can help you decide whether you want to invest more or less in a given security.

Graphing with Quicken **247**

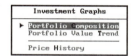

Figure 12.9
The Investment submenu lets you create graphs to help you keep track of the growth of your investments.

Creating a Graph

The procedure for creating a graph in Quicken is basically the same for any graph. The following Quick Steps explain how to create a graph in Quicken.

> **NOTE:** When you select the type of graph you want to create, Quicken will ask you to specify which months you want the graph to cover. Try to select 12 months or fewer to keep the graph from being too crowded.

Creating a Graph

1. From the Main menu, choose View Graphs.

   Quicken displays the View Graphs submenu.

2. Choose the type of graph you want to create.

   Quicken displays a dialog box, as shown in Figure 12.10, prompting you to specify which months you want included in the graph.

3. In the Graph months from field, type the first month you want graphed, and press ↵Enter or Tab.

   The cursor moves to the through field.

4. In the through field, type the last month you want included in the graph, and press ↵Enter or click on Graph.

   Quicken creates the selected graph and displays it on-screen.

Figure 12.10
Quicken asks you to specify the range of dates you want the graph to include.

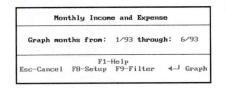

> **TIP:** Although Quicken does not contain a command that allows you to print graphs, you can print the graph using [PrtSc]. Before doing this, however, quit Quicken, change to the drive and directory that contains your DOS files, type **graphics**, and press [⏎Enter]. This allows DOS to print graphics screens. You can now press [PrtSc] or [⇧Shift]-[PrtSc] to print the graph. (*Note:* Some of the lighter colors, such as yellow, may not print.)

Changing Display Options for the Graph Feature

By default, Quicken assumes you want to see more graph and less text on your graphs, so Quicken reduces the print size of any text that appears on the graph and in the legend. However, you can choose to have the text displayed in a larger type size, by using the Graphics Drivers Options dialog box shown in Figure 12.11. You can display this dialog box in either of two ways:

- From the Main Menu, select **P**references, **S**creen Settings, and **S**creen **G**raphics.

- From the View Graphs menu, select the type of graph you want to create, and then press [F8] or click on Setup.

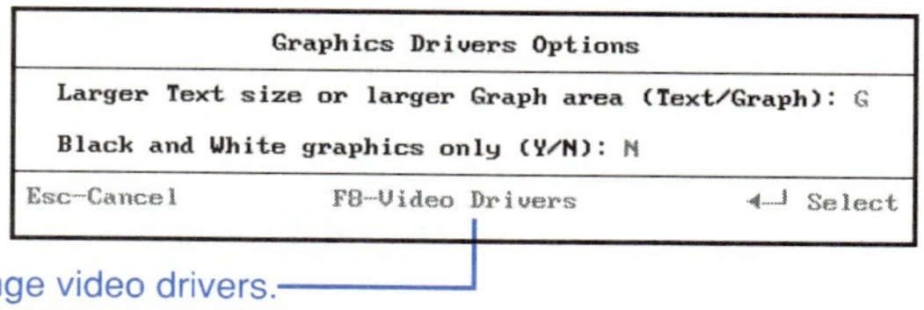

Figure 12.11
The Graphics Drivers Options dialog box.

Press F8 to change video drivers.

To display larger text, type T in the Larger Text size or larger Graph area field. You can also type Y in the Black and White graphics only field to display the graphs in black-and-white instead of color. If the graphs are not displayed correctly on-screen, press F8 or click on Video Drivers and select a different video driver from the list.

Graphing Selected Data

Just as you can filter data to include only selected data in a report, you can filter data when creating graphs. The graph will then include only the specified data. To filter data, perform the following steps:

1. From the Main menu, select View Graphs, and then select the type of graph you want to create. A dialog box appears, asking you to type the range of dates you want to graph.

2. Type the range of dates, and then press F9 or click on Filter. A Filters window appears. The options in this window will vary depending on the type of graph. The Filters window for an Income and Expense graph is shown in Figure 12.12.

3. Complete the fields as desired to specify the data that you want to include in the graph.

4. Press Ctrl-Enter or click on Continue.

5. Press Enter or click on Graph to create the graph.

Figure 12.12
The Income and Expenses Filter Window.

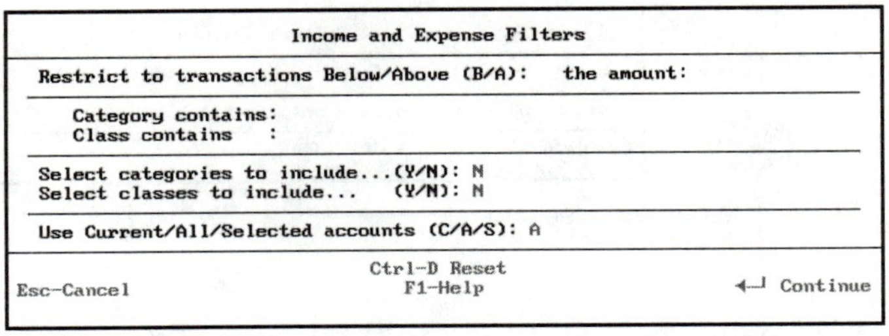

```
                        Income and Expense Filters
 Restrict to transactions Below/Above (B/A):    the amount:
      Category contains:
      Class contains   :
 Select categories to include...(Y/N): N
 Select classes to include...   (Y/N): N
 Use Current/All/Selected accounts (C/A/S): A

                          Ctrl-D Reset
 Esc-Cancel                 F1-Help                      ←┘ Continue
```

In This Chapter

Planning for Your Taxes

Setting Up Categories for Taxes

Creating Tax Reports

Exporting Tax Data

Setting Up Tax-Related Categories

1. At the account register, pull down the Shortcuts menu and select Categorize/Transfer.
2. Select <New Category>.
3. Enter the name, type, and description of the category, and then press Tab.
4. Type **Y**.
5. Press F9 or click on Tax Schedules.
6. Select the desired tax schedule.
7. Select the desired tax line.
8. Press Ctrl-Enter or click on Setup.

Generating a Tax Schedule Report

1. Select Create Reports from the Main menu or pull down the Reports menu.
2. Select Personal Reports.
3. Select Tax Schedule.
4. Enter a report title (optional) and the dates for the report.
5. Press Ctrl-Enter or click on Continue to create the report.

Chapter 13
Using Quicken at Tax Time

In this chapter, you'll see how Quicken can help prepare your federal income tax return. If you prepare your own return, Quicken can greatly reduce the time you spend on the return because it summarizes and organizes your tax data. If someone else prepares your return, Quicken can save you money because the tax service won't have to go through all your records. Finally, if you use a tax preparation program, Quicken can export your tax data in a format that the program can read.

Planning for Taxes

Before Quicken can help you save time doing your taxes, you must understand how Quicken and the IRS organize tax information. Take a look at the individual line items on Schedule C (see Figure 13.1):

Line 1 Gross receipts or sales.

Line 8 Advertising.

Line 18 Office expense.

Figure 13.1

Schedule C income tax form.

Quicken categories

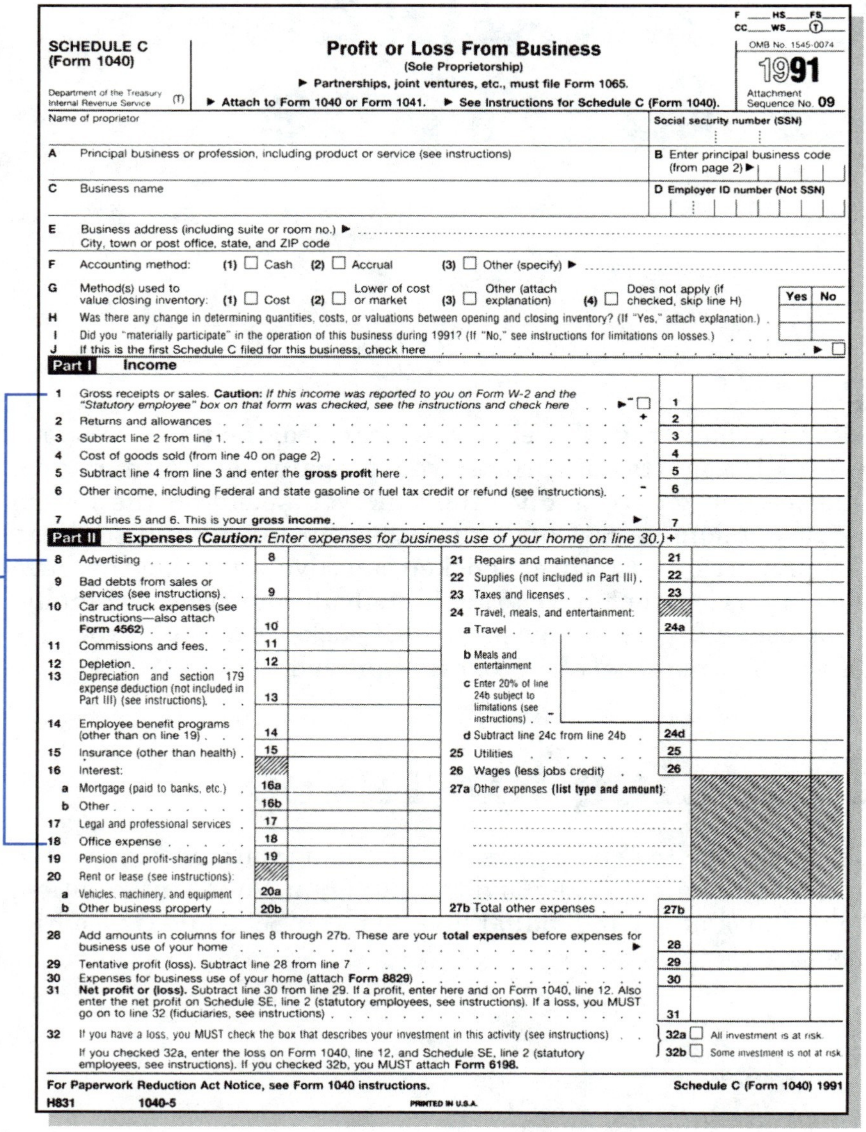

SCHEDULE C (Form 1040)

Department of the Treasury Internal Revenue Service (T)

Profit or Loss From Business

(Sole Proprietorship)

▶ Partnerships, joint ventures, etc., must file Form 1065.

▶ Attach to Form 1040 or Form 1041. ▶ See Instructions for Schedule C (Form 1040).

F ___ HS ___ FS ___ CC ___ WS ___ (T)

OMB No. 1545-0074

1991

Attachment Sequence No. 09

Name of proprietor | Social security number (SSN)

A Principal business or profession, including product or service (see instructions) | B Enter principal business code (from page 2) ▶

C Business name | D Employer ID number (Not SSN)

E Business address (including suite or room no.) ▶ City, town or post office, state, and ZIP code

F Accounting method: (1) ☐ Cash (2) ☐ Accrual (3) ☐ Other (specify) ▶

G Method(s) used to value closing inventory: (1) ☐ Cost (2) ☐ Lower of cost or market (3) ☐ Other (attach explanation) (4) ☐ Does not apply (if checked, skip line H) | Yes | No

H Was there any change in determining quantities, costs, or valuations between opening and closing inventory? (If "Yes," attach explanation.)

I Did you "materially participate" in the operation of this business during 1991? (If "No," see instructions for limitations on losses.)

J If this is the first Schedule C filed for this business, check here ▶ ☐

Part I Income

1 Gross receipts or sales. **Caution:** *If this income was reported to you on Form W-2 and the "Statutory employee" box on that form was checked, see the instructions and check here* ▶ ☐ | 1

2 Returns and allowances | 2

3 Subtract line 2 from line 1 | 3

4 Cost of goods sold (from line 40 on page 2) | 4

5 Subtract line 4 from line 3 and enter the **gross profit** here | 5

6 Other income, including Federal and state gasoline or fuel tax credit or refund (see instructions) | 6

7 Add lines 5 and 6. This is your **gross income** ▶ | 7

Part II Expenses (*Caution: Enter expenses for business use of your home on line 30.*)

8 Advertising | 8

9 Bad debts from sales or services (see instructions) | 9

10 Car and truck expenses (see instructions—also attach **Form 4562**) | 10

11 Commissions and fees | 11

12 Depletion | 12

13 Depreciation and section 179 expense deduction (not included in Part III) (see instructions) | 13

14 Employee benefit programs (other than on line 19) | 14

15 Insurance (other than health) | 15

16 Interest:

a Mortgage (paid to banks, etc.) | 16a

b Other | 16b

17 Legal and professional services | 17

18 Office expense | 18

19 Pension and profit-sharing plans | 19

20 Rent or lease (see instructions):

a Vehicles, machinery, and equipment | 20a

b Other business property | 20b

21 Repairs and maintenance | 21

22 Supplies (not included in Part III) | 22

23 Taxes and licenses | 23

24 Travel, meals, and entertainment:

a Travel | 24a

b Meals and entertainment

c Enter 20% of line 24b subject to limitations (see instructions)

d Subtract line 24c from line 24b | 24d

25 Utilities | 25

26 Wages (less jobs credit) | 26

27a Other expenses (**list type and amount**):

27b Total other expenses | 27b

28 Add amounts in columns for lines 8 through 27b. These are your **total expenses** before expenses for business use of your home ▶ | 28

29 Tentative profit (loss). Subtract line 28 from line 7 | 29

30 Expenses for business use of your home (attach **Form 8829**) | 30

31 **Net profit or (loss).** Subtract line 30 from line 29. If a profit, enter here and on Form 1040, line 12. Also enter the net profit on Schedule SE, line 2 (statutory employees, see instructions). If a loss, you MUST go on to line 32 (fiduciaries, see instructions) | 31

32 If you have a loss, you MUST check the box that describes your investment in this activity (see instructions). If you checked 32a, enter the loss on Form 1040, line 12, and Schedule SE, line 2 (statutory employees, see instructions). If you checked 32b, you MUST attach **Form 6198**. | 32a ☐ All investment is at risk. | 32b ☐ Some investment is not at risk.

For Paperwork Reduction Act Notice, see Form 1040 instructions. **Schedule C (Form 1040) 1991**

H831 1040-5 PRINTED IN U.S.A.

When you fill out a tax return, what you're really doing is *categorizing* your income and expenses for the IRS. In other words, you are using *categories,* and many of the categories that the IRS uses on its tax forms have matching categories in Quicken.

With Quicken, you can assign the appropriate tax schedule and tax line to each tax-related category, so all you need to do is specify the proper category whenever you enter a transaction. At the end of the year, you can create a report (sorted by tax forms) showing the subtotals for each line on the form. All you do is transfer the appropriate totals from the report to the corresponding lines on your tax forms.

This is pretty handy, but getting the most out of this system requires some planning and discipline on your part. Basically, there are three things you must do:

1. Examine each of the tax forms you fill out and make a note of every line you might use.

2. Check to see if a Quicken category exists for each of the lines you marked in step 1. If one doesn't exist, create it and assign it the appropriate tax schedule and line.

3. Categorize your transactions as you enter them.

Using Tax-Related Categories

Most of the work involved in setting up the tax schedule information for categories has already been done for you. Quicken has assigned tax schedules and tax form lines to many of the predefined home and business categories. Table 13.1 shows the standard Quicken business categories and their corresponding tax forms and lines (from the 1991 tax year).

Table 13.1
Quicken Business Categories and Corresponding Tax Schedules

Category	Form	Line
Income categories		
Gr Sales	C	Gross receipts or sales
Other Inc	1040	Other income
Rent Income	E	Rents received
Expense categories		
Ads	C	Advertising
Car	C	Car and truck expenses
Commission	C	Commissions and fees
Freight	C	Other expenses
Int Paid	C	Interest:Other
L&P Fees services	C	Legal and professional
Late Fees	C	Other expenses
Office	C	Office expense
Rent Paid property	C	Rent:Other business
Repairs	C	Repairs and maintenance
Returns	C	Returns and allowances
Tax	C	Taxes and licenses
Travel	C	Travel
Wages	C	Wages

Figure 13.2 shows Schedule A, the general form used by individuals to declare itemized deductions. Again, many of the lines you see on this form have corresponding categories in Quicken. Table 13.2 lists the tax-related home categories with their corresponding schedules and lines.

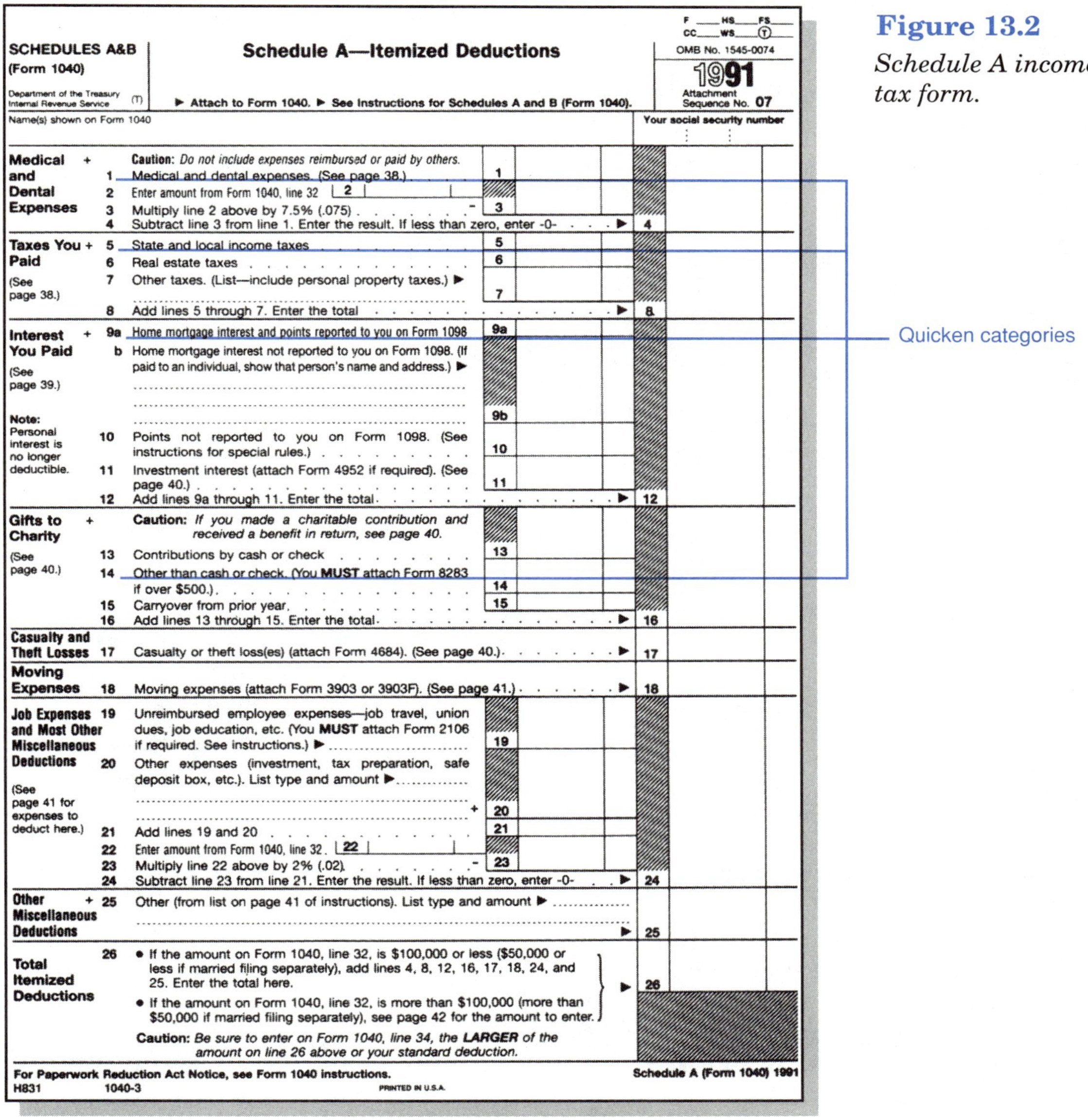

Using Quicken at Tax Time   257

Figure 13.2
Schedule A income tax form.

Table 13.2
Tax-Related Home Categories

Category	Form	Line
Income categories		
Bonus	W-2	Salary
Div Inc	B	Dividend income
Int Inc	B	Interest income
Invest Inc	1040	Other income
Old Age Pension	W-2P	Pensions and annuities—gross
Other Inc	1040	Other income
Salary	W-2	Salary
Expense categories		
Charity	A	Contributions by cash or check
Int Exp	A	Personal interest you paid
Invest Exp	A	Other expenses
Medical	A	Medical and dental
Mort Int	A	Deductible home mortgage interest
Other Exp	C	Other expenses
Supplies	C	Office expenses
Tax	C	Taxes and licenses
UIC	A	State and local income taxes

Table 13.3 shows the tax-related investment categories and their corresponding tax schedules and lines.

Table 13.3
Tax-Related Investment Categories

Category	Form	Line
_DivInc	B	Dividend income
_IntInc	B	Interest income
_LT CapGnDst	D	Long-term capital gains and losses
_ST CapGnDst	D	Short-term capital gains and losses
IntExp	4952	Investment interest

Setting Up Tax-Related Categories

In Chapter 4, you learned how to set up and work with categories. In this section, we will review the steps for assigning tax information to a category. As an example, create the following expense category for the BOOKSHOP account file:

Name	Emp Benefits
Type	Expense
Description	Employee benefits expense
Tax-related	Y
Tax Schedule	C
Tax Line	Employee benefits progs.

Follow these steps to set up tax-related categories:

1. At the account register, press Ctrl-C or pull down the Shortcuts menu and select Categorize/Transfer. The Category and Transfer List appears.

2. Select <New Category>. Quicken displays the Set Up Category window.

3. Enter the name, type, and description of the category (press Tab or Enter to move from one field to the next). Press Tab or click on the Tax-related field.

4. Type Y.

5. Press F9 or click on Tax Schedules. The Tax Schedule menu appears, as shown in Figure 13.3.

6. Use the arrow keys to highlight the appropriate schedule and press Enter, or double-click on the schedule. The Tax Line menu appears, as shown in Figure 13.4.

7. Use the arrow keys to highlight the appropriate tax line and press Enter, or double-click on the line.

8. For schedules where you can file multiple copies (such as Schedule C), a Schedule Copy Number window appears. Enter the number of copies you're going to file and press `Enter` or click on Continue. Quicken returns you to the Set Up Category window.

9. To finish setting up the category, press `Ctrl`-`Enter` or click on Setup.

Figure 13.3
The Tax Schedule menu.

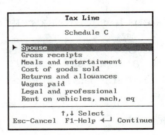

Figure 13.4
The Tax Line menu.

NOTE: If you assign tax form information to a category that has subcategories, the tax information *does not* automatically apply to each of the subcategories. You must define the tax schedule and tax line separately for each subcategory.

Marking an Existing Category as Tax-Related

If you created a category but have not yet marked it as tax-related, you can edit the existing category. To mark a category as tax-related, take the following steps:

1. At the account register, press Ctrl-C or pull down the Shortcuts menu and select Categorize/Transfer.
2. Highlight the category you want to mark, and press Ctrl-E or click on Edit.
3. Tab to or click on the Tax-related field.
4. Type Y.
5. Press F9 or click on Tax Schedules.
6. Use the arrow keys to highlight the appropriate schedule and press Enter, or double-click on the schedule.
7. Use the arrow keys to highlight the appropriate tax line and press Enter, or double-click on the line.
8. If a Schedule Copy Number window appears, enter the number of copies you're going to file and press Enter or click on Continue.
9. Press Ctrl-Enter or click on Setup.

Searching for Additional Categories

Carefully examine each of the tax forms you use and look for line items that aren't on the list of Standard Home and Business categories. If you find a tax line you think you'll use, create a category. If you're a farmer, for example, you'll probably want to create categories for most of Schedule F (Farm Income and Expenses). To get you started, Table 13.4 shows some line items that could be made into categories.

Table 13.4 *Additional Category Suggestions from the Tax Forms*

Tax Form	Income Line	Expense Line
1040	Alimony received	Alimony paid
	IRA distributions	IRA deductions
	Unemployment compensation	

continues

Table 13.4
Continued.

Tax Form	Income Line	Expense Line
Schedule A	Deductible points	Gifts to charity other than by cash or check
		Casualty or theft losses
		Moving expenses
Schedule C		Bad debts
		Depletion
		Depreciation
		Meals and entertainment
Schedule E	Royalties received	

Using Classes

Although you can't assign tax-related information to classes, you can use them to refine your tax reporting. In a home office, for example, there will be such categories as Supplies, where some transactions are for personal use (non-tax-related) and some are for business use (tax-related). The best way to handle this is to set up classes to separate the two kinds of transactions. In Chapter 4, you set up Personal and Business classes for the Johnsons' HOME file. Another approach would be to set up classes called *Tax-related* and *Non-tax-related*. To get the proper information at tax time, you filter your tax reports to exclude classes of transactions that you classified as Personal or Non-tax-related.

Setting Up Tax-Related Accounts

In addition to assigning tax information to categories, Quicken lets you define entire accounts as tax-related. This is useful if you have your IRA or Keogh plan in a Quicken investment account. In certain cases, you can use contributions to these accounts to claim a deduction on your 1040 (see Figure 13.5). By defining a tax schedule and tax line for these accounts, your total contributions (and your total withdrawals) will appear on your tax reports, and you can proceed with the deduction calculation.

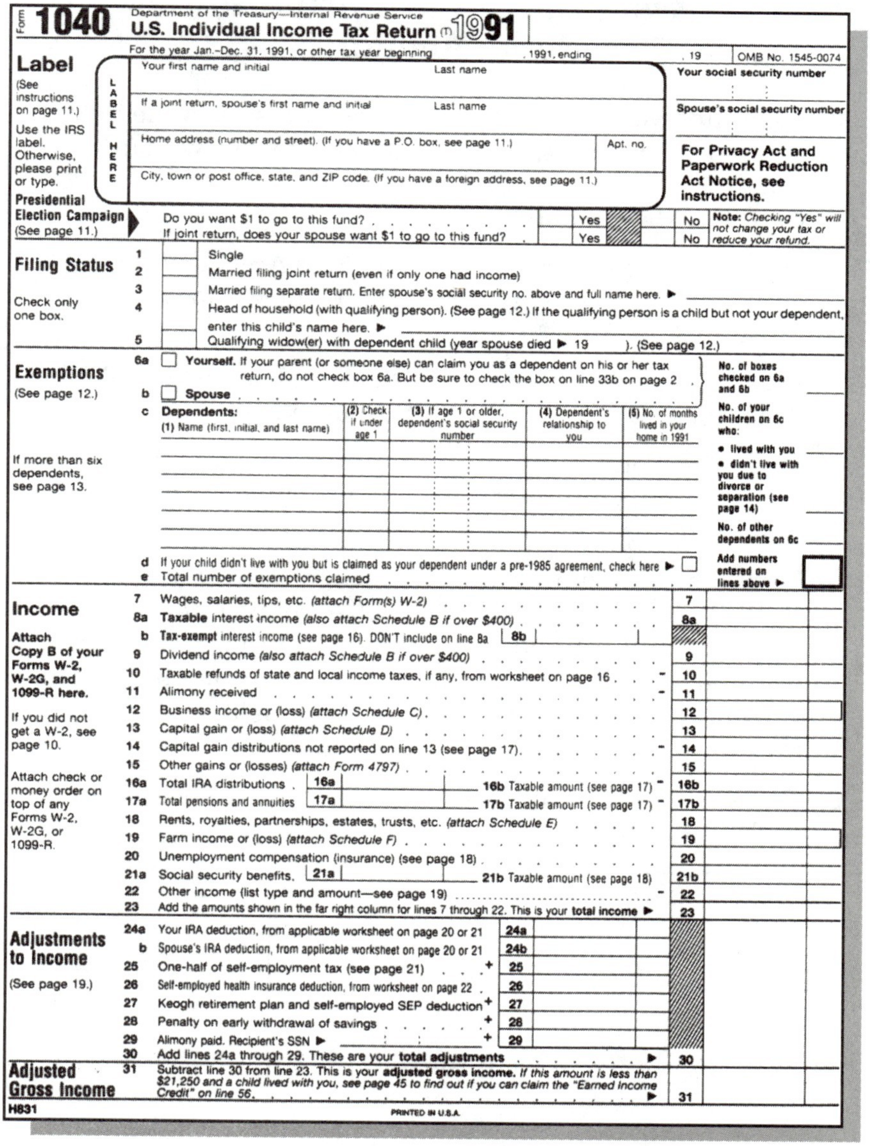

Form 1040 Department of the Treasury—Internal Revenue Service
U.S. Individual Income Tax Return 1991

For the year Jan.–Dec. 31, 1991, or other tax year beginning , 1991, ending , 19 OMB No. 1545-0074

Label (See instructions on page 11.) Use the IRS label. Otherwise, please print or type.
LABEL HERE
Your first name and initial | Last name | Your social security number
If a joint return, spouse's first name and initial | Last name | Spouse's social security number
Home address (number and street). (If you have a P.O. box, see page 11.) | Apt. no.
City, town or post office, state, and ZIP code. (If you have a foreign address, see page 11.)
For Privacy Act and Paperwork Reduction Act Notice, see instructions.

Presidential Election Campaign (See page 11.)
Do you want $1 to go to this fund? Yes No
If joint return, does your spouse want $1 to go to this fund? Yes No
Note: *Checking "Yes" will not change your tax or reduce your refund.*

Filing Status
Check only one box.
1 Single
2 Married filing joint return (even if only one had income)
3 Married filing separate return. Enter spouse's social security no. above and full name here. ▶
4 Head of household (with qualifying person). (See page 12.) If the qualifying person is a child but not your dependent, enter this child's name here. ▶
5 Qualifying widow(er) with dependent child (year spouse died ▶ 19). (See page 12.)

Exemptions
(See page 12.)
6a **Yourself.** If your parent (or someone else) can claim you as a dependent on his or her tax return, do not check box 6a. But be sure to check the box on line 33b on page 2
b **Spouse**
No. of boxes checked on 6a and 6b
c **Dependents:** (1) Name (first, initial, and last name) | (2) Check if under age 1 | (3) If age 1 or older, dependent's social security number | (4) Dependent's relationship to you | (5) No. of months lived in your home in 1991
No. of your children on 6c who: • lived with you • didn't live with you due to divorce or separation (see page 14)
No. of other dependents on 6c
If more than six dependents, see page 13.
d If your child didn't live with you but is claimed as your dependent under a pre-1985 agreement, check here ▶
e Total number of exemptions claimed
Add numbers entered on lines above ▶

Income
Attach Copy B of your Forms W-2, W-2G, and 1099-R here.
If you did not get a W-2, see page 10.
Attach check or money order on top of any Forms W-2, W-2G, or 1099-R.
7 Wages, salaries, tips, etc. *(attach Form(s) W-2)* 7
8a **Taxable** interest income *(also attach Schedule B if over $400)* 8a
b **Tax-exempt** interest income (see page 16). DON'T include on line 8a 8b
9 Dividend income *(also attach Schedule B if over $400)* 9
10 Taxable refunds of state and local income taxes, if any, from worksheet on page 16 10
11 Alimony received 11
12 Business income or (loss) *(attach Schedule C)* 12
13 Capital gain or (loss) *(attach Schedule D)* 13
14 Capital gain distributions not reported on line 13 (see page 17) 14
15 Other gains or (losses) *(attach Form 4797)* 15
16a Total IRA distributions 16a | 16b Taxable amount (see page 17) 16b
17a Total pensions and annuities 17a | 17b Taxable amount (see page 17) 17b
18 Rents, royalties, partnerships, estates, trusts, etc. *(attach Schedule E)* 18
19 Farm income or (loss) *(attach Schedule F)* 19
20 Unemployment compensation (insurance) (see page 18) 20
21a Social security benefits 21a | 21b Taxable amount (see page 18) 21b
22 Other income (list type and amount—see page 19) 22
23 Add the amounts shown in the far right column for lines 7 through 22. This is your **total income** ▶ 23

Adjustments to Income
(See page 19.)
24a Your IRA deduction, from applicable worksheet on page 20 or 21 24a
b Spouse's IRA deduction, from applicable worksheet on page 20 or 21 24b
25 One-half of self-employment tax (see page 21) 25
26 Self-employed health insurance deduction, from worksheet on page 22 26
27 Keogh retirement plan and self-employed SEP deduction 27
28 Penalty on early withdrawal of savings 28
29 Alimony paid. Recipient's SSN ▶ 29
30 Add lines 24a through 29. These are your **total adjustments** ▶ 30

Adjusted Gross Income
31 Subtract line 30 from line 23. This is your **adjusted gross income.** *If this amount is less than $21,250 and a child lived with you, see page 45 to find out if you can claim the "Earned Income Credit" on line 56.* ▶ 31

H831 PRINTED IN U.S.A.

Figure 13.5
The Form 1040 individual income tax return.

Chapter 13

Follow these Quick Steps to assign tax-related information to an account.

Assigning Tax Information to an Account

1. Assuming you've already created the account, choose Select Account from the Main menu.

   Quicken displays the Select Account to Use window.

2. Highlight the desired account and press Ctrl-E or click on Edit.

   The Edit Account Information window appears.

3. Press F9 or click on Tax Schedules.

   Quicken displays the Tax Schedule menu.

4. Highlight Form 1040 and press Enter or click on Continue.

   Quicken displays the Form 1040 submenu, as shown in Figure 13.6.

5. Highlight the appropriate tax line. (For example, highlight IRA contribs-deductible for an IRA.) Press Enter or click on Continue.

   Quicken returns you to the Edit Account Information window with the tax information displayed in the Tax Schedule field.

6. Press Ctrl-Enter or click on Continue.

   Quicken records the information.

Figure 13.6
The Form 1040 menu.

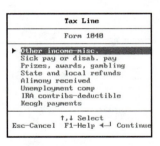

Creating Tax Reports

The fruits of your year-round tax-preparation labor finally come at tax time, when you print out your reports and see all your tax information neatly laid out for you. You can create two tax reports: the Tax Summary Report and the Tax Schedule Report.

The Tax Summary Report lists tax-related income and expenses by category, providing you with a thorough record of all tax-related transactions. The Tax Schedule Report groups transactions from all your accounts according to the tax schedule (Schedule A, Schedule C, and so on) and then by the tax form line description. The Tax Schedule Report is more useful for completing your tax forms at the end of the year.

The following steps explain how to create and customize a Tax Schedule Report:

1. From the main menu select **Create Reports** or, from any register, pull down the **Reports** menu.

2. Select **Personal Reports**. The Personal Reports submenu appears.

3. Select **Tax Schedule**. The Tax Schedule Report window appears, as shown in Figure 13.7.

4. Enter a report title (optional) and the dates for the report (use `Tab` to move from field to field).

5. (Optional) Press `F7` or click on **Layout** to customize the report layout. Use this option to restrict the accounts your report uses. Press `Esc` or click on **Cancel** to return to the Tax Schedule Report window.

6. (Optional) Press `F8` or click on **Options** to customize the organization and appearance of your report. If you want to suppress the transaction detail, type Y in the Show totals only field. If you've set up an account as tax-related, make sure that the **Include all** option is selected in the Transfers field. Press `Ctrl`-`↵Enter` or click on **Continue** to return to the Tax Schedule Report window.

7. Press F9 or click on Filter to filter the transactions that appear in your report. If you used classes to differentiate between tax-related and non-tax-related in some categories, type Y in the Select classes to include field and then exclude the non-tax-related classes. Press Ctrl-Enter or click on Continue to return to the Tax Schedule Report window.

8. Press Ctrl-Enter or click on Continue to create the report.

Figure 13.7
The Tax Schedule Report window.

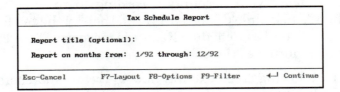

Figure 13.8 shows a sample tax schedule report for Mrs. Johnson's home business. The transaction detail has been suppressed, and transactions classified as Personal have been filtered out. Like all Quicken reports, the tax schedule reports can be printed. See Chapter 10 for details.

Using Quicken at Tax Time

```
                    1992 Tax Schedule Report
                    1/ 1/92 Through 12/31/92
HOME-All Accounts
Page 1
4/ 3/92

                Description                         Amount

    Form 1040

        Other income-misc.                       28,075.00

        IRA contribs-deductible                  -2,000.00

    Schedule A

        Cash charity contributions                 -200.00

    Schedule C

        Other business expense                     -744.91

        Advertising                                -883.47

        Office expense                           -2,707.73

        Travel                                     -312.21
```

Figure 13.8
A sample tax schedule report.

NOTE: If you use a tax preparation program such as TurboTax or TaxCut, you can print the Tax Schedule Report to disk and then import the data into your tax preparation program. For details on how to print a report to disk, see Chapter 10. For details on how to use the data on disk in your tax preparation program, refer to the documentation that came with the tax preparation program.

In This Chapter

Cash versus Accrual Accounting Methods

Cash Accounting with Quicken

Payables and Receivables with Cash Accounting

Accrual Accounting with Quicken

Accruing Payables and Receivables

Producing Business Reports

Recording an Invoice

1. At the accounts receivable register, select a blank transaction.
2. In the Date field, enter the date you expect the invoice to be paid, and press Tab.
3. Enter the invoice number, and press Tab.
4. Enter the payee's name, and press Tab three times.
5. Enter the invoice amount, and then press Enter.
6. Type the date you issued the invoice, and press Enter.
7. Select an income category for the invoice.
8. Press Ctrl-Enter.

Creating a Business Report

1. From the Main menu, select Create Reports, or pull down the Reports menu.
2. Select Business Reports.
3. Select the report you want to produce.
4. Enter a title for the report.
5. Enter the date for the report, as needed.
6. Press Ctrl-Enter or click on Continue.

Chapter 14

Setting Up a Business Accounting System

This chapter covers the fundamentals for creating a complete business accounting system with Quicken. You'll learn the differences between cash accounting and accrual accounting, and you'll learn how to set up your payables and receivables using both methods, and you'll learn how to produce business reports.

Cash Versus Accrual Accounting

When you set up an accounting system for your business, one of the first decisions you have to make is when to record your transactions. You can record a transaction either at the time it occurs or when you first know the transaction will take place. For example, if you receive an invoice for an insurance payment due on June 1, you can record the payment on June 1 (or when you print the check), or you can record it as a future payment. The first method is called *cash accounting*, and the second method is called *accrual accounting*.

The method you use depends on the type of business you have. If your business is a corporation, for example, you must use the accrual system. On the other hand, for a small service-based business, the simpler cash-basis method is usually sufficient. The key point is the timing of your financial activity. You should use the cash method if

- You bill and collect payments from your customers around the time your product or service is delivered.
- You don't carry a regular inventory of goods.
- Your vendors are invoicing and collecting payments from you close to when the product or service is delivered.

You should use the accrual method if

- You bill and collect payments from your customers over several weeks or months.
- You regularly carry an inventory of goods.
- Your vendors are invoicing and collecting payments from you over several weeks or months.

Completing Your Chart of Accounts

A *chart of accounts* is a list of codes used to classify each of your company's income and expense transactions (Table 14.1 shows a simple chart of accounts). These correspond, roughly, to the categories you create when you record transactions in your Quicken registers. To set up a working accounting system for your business, you must first make sure that your chart of accounts is complete.

Table 14.1
A Sample Chart of Accounts

Description	Account Code
Income	
Gross Sales	505
Returns	510
Other Income	515
Expenses	
Advertising	605
Freight	610
Utilities	615

The standard business categories supplied by Quicken are a good place to start. Using the methods you learned in Chapter 4, "Using Categories and Classes," you can either modify the existing list or add other categories that you might need. The best approach is to talk to an accountant and have him or her determine the specific categories that best suit your type of business.

If you already have a chart of accounts, you should restructure your categories to follow your current system. In most cases, you have (or your accountant has) assigned a number for each type of income and expense. For example, Gross Sales might be 1005, Bad Debt Allowance might be 2020, and so on. Edit the standard categories so the names and descriptions reflect your numbering system.

It is very important to categorize every one of your transactions. Without categorizing all your income and expenses, you won't be able to effectively manage and report your finances. If you're not disciplined when it comes to entering categories, you can have Quicken remind you to select a category before a transaction is recorded. To do this, follow these steps:

1. From the Main menu, select Set Preferences. Quicken displays the Set Preferences menu.

2. Select Transaction Settings. The Transaction Settings window appears, as shown in Figure 14.1.

Chapter 14

3. Type **Y** in the Warn if a transaction has no category field.
4. Press [Ctrl]-[↵Enter] or click on Continue.

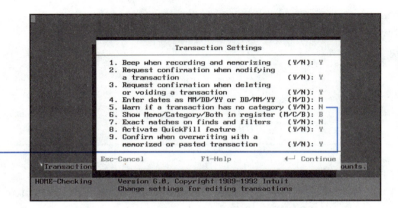

Figure 14.1
The Transaction Settings window.

Change this field to a "Y" to have Quicken remind you to enter a category.

Tracking Accounts Receivable—Cash Method

To track accounts receivable, set up an asset account to record all your outstanding invoices. Tracking accounts receivable involves three steps:

1. When you bill your customers, enter the invoice information in the asset register along with the appropriate income category.

2. When you receive the check, split the original invoice transaction to decrease the receivables balance and transfer the check amount to your bank account.

3. Run periodic reports to monitor your receivables. (Business reporting is covered later in this chapter.)

Setting Up an Accounts Receivable Asset Register

Before you can start tracking accounts receivable, you must set up a separate account, as explained in Chapter 3. For practice, you can set up the following accounts receivable system for Mrs. Johnson's home-based desktop publishing business. To begin, make sure the Home account file is active; then, press Ctrl-A, select <New Account>, and enter the following information:

Type	Other Asset
Name	Accts Rec
Balance	$0.00
Date	Today
Description	Accounts Receivable

Entering Invoices

After you generate an invoice to send to your customer, you can record the information in your accounts receivable asset register. If you expect to be paid in several installments, enter the appropriate number of transactions. Follow these Quick Steps to enter invoices in your accounts receivable register.

Quick Steps

Recording Accounts Receivable Invoices

1. At the accounts receivable register, select a blank transaction.

2. In the Date field, enter the date you expect the invoice to be paid. Press Tab or click on the Ref field.

    The cursor moves to the Ref field (see Figure 14.2).

continues

continued

3. Enter the invoice number (if your invoice numbers are more than five characters long, use the Memo field). Press `Tab` or click on the Payee field.	The cursor moves to the Payee field.
4. Enter the payee's name. Press `Tab` three times or click on the Increase field.	The cursor moves to the Increase field.
5. Enter the invoice amount, and then press `↵Enter` or click on the Memo field.	The cursor moves to the Memo field.
6. Enter the date you issued the invoice. Press `↵Enter` or click on the Cat field.	The cursor moves to the Cat field.
7. Press `Ctrl`-`C` and select an income category for the invoice.	
8. Press `Ctrl`-`↵Enter` or click on Record.	Quicken records the transaction in the register.

Figure 14.2
The accounts receivable register showing a sample invoice.

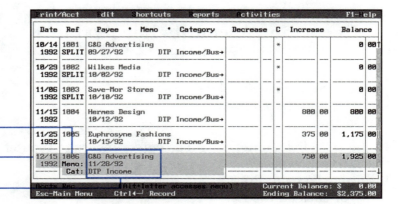

Invoice number
Date payment is expected
Invoice data

New invoices increase the amount of money owed to you, so you always record invoice amounts in the Increase field. The exception is when you issue a credit invoice for returned goods. The amount on a credit invoice is entered in the Decrease field.

Entering Payments

Eventually (you hope), your customers will pay you. When this happens, record two things:

- The decrease in value of your receivables.
- The increase in value of your bank account.

To do this, split the original invoice transaction so that a transfer from the accounts receivable account—equal in value to the payment—is recorded to your bank account. Figure 14.3 shows an example of this technique. Notice that, by splitting the original invoice transaction, you preserve the income category information (DTP Income in Figure 14.3) and record the cash received (the Checking transfer in Figure 14.3). Follow these Quick Steps to record a payment.

Recording Accounts Receivable Payments

1. In the accounts receivable register, highlight the original invoice.

2. Change the transaction date to the date of the payment.

3. Press Ctrl-S or pull down the Edit menu and select Split Transaction. — Quicken displays the Split Transaction window, which shows the original category information for the invoice.

continues

continued

4. In the first empty Category field, press Ctrl-C and select the bank account to which the funds are to be transferred. Press ↵Enter twice or click on the Amount field.	The cursor moves to the Amount field.
5. Type the payment amount with a negative sign, but don't press ↵Enter.	
6. Press F9 or click on Recalc Transaction Total to recalculate the transaction amount in the accounts receivable register.	The value of the transaction is decreased by the amount of the payment.
7. Press Ctrl-↵Enter or click on Done.	Quicken records the transfer and returns you to the accounts receivable register.
8. If the payment was for the full amount of the invoice, type an asterisk (*) in the C (Cleared) column and press Ctrl-↵Enter or click on Record.	Quicken records the transaction and adjusts the accounts receivable register balance to reflect the payment.

Figure 14.3 shows the split transaction used to record the payment for the invoice entered in the last section.

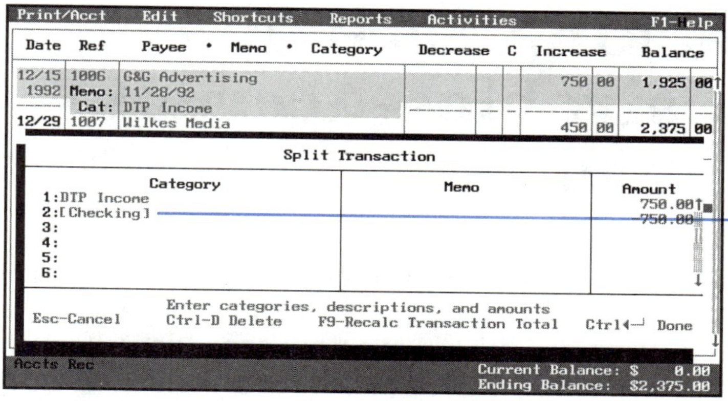

Figure 14.3
Accounts receivable payments are recorded as transfers in a split transaction.

Payment is transferred to the checking account.

Tracking Accounts Payable—Cash Method

Monitoring your payables is even easier than monitoring your receivables. You don't need to set up an extra account; you can do it all within your checking account. The idea is very simple: every time you get a bill, write a check and *postdate* it to when the bill is due. As long as you don't print the check, the current balance in your account isn't affected. You print the check only when the due date arrives, and only then is the current balance updated.

> **TIP:** Most businesses don't mind if an invoice that is payable in 30 days arrives two or three days late, but there are times when a late payment can cost you money. In such cases, you should postdate your check a few days before payment is due to allow enough time for the check to arrive at its destination.

Tracking Accounts Receivable—Accrual Method

With accrual accounting, you're more concerned with the balance sheet of your business. You want to monitor not just cash but the net total of all your assets (cash, receivables, inventory, capital) minus all your liabilities (payables, loans, payroll). With the accrual method, therefore, you reflect your income and expenses in your accounts as soon as you know about them.

To track accounts receivable with the accrual method, set up an asset account that you'll use to record all your outstanding invoices. Tracking accounts receivable involves three steps:

1. When you bill your customers, enter the invoice information in the receivables asset register along with the appropriate income category.

2. When you receive the check, enter another transaction in the receivables account to decrease the receivables balance and transfer the check amount to your bank account.

3. Run periodic reports to monitor your receivables. (Business reporting is covered later in this chapter.)

Setting Up an Accounts Receivable Asset Register

Before you can start tracking accounts receivable, you must set up a separate account, as explained in Chapter 3. For practice, you can set up the following accounts receivable system for Book City, if you haven't already done so. To begin, make sure the BookShop file is active; then, press Ctrl-A, select <New Account>, and enter the following information:

Type	Other Asset
Name	Acct Rec
Balance	$0.00
Date	Today
Description	Accounts Receivable

Entering Invoices

To enter an invoice, follow the same steps you followed for the cash-basis method. The only difference is that you enter *the actual invoice date* in the Date field. Remember, in accrual accounting, you reflect the transaction in your account on the date you send or receive an invoice.

Figure 14.4 shows the receivables register containing a sample entry for Book City. (Normally, you would also enter an offsetting entry in an inventory account to show the decrease in inventory.)

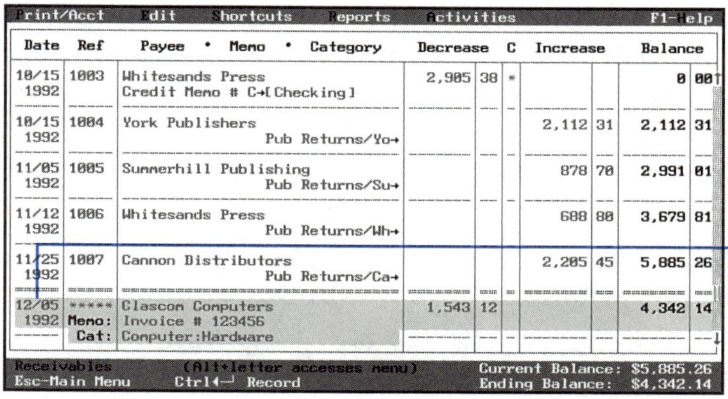

Figure 14.4
Receivables register showing a sample invoice.

Check is postdated to when the bill is due.

Entering Payments

As in cash accounting, when your receivables are paid, you record two things:

- The decrease in value of your receivables.
- The increase in value of your bank account.

To do this, you need to enter a second transaction equal to the value of the payment. This transaction is a transfer from the accounts receivable account to your bank account. Follow these steps to record a payment in your receivables account:

1. In the accounts receivable register, go to a blank transaction.
2. In the Date field, enter the date you received the payment. Press `Tab` twice or click on Payee.
3. Enter the customer's name. Press `Tab` or click on Decrease.
4. Enter the payment amount. Press `Tab` or click on the C (Cleared) field.
5. Enter an asterisk (*) to clear the payment. Press `Tab` twice or click on Memo.
6. Enter the invoice numbers that the payment covers. Press `Tab` or click on Cat.
7. Press `Ctrl`-`C` and select the bank account to which the funds are to be transferred. Press `Ctrl`-`Enter` or click on Record to record the transaction.
8. Highlight the invoice transaction in the receivables register.
9. Enter an asterisk (*) in the C (Cleared) field. Then go to the Memo field.
10. Enter the date the invoice was paid. Press `Ctrl`-`Enter` or click on Record to record the changes.

Tracking Accounts Payable—Accrual Method

With the accrual accounting method, you track accounts payable using a separate liability account. This way, your payables show up as liabilities on your balance sheet. Like your receivables, tracking accounts payable involves three steps:

1. When you receive a bill, enter the information in the payables liability register along with the appropriate expense category.

2. When you pay the bill, write a check in your checking account and transfer the check amount to your payables account to decrease your liability.

3. Run periodic reports to monitor your payables.

Setting Up an Accounts Payable Liability Register

Before you can start tracking accounts payable, you must set up a separate account, as explained in Chapter 3. For practice, you can set up the following accounts payable system for Book City, if you haven't already done so. To begin, make sure the BookShop file is active; then, press Ctrl-A, select <New Account>, and enter the following information:

Type	Other Liability
Name	Payables
Balance	$0.00
Date	Today
Description	Accounts Payables

Entering a Bill

When you get a bill, record the information in your payables account as follows:

1. In the accounts payable register, go to a blank transaction.

2. In the Date field enter the date you received the bill. Press `Tab` or click on Ref.

3. Enter the invoice number from the bill. If the number is longer than five characters, use the Memo field. Press `Tab` or click on Payee.

4. Enter the supplier's name. Press `Tab` or click on Increase.

5. Enter the bill amount. Press `Tab` four times or click on Cat.

6. Enter an expense category. Press `Ctrl`-`Enter` or click on Record to record the transaction.

Entering Your Payment

To record your bill payments, write a check and transfer the amount to the payables account. To track your payables due, use the postdated check method described in the section "Tracking Accounts Payable—Cash" earlier in this chapter. Follow these steps to record your bill payments:

1. In the check register or the Write Checks screen, enter a check for the bill.

2. In the Category field, enter the name of your payables account.

3. Press `Ctrl`-`Enter` or click on Record to record the check.

4. Go to the accounts payable register and enter an asterisk (*) in the C (Cleared) field to clear the payment.

5. Press `Ctrl`-`Enter` or click on Record to save your changes.

Producing Business Reports

In addition to helping you keep track of your daily business transactions, Quicken can help you keep track of the health of your business by creating business reports. In addition to a number of predefined reports, you can produce your own custom reports using the procedures discussed in Chapter 10. Following is a list of the eight predefined business reports:

P & L (profit and loss) Statement   Summarizes your income and expenses by month. Quicken uses all your accounts to compile the report but does not include transfers, because these have no effect on your profit or loss.

Cash Flow report   Shows the inflow of money to your accounts and the outflow of money from your accounts. Quicken uses only transactions from your bank, cash, and credit card accounts. A sample cash flow report is shown in Figure 14.5.

A/P (accounts payable) by Vendor report   Lists your unprinted checks by payee from your bank, cash, and credit card accounts. The report shows a separate column for each month in which there are unprinted checks.

A/R (accounts receivable) by Customer report   Lists the outstanding balances for each of your customers by month. You'll need to tell Quicken to use only your A/R asset account (otherwise, Quicken selects all your Other Asset accounts for the report).

Job/Project Report   Summarizes your income and expenses for each class. Quicken uses transactions from all accounts.

Payroll Report   Summarizes income and expenses for each employee. Quicken uses all accounts but only the transactions categorized as Payroll.

Balance Sheet Shows the balances from all your accounts and compares your current assets and liabilities.

Missing Check report Lists all your checks in check number order and flags gaps in the check number sequence as well as duplicated check numbers.

Figure 14.5
Book City cash flow report.

```
                    Book City October Cash Flow Report
                         10/ 1/92 Through 10/31/92
     BOOKSHOP-Bank,Cash,CC Accounts                       Page 1
     11/28/92
                                                        10/ 1/92-
                        Category Description            10/31/92

                    INFLOWS
                      Gross Sales                       155,577.71
                      FROM Receivables                    8,450.80
                                                        ----------
                    TOTAL INFLOWS                       164,028.51

                    OUTFLOWS
                      Advertising                         2,567.10
                      Freight                             1,544.41
                      Insurance                             424.50
                      Miscellaneous Expenses                424.50
                      Office Expenses                       427.31
                      Payroll:
                        Company FICA contribution   1,426.68
                        Company FUTA contribution     369.37
                        Company Medicare contrib      335.04
                        Compensation to employee   11,421.70
                                                   ----------
                      Total Payroll                      13,552.79
                      Rent Paid                           2,325.00
                      Repairs                               283.88
                      Returns & Allowances                3,131.14
                      Telephone Expense                     251.66
                      Utilities                             155.10
                      TO Payables                       127,082.73
                                                        ----------
                    TOTAL OUTFLOWS                      152,170.12

                                                        ----------
                    OVERALL TOTAL                        11,858.39
                                                        ==========
```

To have Quicken create one of these predefined reports, perform the following steps:

1. From the Main menu, select the Create Reports option, or pull down the Reports menu from any register or from the Write Checks screen.

2. Select Business Reports. Quicken displays the menu shown in Figure 14.6.

3. Select the report you want to produce. Quicken displays a setup window for the report. Figure 14.7 shows the setup window for the P & L statement.

4. (Optional) Enter a title for the report. If you leave this field blank, Quicken uses the report type as the title (for example, Profit & Loss Statement).

5. Enter the date for the report, as needed. Most of the predefined business reports ask you to specify a date range for the report. The exceptions are the balance sheet report, which asks only for a single date, and the A/P by vendor report and the A/R by customer report, which don't ask for a date at all.

6. Press Ctrl-Enter or click on Continue. Quicken assembles the report and displays it on-screen.

Figure 14.6

The Business Reports submenu.

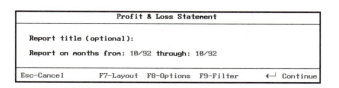

Figure 14.7

The P & L setup window.

In This Chapter

Using Quicken to Do Your Payroll

Setting up a Simple Inventory System

Managing Rental Properties

Using Asset Accounts to Track Personal Belongings

Tracking Home Repairs and Improvements

Managing a Payroll

1. Set up a payroll system with Quicken's payroll assistant.
2. Write your payroll checks.
3. Run reports to summarize wages paid, taxes withheld, and employer contributions.

Setting Up a Payroll System

1. Select the account you want to use for paying your workers.
2. From the Main menu, select Use Tutorials/Assistants.
3. Select Create Payroll Support.
4. Press ⏎Enter or click on Continue.
5. Enter the abbreviation for your state, and press ⏎Enter.
6. Press ⏎Enter or click on Continue.

Creating a Home Inventory

1. Create one general-purpose account for one-of-a-kind items such as your VCR and microwave oven.
2. Set up individual asset accounts for multiple items of the same type, such as videos, books, and stamps.
3. For each item, enter the purchase date, a description of the item, and its worth.

Chapter 15

Quicken Applications

In this chapter, you'll examine several common business situations and learn how to use Quicken to make them easier to manage. Specifically, you'll look at preparing payroll, tracking inventory, and managing properties.

For home users, you'll examine how to use Quicken asset accounts to itemize your personal belongings. You'll also learn a system for recording home improvements that affect your home basis (the original value of your home plus any improvements you've made).

Preparing Payroll

Preparing payroll is a complicated business no matter what size your company is, but it can be broken down into three basic steps:

1. *Set up a payroll system.* With Quicken, you have to do two things: create categories to expense your payroll tax contributions (*expensing* means that you enter an expense

transaction in the register) and set up liability accounts to accrue both taxes withheld from employees and your own payroll tax liabilities.

2. *Write your payroll checks*. When you split each check to show the various payroll deductions for each employee, Quicken expenses your contributions and updates your payroll liability accounts.

3. *Run reports* to summarize wages paid, taxes withheld, and employer contributions. Use these reports to fill out the required government forms.

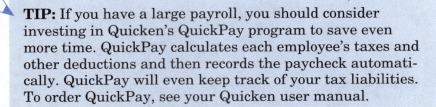

TIP: If you have a large payroll, you should consider investing in Quicken's QuickPay program to save even more time. QuickPay calculates each employee's taxes and other deductions and then records the paycheck automatically. QuickPay will even keep track of your tax liabilities. To order QuickPay, see your Quicken user manual.

Setting Up a Payroll System

Before you write your first payroll check, you need to set up a few categories and accounts for your payroll transactions. The categories you'll set up are used to track such things as each employee's gross salary, your matching FICA (Federal Insurance Contributions Act) payments, and your contributions for FUTA (Federal Unemployment Tax Act), Medicare, and SUI (State Unemployment Insurance). These are all business expenses and need to be categorized as such.

The accounts you create are used to record your accrued liabilities for things like the deductions withheld from your employees' paychecks and your own payroll tax contributions.

To set up your payroll system, you will use one of Quicken's assistants (*assistants* are a feature of Quicken that makes the software easier to use by automating certain tasks). To run the payroll assistant, follow these steps:

1. If you use more than one account file, make sure that the current file is the one you'll use to do your payroll.

2. From the Main menu, select Use Tutorials/Assistants. Quicken displays the Tutorials and Assistants menu, as shown in Figure 15.1.

3. Select Create Payroll Support. Quicken displays a message telling you what it is about to do.

4. Press ↵Enter or click on Continue. Quicken asks you to enter your state's two-letter abbreviation.

5. Enter the abbreviation for your state. If you're not sure what the proper abbreviation is, press ↵Enter or click on Continue. Quicken will pop up a list of the two-letter codes. Highlight the correct abbreviation and press ↵Enter or double-click on it.

6. Press ↵Enter or click on Continue. Quicken creates the necessary payroll categories and accounts. A message appears when the process is complete. Press ↵Enter or click on Continue to return to the Main menu.

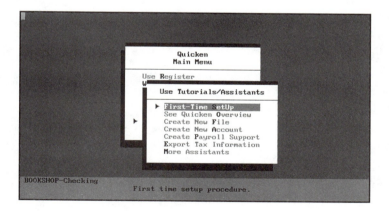

Figure 15.1
The Use Tutorials/Assistants menu.

The payroll assistant creates a payroll expense category and a number of subcategories. These subcategories are listed in Table 15.1.

Table 15.1
Categories Created by the Payroll Assistant

Subcategory Name	Description
Comp FICA	Company FICA contribution
Comp FUTA	Company FUTA contribution
Comp MCARE	Company Medicare contribution
Comp SUI	Company SUI contribution
Gross	Compensation to employee

You use the general payroll category to expense transactions related to the payroll process (such as the cost of payroll voucher checks). You use the payroll subcategories to expense the contributions your company makes for each employee. For example, you categorize the employee's gross salary or wage as Payroll:Gross, the company's matching FICA contribution as Payroll:Comp FICA, and so on.

If you have a company dental plan, pension plan, or any other deduction, you'll have to add the appropriate payroll subcategories. Use the same format that the payroll assistant used when setting up these categories. For example, you'd set up your dental plan subcategory as Comp Dental.

The payroll assistant also sets up a number of liability accounts. These are listed in Table 15.2.

Table 15.2
Liability Accounts Created by the Payroll Assistant

Account	Description
Payroll—FICA	FICA contributions
Payroll—FUTA	Federal unemployment tax
Payroll—FWH	Federal income tax
Payroll—MCARE	Medicare contribution
Payroll—SDI	State disability insurance
Payroll—SUI	State unemployment tax
Payroll—SWHIN	State income tax

These accounts track both the earnings withheld from each employee and your company's contributions. They are all liability accounts because the withholdings and contributions are funds that you owe to the government or another agency. By recording each liability at the time you process the payroll, you always have an accurate picture of what you owe.

If you've created extra subcategories to handle other payroll deductions, you need to set up corresponding liability accounts for each one. You must be sure to start the name of each payroll liability account with Payroll so Quicken knows to use the account when gathering information for reports. For example, if you set up a subcategory for a company dental plan, create a liability account called Payroll—Dental.

Writing Payroll Checks

After you set up all your payroll categories and liability accounts, you can write checks for your employees. This is a four-step process:

1. Determine the employee's gross earnings: use the gross salary for salaried employees and the total wages for hourly workers.

2. Determine the deductions to be withheld from the gross earnings.

3. Split the check transaction and enter the gross salary and the deductions calculated in step 2.

4. Enter offsetting splits for your company's accrued tax liabilities.

Follow these Quick Steps to record a payroll check.

Recording a Payroll Check

1. At the Write Checks screen, select a blank check.

continues

continued

2. Fill in the date and the employee's name.

3. Press `Ctrl`-`S` or pull down the Edit menu and select Split Transaction.

   Quicken displays the Split Transaction window.

4. On the first split line, type `Payroll:Gross` in the Category field, `Gross salary` in the Memo field, and the employee's gross pay in the Amount field.

5. Split each deduction by typing the corresponding liability account in the Category field and the deduction amount in the Amount field. Be sure to enter the deduction as a *negative* amount.

   Figure 15.2 shows the complete deductions for a Book City employee.

6. Move to split line 17.

7. Type `Payroll:Comp FICA` in the Category field and enter your company's FICA contribution as a *positive* number in the Amount field.

   This categorizes your FICA contribution expense.

8. On the next line, type `[Payroll-FICA]` in the Category field and your company's FICA contribution as a *negative* number in the Amount field.

   This transfers your FICA liability to the FICA account. The two amounts cancel each other out, so the check amount will not be affected.

Quicken Applications

9. Repeat steps 7 and 8 for your FUTA, SUI, Medicare, and any other contributions your company makes.

   Figure 15.3 shows a Book City example.

10. Press Ctrl-↵Enter or click on Done to save the split.

    Quicken returns you to the Write Checks screen.

11. Press Ctrl-↵Enter or click on Record to record the check.

    Quicken records the check.

Figure 15.2
Splitting a payroll check to withhold deductions.

Withholdings are accrued in your payroll liability accounts.

Enter deductions as negative numbers.

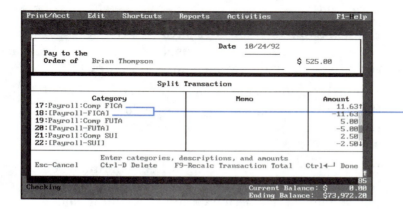

Figure 15.3
Entering your company contributions.

Categorize each contribution expense AND accrue an offsetting amount in your payroll liability accounts.

Memorizing Payroll Checks

When you record your employees' paychecks for the first time, memorize each one for later use. If you have salaried employees, you can memorize the entire check because the amounts won't generally change from paycheck to paycheck. If you have hourly workers, their gross pay will probably vary, so just memorize the splits without the amounts.

To make life even easier, you can create a transaction group to process your entire payroll at once. To do so, follow these steps:

1. At any register or the Write Checks screen, pull down the Shortcuts menu and select Transaction Groups, or press Ctrl-J. Quicken displays the Select Transaction Group to Recall window.

2. Highlight the next available <unused> group and press Enter or click on Continue. The Describe Group window appears, as shown in Figure 15.4.

3. Type **Payroll** for the group name. Press Tab or click on Account to load before executing.

4. Enter the name of the account that you use for payroll. Quicken will load this account before recording the payroll checks. Press Tab or click on the Frequency field.

5. Select a reminder frequency for the group. Press Tab, and Quicken enters the current date in the Next scheduled date field.

6. Enter the date of your next payday. Press Ctrl-Enter or click on Continue. Quicken displays the Assign Transactions to Group window, as shown in Figure 15.5.

7. Select the payroll checks you memorized by highlighting them and pressing the Space bar or by double-clicking on them. Each time you select a check, the group number appears in the Grp column.

8. Press Enter or click on Done when you finish selecting transactions. Quicken creates the group and returns you to the Select Transaction Group to Recall window.

When payday arrives, select the Payroll group from the group list. Quicken records each check automatically. If you need to make any changes or if you need to enter amounts for hourly workers, just edit the checks as you normally would.

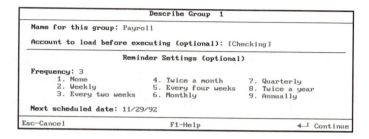

Figure 15.4
The Describe Group window.

Figure 15.5
The Assign Transactions to Group window.

Paying Payroll Taxes

Eventually, you need to pay both the deductions withheld from your employees and your company's contributions. This will reduce the accrued liabilities in your payroll accounts. To do this, write a check to the appropriate agency and enter the liability account in the Cat field. Figure 15.6 shows an example payment for federal taxes withheld.

Producing Payroll Reports

Quicken comes with a predefined payroll report that summarizes your payroll expenses and transfers to and from your payroll liability accounts. Figure 15.7 shows an example from Book City.

Figure 15.6

A check to pay federal taxes withheld from employees.

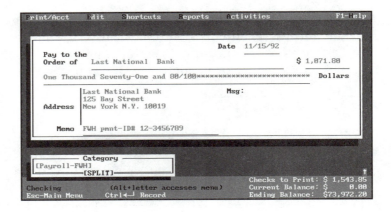

The first part of the report shows payroll expenses listed by employee. The second part shows the liability account transfers. The TRANSFERS TO items are your payroll tax payments that reduce your accrued liability. The TRANSFERS FROM items are the amounts withheld from your employees and the company contributions that increase your accrued liability.

Tracking Business Inventory

If you have a manufacturing business or any kind of retail operation, you probably keep inventory that you need to track. An ideal inventory system would tell you, at any given moment, how many units of a particular item you have and the total dollar cost of the stock. Unfortunately, Quicken deals with dollar amounts only, so you can't use it to track individual units. However, you can still set up a system to monitor inventory figures for use on your balance sheet. This section will show you how to create such a system.

An inventory system has to be able to handle four different situations:

- Goods received from suppliers (inventory increase).
- Goods sold to customers (inventory decrease).
- Goods returned from customers (inventory increase).
- Goods returned to suppliers (inventory decrease).

Figure 15.7
Book City Payroll Report.

```
                              Book City Payroll Report
                               11/ 1/92 Through 11/30/92
BOOKSHOP-All Accounts
12/ 1/92                                                                           Page 2
                                                                                 OVERALL
   Category Description    Brian Thompson  Emily Renaud  Sylvain Sylvain  Vince Durbin  TOTAL
INCOME/EXPENSE
  EXPENSES
    Payroll:
      Company FICA contribution       23.26       25.84       15.50       77.52      962.08
      Company FUTA contribution       10.00       10.00       10.00       40.00      470.00
      Company Medicare contrib         5.00        5.00        5.00       20.00      235.00
      Company SUI contribution         5.00        5.00        5.00       20.00      235.00
      Compensation to employee       360.00      400.00      240.00    1,200.00   14,828.78

    Total Payroll                    403.26      445.84      275.50    1,357.52   16,730.86

  TOTAL EXPENSES                     403.26      445.84      275.50    1,357.52   16,730.86

TOTAL INCOME/EXPENSE                -403.26     -445.84     -275.50   -1,357.52  -16,730.86

TRANSFERS
  TO Payroll-FICA                      0.00        0.00        0.00        0.00     -947.18
  TO Payroll-FUTA                      0.00        0.00        0.00        0.00     -235.00
  TO Payroll-FWH                       0.00        0.00        0.00        0.00   -1,071.80
  TO Payroll-MCARE                     0.00        0.00        0.00        0.00     -209.87
  TO Payroll-SUI                       0.00        0.00        0.00        0.00     -117.50
  TO Payroll-SWHNY                     0.00        0.00        0.00        0.00      -69.17
  FROM Payroll-FICA                   46.52       51.68       31.00      155.04    1,924.16
  FROM Payroll-FUTA                   10.00       10.00       10.00       40.00      470.00
  FROM Payroll-FWH                    54.00       60.00       36.00      180.02    2,234.22
  FROM Payroll-MCARE                  10.42       11.02        8.62       38.06      459.14
  FROM Payroll-SUI                     5.00        5.00        5.00       20.00      235.00
  FROM Payroll-SWHNY                   3.72        4.14        2.48       12.40      153.90

TOTAL TRANSFERS                      129.66      141.84       93.10      445.52    2,825.90

OVERALL TOTAL                       -273.60     -304.00     -182.40     -912.00  -13,904.96
```

You begin your inventory system by creating an asset account (you can call it Inventory) that you'll use to record these four kinds of transactions. Use your current inventory as a starting balance. The only other thing you'll need is a category to expense the cost of your goods (call it Cost of Goods).

Here's how this system handles each of the four types of inventory transactions:

Goods received from suppliers If you paid cash for the goods, enter the payment in your checking account (or whatever you use) and categorize it as a transfer to the Inventory account. This increases the value of the inventory by the amount of the payment. If your vendor has extended you credit, enter the transaction in your payables register and categorize it as a transfer to the Inventory account.

Goods sold to customers Calculate your cost of the goods sold and enter that amount in the Decrease column of the Inventory register. Categorize the transaction as Cost of Goods.

Goods returned from customers Again, calculate your cost of the goods returned and enter that amount in the Increase field of the Inventory account. Use the Cost of Goods category.

Goods returned to suppliers If you receive cash for the return, enter the deposit in your checking account and transfer the amount to Inventory. This decreases the value of the inventory by the amount of the deposit. If you have to wait for the money, enter the transaction in your receivables register and transfer the amount to Inventory.

Some Inventory Examples

Look at some inventory examples. The Book City inventory account has a $100,000 starting balance. Figure 15.8 shows several purchases from publishers recorded in the payables account. Each purchase is categorized as a transfer to the inventory account. Figure 15.9 shows how each of these transactions increases the inventory balance.

Figure 15.10 shows the Book City checking account. Notice, in particular, the two Daily Sales transactions on October 8 and 9. These represent total sales to customers on those two days. To make the inventory adjustment, you need to calculate the cost of the books sold. Assume that Book City buys all its books at 40% off the publisher's list price. Thus, you have the following:

	October 8	October 9
Daily Sales	$2,921.73	$2,655.98
Less 40%	1,168.69	1,062.39
Cost of Goods	1,753.04	1,593.59

Now all that remains is to record the two inventory adjustments. Figure 15.11 shows the Book City Inventory account. The two Daily Sales transactions reduce the inventory by the already calculated costs, and these are expensed to the Cost of Goods category.

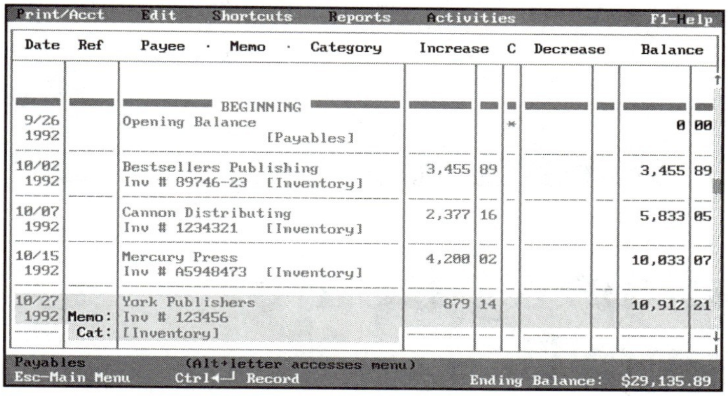

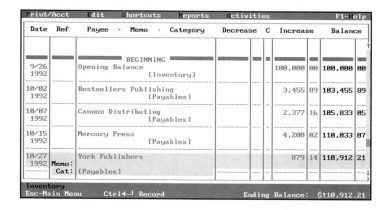

Figure 15.8

Purchases recorded in the payables account.

Figure 15.9

Corresponding increases in Inventory.

Figure 15.10
Book City checking account showing Daily Sales.

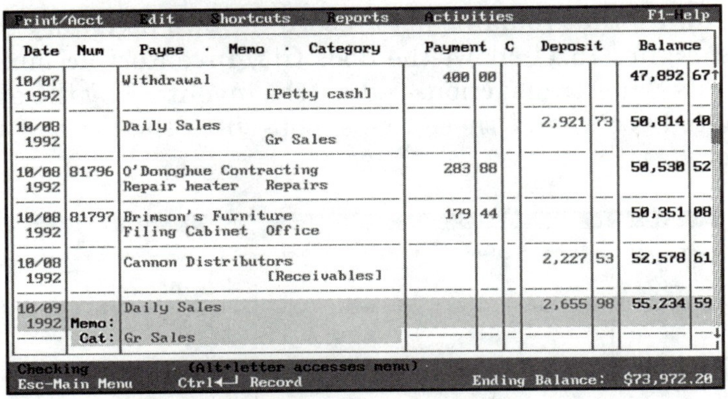

Managing Rental Properties

When you start a property management system, you need to set up categories for your rental income and expenses, and you need to establish a class for each property.

Figure 15.11
Cost of goods inventory adjustments.

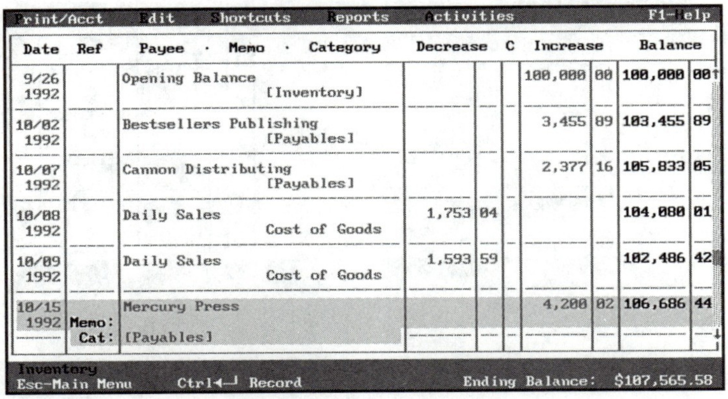

Almost all of the categories you'll need are already listed in the standard Quicken Category List—simply add to or edit the categories to suit your needs. Most of the work you need to do involves changing the tax schedule information for these categories because you'll be filing your rental income and expenses on tax schedule E (Supplemental Income and Loss). Follow the instructions given in Chapter 13, "Using Quicken at Tax Time," to change category tax information.

Once you have your category information in place, you need to set up a class for each rental property. This will allow you to keep track of income and expenses for each location. It also saves time when you do your taxes because the IRS requires you to enter separate income and expense amounts for each property.

For this section, set up a system to manage two properties: a house (16 Michigan Avenue) and a duplex (74 Howser Street). You must set up a new account file called RENTALS. This file includes the following accounts: checking, petty cash, asset accounts for each property, and liability accounts for each mortgage. You must also set up a class for each location and a subclass for the two units in the Howser St. building:

Class	Description
Michigan	16 Michigan Ave.
Howser	74 Howser St. building
Upper	Howser upper apartment
Lower	Howser lower apartment

Entering Transactions

When you record your income and expense transactions, enter a category for each one followed by the class name of the property involved. For example, if you receive rent from the Michigan Avenue property, enter the amount as usual in your checking account and type the following in the Category field: `Rent Inc/Michigan`. Record expense transactions in the same way. Figure 15.12 shows several transaction examples.

Use the techniques you've learned throughout this book to record other types of transactions. For example, you should split mortgage payments to categorize the interest as Mort Int and the principal transferred to the appropriate mortgage liability account.

Figure 15.12

Property management transaction examples.

Date	Num	Payee · Memo · Category	Payment	C	Deposit	Balance
10/01 1992		Deposit October rent Rent Income/Ho→			650 00	25,650 00
10/01 1992		Deposit October rent Rent Income/Mi→			1,200 00	26,850 00
10/01 1992		Deposit October rent Rent Income/Ho→			600 00	27,450 00
10/03 1992	1000	Wilkes Plumbing Memo: Cat: Repairs/Howser:Upper	357 88			27,092 12
10/08 1992	1001	Evanson Cleaners Cleaning/Michi→	150 00			26,942 12
10/15 1992	***** SPLIT	Last National Bank October mortgag→Mort Int/Howser	868 32			26,073 80

Checking   (Alt+letter accesses menu)
Esc–Main Menu   Ctrl↵ Record   Ending Balance: $25,159.35

If you write a check that covers expenditures for more than one property, split the transaction to show the separate expense items. For example, suppose you hire a contractor to perform heating system maintenance for both properties and pay him with one check. Figure 15.13 shows the split transaction you'd use to separate the expense.

Figure 15.13

Expensing separate items by property.

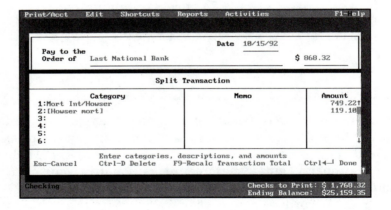

Producing Property Management Reports

Use the job/project report to see your rental income and expenses by property. (This report is available from the Business Reports menu.) Figure 15.14 shows a report summarizing the income and expenses for the Howser Street property. This is a job/project report that has been filtered to include only the transactions that use the Howser class.

```
                    Howser Street Building - Oct. Report
                        10/ 1/92 Through 10/31/92
RENTALS-All Accounts
                                                                    Page 1
12/ 1/92
                        Howser St bldg Howser St bldg Howser St bldg Howser St bldg
     Category Description   Lower apt      Upper apt       Other         TOTAL

INCOME/EXPENSE
  INCOME
    Rent Income              650.00         600.00          0.00       1,250.00

  TOTAL INCOME               650.00         600.00          0.00       1,250.00

  EXPENSES
    Cleaning                   0.00           0.00          0.00           0.00
    Mortgage Interest Exp      0.00           0.00        749.22         749.22
    Repairs                    0.00         357.88        400.00         757.88
    Water, Gas, Electric:
      Gas and Electricity      0.00           0.00         14.45          14.45

    Total Water, Gas, Electric 0.00           0.00         14.45          14.45

  TOTAL EXPENSES               0.00         357.88      1,163.67       1,521.55


TOTAL INCOME/EXPENSE         650.00         242.12     -1,163.67        -271.55

TRANSFERS
  TO Howser mort               0.00           0.00          0.00           0.00
  FROM Checking                0.00           0.00          0.00           0.00

TOTAL TRANSFERS                0.00           0.00          0.00           0.00


OVERALL TOTAL                650.00         242.12     -1,163.67        -271.55
```

Figure 15.14
Income and expenses for the Howser Street property.

Tracking Personal Belongings

Most people know, more or less, *what* they have in their homes or apartments, but how many actually know the *total value* of these personal belongings? For example, did you know that even a medium-sized bookcase contains, conservatively, around two or three *thousand* dollars worth of books? Sure, you probably remember what you paid for your VCR or your stereo or your computer, but what about all those videos and CDs and games? What about your tools, your furniture, and your clothes? All of these things are tangible assets, and if you don't take them into account, you're understating your net worth. What's worse, in the event of a fire, burglary, or other catastrophe, if *you* don't know the value of your possessions, how is your insurance company going to know?

To track your personal belongings, you can use Quicken asset accounts to act as databases for your records. You'll need one general-purpose account for one-of-a-kind items such as your VCR and microwave oven. Then you can set up individual asset accounts for multiple items of the same type, such as videos, books, and stamps. Table 15.3 shows some examples of accounts you could create.

Table 15.3
Example Asset Accounts for Your Personal Belongings

Account	Description
Belongings	Furniture, electronics
Videos	Films, home movies
Stereo	CDs, albums, tapes
Books	Hardcovers, paperbacks
Clothes	Clothes, shoes, hats
Hardware	Tools, equipment
Stamps	Stamp collection
Computer	Software, hardware

Once you have your accounts in place, you can begin the process of cataloging what you own. This is not a project you'll finish in an afternoon. Depending on what level of detail you want for your assets record, you could easily have hundreds of items to record. The best approach is to do a little at a time. You'll be more thorough and less inclined to make mistakes.

For each item, fill in the register fields as follows:

Date Enter the date of purchase. If you don't remember, you can use the current date.

Payee Enter a brief description of the item, such as VCR or War and Peace.

Memo Enter any additional description needed to identify the item.

Increase Enter the value of the item. This is probably the most important piece of information, so you should try to use an accurate amount. For most items, you can use the original purchase price. For valuables such as antiques and jewelry, use the most recent appraised value.

Notice that you don't need to use categories because you've set up separate accounts for each type of asset. Figure 15.15 shows some example entries in the stereo register. Note the use of the Ref field to distinguish between CDs, LPs, and tapes.

When you finish entering your belongings, create two reports: an account balance report to show the total value of your assets and a transaction report detailing the individual items in each account. In both cases, you should filter the report to include only entries in the asset accounts you created in this section. Run two copies of each report and store one copy in a safety deposit box or somewhere else outside your home. This will ensure that you have a record of your belongings should a fire or some other disaster befall your house.

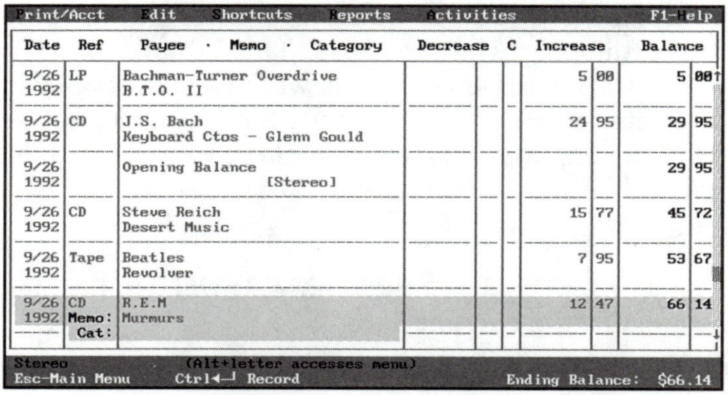

Figure 15.15
The stereo asset register.

Tracking Home Repairs and Improvements

If you're like most people, your house is by far the single largest investment you'll ever make. You begin by scraping together a few tens of thousands of dollars for a down payment. Then come the monthly mortgage payments, those ever-increasing property taxes, and the inevitable repair expenses. Add to all this the costs of your periodic home improvements (new carpeting, an extra bathroom), and you can see why a house is called a money pit.

The good news, however, is that while all this is going on, your house is probably appreciating in value. What you hope will happen is that, when you eventually sell your home, you'll make enough of a profit to recoup your costs. The problem is that the government taxes you on any capital gains you realize when you sell. In this section, you'll see how to reduce the tax you pay by simply keeping accurate records of the improvements you make to your home.

Here's how it works. Suppose you purchased your house for $150,000, and over the years you made a couple of major improvements: a new bathroom for $5,000 and a swimming pool for $15,000. If you sell the house later on for $200,000, you might at first think that your capital gain is $50,000, the difference between your purchase price ($150,000) and your selling price ($200,000). This isn't the case, however. The capital gain is actually the difference between the *adjusted basis* of your home and your selling price. The adjusted basis is your original purchase price plus any improvements that increase the value of the property. In the example, you'd calculate the home basis as follows:

	Purchase price	$150,000
	Swimming pool	15,000
+	**Bathroom**	5,000
	Home basis	170,000

So your taxable gain is actually only $30,000. Congratulations, you've just saved yourself a few thousand dollars in taxes.

With so much money at stake, keeping a careful record of your home improvements should be a top priority. You can use a Quicken asset register to keep track of each improvement. Set up the account (call it House) and enter the original purchase price of the house as the starting balance. Each time you make an improvement, enter the following information in your checking account (or whatever account you're using to pay the bill):

Date   The date of purchase or completion.

Payee   The store or contractor.

Payment   The total cost of the improvement.

Memo   A description of the improvement.

Category   The House asset account.

By transferring the payments to the House account, you automatically keep track of the adjusted basis of your home. Figure 15.16 shows the House register with a few example improvements.

Figure 15.16
The House asset register.

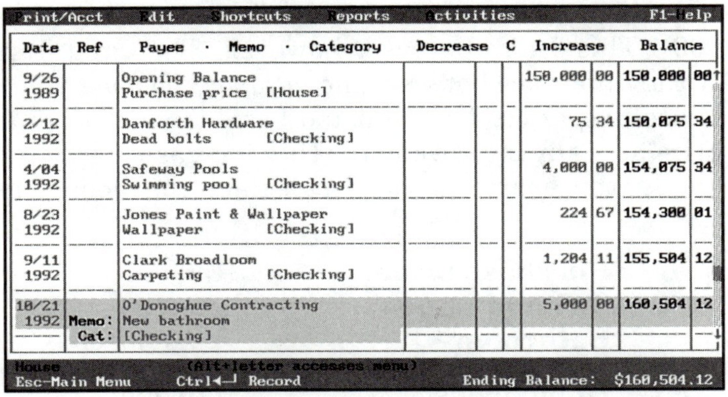

Print/Acct Edit Shortcuts Reports Activities F1-Help

Date	Ref	Payee · Memo · Category	Decrease	C	Increase	Balance
9/26 1989		Opening Balance Purchase price [House]			150,000 00	150,000 00
2/12 1992		Danforth Hardware Dead bolts [Checking]			75 34	150,075 34
4/04 1992		Safeway Pools Swimming pool [Checking]			4,000 00	154,075 34
8/23 1992		Jones Paint & Wallpaper Wallpaper [Checking]			224 67	154,300 01
9/11 1992		Clark Broadloom Carpeting [Checking]			1,204 11	155,504 12
10/21 1992	Memo: Cat:	O'Donoghue Contracting New bathroom [Checking]			5,000 00	160,504 12

House (Alt+letter accesses menu)
Esc-Main Menu Ctrl◄┘ Record Ending Balance: $160,504.12

FYI IDEAS

Maximizing Appraisal Value

An added benefit to keeping track of your home improvements is to help increase the appraised value of your home. If you can show records (and receipts) for each addition to the house, you'll be sure to get full credit for them during an appraisal.

The End

Now that you have finished this book, you are on the way to saving yourself loads of time and taking full control of your finances. Take some time now to enter all your financial records into Quicken, so you can take full advantage of the program. And before you exit, make sure you back up your files.

Appendix

A

Installing Quicken

Before you can use Quicken for the first time, you need to install and configure it to run on your system. The Quicken installation program makes this process as easy as possible. You just answer a few questions about your system and the program handles the rest.

What You Need to Run Quicken

To use Quicken, your system must meet the following hardware requirements:

- An IBM PC XT, AT, PS/1, PS/2, Tandy, or 100% compatible computer.
- A hard disk drive.
- DOS 2.0 or later.
- 512K minimum memory (640K if you want to use IntelliCharge with a modem).

In addition, the following equipment is optional with Quicken:

- Any Microsoft-compatible mouse.
- A printer.
- A modem to send electronic payments through CheckFree or to use IntelliCharge.
- A graphics card and monitor (Hercules graphics, CGA, EGA, or VGA), if you want to view graphs.
- Special checks from Intuit, if you want to print checks.

Before proceeding with the installation, make sure your computer is turned on. (You should see the DOS prompt—C:\ or C:\>).

Quicken Installation

Quicken 6 requires a hard disk. So, before you can use the program, you must install the program files from the floppy disks onto the hard disk. Follow these steps to install Quicken:

1. Insert the Quicken Install Disk 1 in drive A or B, and close the drive door, if necessary.

2. Change to the floppy drive that contains the disk by typing `A:` or `B:` and pressing [Enter]. The DOS prompt for the floppy drive appears.

3. Type `install` and press [Enter]. Quicken displays the Welcome to Quicken Install window, which gives you a brief overview of the installation process.

4. Press [Enter] to continue. Install asks if you have a color screen (see Figure A.1).

5. The default option is Yes, so just press [Enter] if you have a color monitor. If you don't have a color monitor, press [↓] or [2] to highlight the No option, and then press [Enter]. Install prompts you for your name.

Installing Quicken

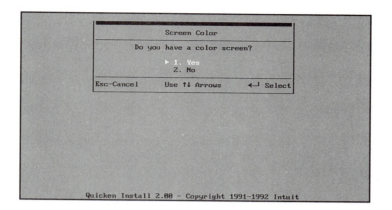

Figure A.1
The installation program asks you to specify the type of screen.

6. Type your name and press ⏎Enter. The Drive and Directory window appears, as shown in Figure A.2. Install will copy the files to drive C in the QUICKEN directory, unless you specify otherwise.

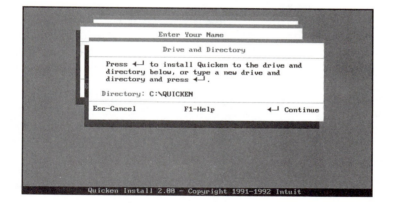

Figure A.2
Quicken suggests a directory for installation.

7. Press ⏎Enter if you want to accept the suggested drive and directory. If you would prefer a different drive or directory, use ←Backspace to erase characters and then type your changes.

8. Press ⏎Enter to continue. The Choose a Printer window appears with a list of the available printers (see Figure A.3).

Figure A.3
The Choose a Printer window.

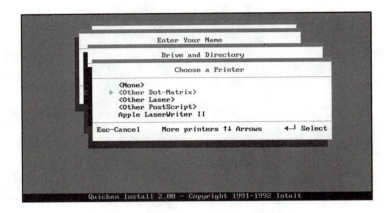

9. Use ↑ and ↓ to highlight your printer. If you don't have a printer, select the <None> option. If you don't see your printer listed, use ↓ to scroll through additional printers on the list. If your printer is not listed, select one of the generic options, such as <Other Dot-Matrix>.

10. Press ↵Enter. Install asks if you want Billminder to load automatically when you start your computer. Billminder is a feature that displays a message on-screen telling you when a bill is due.

11. If you want to use Billminder, press ↵Enter. Otherwise, press ↓ to highlight the Do not use Billminder option and press ↵Enter. (You can always activate it later.) Install displays a summary of the options you have chosen up to this point.

12. Read the summary screen. If you see any errors, press Esc to move back through the installation screens. When you get to the appropriate screen, correct the error and then repeat the necessary installation steps.

13. Press ↵Enter. Install starts to copy the files from the floppy disk to the hard disk. Install notifies you when to insert the next disk.

14. When Install displays a message telling you to switch disks, remove the disk from the floppy drive, insert the next disk, and press ↵Enter.

15. Repeat step 14 for the next disk, if necessary. A message box appears when the installation is complete. Press `Enter` to return to DOS.

Index

Symbols

.. (double period) wild-card
  character, 24
? (question mark) wild-card
  character, 24
1-2-3 files, printing to, 214

A

A/P (accounts payable) by Vendor
  reports, 205, 283
A/R (accounts receivable) by
  Customer reports, 205, 283
accessing registers, 28
Account Balances (Reports menu)
  option, 194, 209
accounting
  accrual, 269-270
    accounts payable,
      tracking, 281-282
    accounts receivable,
      tracking, 278-280
  cash, 269-270
    accounts payable,
      tracking, 277
    accounts receivable,
      tracking, 272-276
accounting tools
  CheckFree (electronic bill-paying
    service), 11
  financial planning calculators,
    11, 232-233
    college planning
      calculator, 236
    investment planning
      calculator, 234-235
    loan calculator, 233-234
    refinance calculator, 237
    retirement planning
      calculator, 235
  graphs, 11
  Intuit electronic credit card, 11
  loan amortization calculator, 11
accounts
  assigning Quick Keys to, 45
  cash, updating, 172-176
  chart of, 270-272
  creating, 28, 36
  credit card, 177-178
    reconciliation, 172, 179-182
    setting up, 178-179
  deleting, 46-47
  editing, 36, 45-46

files, 47-62
    activating, 67
    backing up, 57-60
    copying, 55-56
    creating, 36, 49-51
    deleting, 54-55
    names, 53-54
    placing, 51
    restoring, 61-62
    selecting, 52-53
payroll
    liability, 290-291
    setting up, 288-291
reconciliation, 155
    adjusting unresolved
        differences, 168-169
    balancing errors, 165-169
    completing, 154, 163-164
    credit card accounts, 172,
        179-182
    entering missing
        transactions, 168
    process of, 155-156
    starting, 154, 157-159
selecting, 28, 36, 43-45
setting up, 39
tax-related, setting up, 262-264
types of, 37-39
accounts payable, tracking
    accrual method
        bills, entering, 282
        liability register, setting up,
            281
        payments, entering, 282
    cash method, 277
accounts receivable, tracking
    accrual method
        asset register, setting up,
            278-279
        invoices, entering, 279
        payments, recording, 279-280

cash method, 272-276
    asset register, setting up, 273
    invoices, entering, 273-275
    payments, recording, 275-276
accrual accounting, 269-270
    accounts payable, tracking,
        281-282
    accounts receivable, tracking,
        278-280
activating account files, 67
Activities menu, Calculator option,
    111
Address field, 120
adjusting unresolved differences,
    168-169
alignment
    horizontal, setting, 133
    vertical, setting, 129-133
Alt-keys menu style, 25-26
amortization, 188-190
Amount field, 119
ASCII files, printing to, 213
Asset Composition (Net Worth)
    option, 244
asset register (account receivable),
    setting up, 273
Asset Trend (Net Worth) option,
    244
assets, 39, 184
    closing, 187-188
    entering, 185
    updating, 186-187
Assign Transactions to Group
    screen, 294
assigning
    Quick Keys to accounts, 45
    tax-related information to
        accounts, 262-264
assistants, payroll, running,
    288-289
AutoCreate (Edit menu) option,
    224-225

Index

B

background patterns, customizing, 33
backing up account files, 57-60
Backup Reminder Frequency, setting, 59-60
Backup Reminder Frequency dialog box, 60
Bad command or file name error message, 16
Balance field, 100
Balance Sheet reports, 205, 284
balances
  Checks to Print, 119
  Current, 119
  Ending, 119
balancing reconciliation errors, 165-169
bank accounts, 38-39
Bank Statement Balance field, 160
basic math calculator, 111-112
bills, recording in payables account, 282
Budget (Reports menu) option, 194, 209
Budget and Actual (View Graphs menu) option, 245-246
Budget Composition (Budget and Actual) option, 246
budget graphs, 245-246
budget reports
  custom, 227-231
  generating, 227-231
  monthly, 227-228
  printing, 231
budget setup screen
  key combinations, 219
  layout, changing, 220
  menu options, 219
  transfers, displaying, 226-227
Budget Transfers (Edit menu) option, 226
Budget Trend (Budget and Actual) option, 246
budgets
  copying amounts between months, 221-222
  goals, setting, 220-221
  historical data, using, 225
  income and expense data, copying, 225
  setting up, 218-226
  two-week items, setting up, 223
business accounting
  accounts payable, tracking
    accrual method, 281-282
    cash method, 277
  accounts receivable, tracking
    accrual method, 278-280
    cash method, 272-276
  accrual accounting, 269-270
  business reports, creating, 283-285
  cash accounting, 269-270
  chart of accounts, 270-272
business reports
  A/P (accounts payable) by Vendor, 205, 283
  A/R (accounts receivable) by Customer, 205, 283
  Balance Sheet, 205, 284
  Cash Flow, 205, 283
  Job/Project, 205, 283, 303
  Missing Check, 205, 284
  P & L (profit and loss), 205, 283
  Payroll, 205, 283
Business Reports (Reports menu) option, 205

C

C (cleared) field, 99
Calculator (Activities menu) option, 111

calculators
    financial planning, 11, 232-233
        college planning calculator, 236
        investment planning calculator, 234-235
        loan calculator, 233-234
        refinance calculator, 237
        retirement planning calculator, 235
    loan amortization, 11
Capital Gains reports, 206
cash accounting, 269-270
    accounts payable, tracking, 277
    accounts receivable, tracking, 272-276
cash accounts, 38
    updating, 172-176
Cash Flow reports, 195-197, 205, 283
categories, 4-7
    creating, 64, 74-78
    custom, 66
    deleting, 72-73
    editing, 70-72
    entering, 103
    payroll expense, 289
    payroll, setting up, 288-291
    standard, 66
    subcategories, 7, 78
        creating, 80-81
        deleting, 81
        editing, 81
        naming, 80
        payroll expense, 289
    tax-related, 255-258
        marking as, 260-261
        searching for additional, 261-262
        setting up, 259-260
Categories Over Budget (Budget and Actual) option, 245
Categories Under Budget (Budget and Actual) option, 246

categorizing transactions, 98, 270-272
Category and Transfer List
    columns, 68
    navigating, 69
    printing, 73-74
    viewing, 64, 67-68
Category field, 98-99
Category/Transfer column, 68
chart of accounts, 270-272
Check Number field, 97, 121
CheckFree (electronic bill-paying service), 11
checks, 114-117
    continuous, 116
    deleting, 125-126
    editing, 114, 124-125
    fields
        Address, 120
        Amount, 119
        Check Number, 121
        Date, 118-119
        Memo, 120
    ordering, 116
    payroll
        memorizing, 294-295
        setting up system, 288-291
        writing, 291-293
    printing, 28, 114, 133-136
        preparation, 128-133
        problem solving, 136
        setting up printer, 127-128
    reviewing, 124
    single-sheet, 116
    standard, 116
    voiding, 126-127
    voucher, 116
    wallet, 116
    writing, 28, 114, 121-123
Checks to Print Balance, 119
Class List, viewing, 64, 84
classes, 7, 82-83
    creating, 64, 84-86
    deleting, 87
    editing, 86
    in tax-related categories, 262

Index

classifying transactions, 98
Cleared (X,*) Balance field, 160
cleared transactions, 156
    marking, 154, 160-161
clicking mouse, 32
closing
    assets, 187-188
    liabilities, 187-188
college planning calculator, 236
columns, Category and Transfer List, 68
Comp FICA payroll expense subcategory, 290
Comp FUTA payroll expense subcategory, 290
Comp MCARE payroll expense subcategory, 290
Comp SUI payroll expense subcategory, 290
completing reconciliation, 154, 163-164
context-sensitive Help, 19
continuous checks, 116
copying
    account files, 55-56
    budget amounts between months, 221-222
    income and expense data, 225
    transactions, 105-106
correcting uncleared transactions, 167
Create Budget Report screen, 230
Create Reports (Main menu) option, 28, 194
creating
    account files, 36, 49-51
    accounts, 28, 36
    categories, 64, 74-78
    classes, 64, 84-86
    graphs, 247-248
    memorized transactions, 144-146
    reports, 192
        budget, 227-231
        business, 283-285
        predefined, 206-208
        tax, 265-267
    subcategories, 80-81
    transfers, 108-109
credit card accounts, 38, 177-178
    reconciliation, 172, 179-182
    setting up, 178-179
credit transactions, 99, 107
Current Balance, 119
custom budget reports, 227, 230-231
custom categories, 66
customizing
    reports, 209-210
    screen settings, 33-34

D

Date field, 95-96, 118-119, 305
debit transactions, 99, 107, 165
deleting
    account files, 54-55
    accounts, 46-47
    categories, 72-73
    checks, 125-126
    classes, 87
    memorized transactions, 150
    split transactions, 143
    subcategories, 81
    transactions, 90, 104
Deposit field, 99
Depreciation transactions, 187
Describe Group screen, 294
Description column, 68
Difference field, 160
disk files, printing to, 213-214
display settings, changing, 34
displaying
    budget setup screen, 218
    Graphs menu, 28
    Reports menu, 28
    Set Preferences menu, 28
    text in graphs, 248-249
    transfers, 226
    tutorial programs menu, 29
    View Graphs menu, 240

double bar graphs, 240
double period (..) wild-card character, 24
double-clicking mouse, 32
dragging mouse, 32

E

Edit menu
    AutoCreate option, 224-225
    Budget Transfers option, 226
    Fill Columns option, 222
    Fill Right option, 221-222
    Two Week option, 223
editing
    account file names, 53-54
    accounts, 36, 45-46
    categories, 70-72
    checks, 114, 124-125
    classes, 86
    memorized transactions, 148-149
    split transactions, 143
    subcategories, 81
    transactions, 104
    transfers, 109-110
EGA/VGA 43-line Display (screen setting), customizing, 33
Ending Balance, 119
entering
    assets, 185
    categories, 103
    check numbers, 97
    liabilities, 185
    missing transactions, 168
    split transactions, 141
    transactions, 90, 301
errors, reconciliation, balancing, 165-169
Exit (Main menu) option, 29, 35
exiting Quicken, 29, 35
Expense Composition (View Graphs) option, 243
Expense Trend (View Graphs) option, 244

F

fields, 95
    Bank Statement Balance, 160
    check
        Address, 120
        Amount, 119
        Check Number, 121
        Date, 118-119
        Memo, 120
    Cleared (X,*) Balance, 160
    Difference, 160
    Opening Bal Difference, 160
    register
        Balance, 100
        C (cleared), 99
        Category, 98-99
        Date, 95-96, 305
        Deposit, 99
        Increase, 305
        Memo, 98, 305
        Num (check number), 97
        Payee, 98, 305
        Payment, 99
files
    1-2-3, printing to, 214
    account, 47-56
        activating, 67
        backing up, 57-60
        copying, 55-56
        creating, 36, 49-51
        deleting, 54-55
        names, 53-54
        placing, 51
        restoring, 61-62
        selecting, 52-53
    ASCII, printing to, 213
    saving, 29
    tax, printing to, 214
Fill Columns (Edit menu) option, 222
Fill Right (Edit menu) option, 221-222

Index

filtering
    graph data, 249
    transactions, 199
financial planning calculators, 11, 232-233
    college planning calculator, 236
    investment planning calculator, 234-235
    loan calculator, 233-234
    refinance calculator, 237
    retirement planning calculator, 235
finding, *see* searching
Forms Leader (Print/Acct menu) option, 134
Full Column Width (Layout menu) option, 208

G

graphics, viewing, 34
Graphics Drivers Options dialog box, 248-249
graphs, 11
    budget, 245-246
    creating, 247-248
    display options, changing, 248-249
    double bar, 240
    filtering data, 249
    income and expense, 243-244
    investment, 246
    line, 240
    net worth, 244-245
    pie, 240
    printing, 248
    stacked bar, 240
    text, displaying, 248-249
Graphs menu, displaying, 28
Gross payroll expense subcategory, 290
grouping transactions
    by categories, 7
    by classes, 7-8

H

hardware requirements, 311-312
Help
    context-sensitive, 19
    hypertext links, 21
    index, 20
    key combinations, 24-25
    related topics, viewing, 21
    screens, scrolling through, 21
    searching for topics, 22-25
    table of contents, 20
home repairs/improvements, tracking, 306-308
horizontal alignment, setting, 133
hypertext links, 21

I

Income and Expense (View Graph) option, 243-244
income and expense graphs, 243-244
Income Composition (View Graphs) option, 243
Income Trend (View Graphs) option, 243
Increase field, 305
index, Help, 20
inflows, 195
installing Quicken, 311-315
    hardware requirements, 311-312
Intelli-Charge feature, 183-184
Intuit electronic credit card, 11
inventory
    business, tracking, 296-299
    personal belongings, tracking, 304-305
Investment (View Graphs menu) option, 246
investment accounts, 38
investment graphs, 246
Investment Income reports, 206

Investment Performance reports, 206
investment planning calculator, 234-235
Investment Reports (Reports menu) option, 205-206
investment transactions, recording, 191
Investment Transactions reports, 206
invoices (accounts receivable), recording, 273-275, 279
itemized categories reports, 197

J-K

Job/Project report, 205, 283, 303

key combinations
   budget setup screen, 219
   Help system, 24-25
   pop-up menus, 27
   pull-down menus, 30
   Quick Keys, 30

L

Layout menu, Full Column Width option, 208
liabilities, 39, 184
   closing, 187-188
   entering, 185
   updating, 186-187
liability accounts (payroll), 290-291
Liability Composition (Net Worth) option, 245
liability register (accounts payable), setting up, 281
Liability Trend (Net Worth) option, 245
line graphs, 240
links, 21

lists
   Category and Transfer columns, 68
   navigating, 69-70
   printing, 73-74
   viewing, 64, 67-68
   Class, viewing, 64, 84
loan amortization calculator, 11, 233-234

M

Main menu, 28-29
   Create Reports option, 28, 194
   Exit option, 29, 35
   Select Account option, 28
   Set Preferences option, 28
   Use Register option, 28, 93
   Use Tutorials/Assistants option, 29
   View Graphs option, 28
   Write/Print Checks option, 28
marking
   cleared transactions, 154, 160-161
   uncleared transactions, 161
Memo field, 98, 120, 305
Memorized Reports (Reports menu) option, 194
memorized transactions, 144-150
   creating, 144-146
   deleting, 150
   editing, 148-149
   recalling, 138, 146-147
memorizing
   payroll checks, 294-295
   split transactions, 147
   transactions, 138, 144-146
Menu Access (screen setting), customizing, 34
menu styles, 25-26

Index

menus
  Edit
    AutoCreate option, 224-225
    Budget Transfers option, 226
    Fill Columns option, 222
    Fill Right option, 221-222
    Two Week option, 223
  Main, 28-29
    Create Reports option, 28, 194
    Exit option, 29, 35
    Select Account option, 28
    Set Preferences option, 28
    Use Register option, 28, 93
    Use Tutorials/Assistants option, 29
    View Graphs option, 28
    Write/Print Checks option, 28
  pop-up, 26-27
  Print/Acct
    Forms Leader option, 134
    Number of additional copies option, 134
    Print All/Selected checks option, 133
    Print checks dated through option, 133
    Print to option, 133
    Type of checks to print on option, 134
  pull-down, 29-30
  Reports, 193-194
    Account Balances option, 194, 209
    Budget option, 194, 209
    Business Reports option, 205
    displaying, 28
    Investment Reports option, 205-206
    Memorized Reports option, 194
    Personal Reports option, 194-202
    Summary, 194, 209
    Transaction option, 194, 209
    Tax Schedule, 259
  View Graphs, 240
    Budget and Actual option, 245-246
    Income and Expense option, 243-244
    Investment option, 246
    Net Worth option, 244-245
Missing Check reports, 202-205, 284
Monitor Display (screen setting), customizing, 33
Monthly Actual Less Budget (Budget and Actual) option, 245
Monthly Assets and Liabilities (Net Worth) option, 244
Monthly Assets Less Liabilities (Net Worth) option, 244
Monthly Budget and Actual (Budget and Actual) option, 245
Monthly Budget Report screen, 228
monthly budget reports, 197, 227-228
Monthly Income and Expense (View Graphs) option, 243
Monthly Income Less Expense (View Graphs) option, 243
mouse
  clicking, 32
  double-clicking, 32
  dragging, 32
  pointing, 32
  toggling fields, 72
moving within Quicken, 25-26

N

naming subcategories, 80
navigating
  Category and Transfer List, 69
  Register screen, 93-94
net worth, 184
  graphs, 244-245
  reports, 199-202

Net Worth (View Graphs menu) option, 244-245
Num (check number) field, 97
Number of additional copies (Print/Acct menu) opti, 134

O

on-line Help, *see* Help
opening registers, 90-93
Opening Bal Difference field, 160
options
   Account Balances (Reports menu), 194, 209
   Asset Composition (Net Worth menu), 244
   Asset Trend (Net Worth menu), 244
   AutoCreate (Edit menu), 224-225
   Budget (Reports menu), 194, 209
   Budget and Actual (View Graphs menu), 245-246
   Budget Composition (Budget and Actual menu), 246
   Budget Transfers (Edit menu), 226
   Budget Trend (Budget and Actual menu), 246
   Business Reports (Reports menu), 205
   Calculator (Activities menu), 111
   Categories Over Budget (Budget and Actual menu), 245
   Categories Under Budget (Budget and Actual menu), 246
   Create Reports (Main menu), 28, 194
   description of, viewing, 27
   Exit (Main menu), 29, 35
   Expense Composition (View Graphs menu), 243
   Expense Trend (View Graphs menu), 244
   Fill Columns (Edit menu), 222
   Fill Right (Edit menu), 221-222
   Forms Leader (Print/Acct menu), 134
   Full Column Width (Layout menu), 208
   Income and Expense (View Graphs menu), 243-244
   Income Composition (View Graphs menu), 243
   Income Trend (View Graphs), 243
   Investment (View Graphs menu), 246
   Investment Reports (Reports menu), 205-206
   Liability Composition (Net Worth menu), 245
   Liability Trend (Net Worth menu), 245
   Memorized Reports (Reports menu), 194
   Monthly Actual Less Budget (Budget and Actual menu), 245
   Monthly Assets and Liabilities (Net Worth menu), 244
   Monthly Assets Less Liabilities (Net Worth menu), 244
   Monthly Budget and Actual (Budget and Actual menu), 245
   Monthly Income and Expense (View Graphs menu), 243
   Monthly Income Less Expense (View Graphs menu), 243
   Net Worth (View Graphs menu), 244-245
   Number of additional copies (Print/Acct menu), 134
   Personal Reports (Reports menu), 194-202
   Portfolio Composition (Investment menu), 246
   Portfolio Value Trend (Investment menu), 246

Index

Price History (Investment menu), 246
Print All/Selected checks (Print/Acct menu), 133
Print checks dated through (Print/Acct menu), 133
Print to (Print/Acct menu), 133
Select Account (Main menu), 28
selecting, 25-26
   from pull-down menus, 30
Set Preferences (Main menu), 28
Summary (Reports menu), 194, 209
Transaction (Reports menu), 194, 209
Two Week (Edit menu), 223
Type of checks to print on (Print/Acct menu), 134
Use Register (Main menu), 28, 93
Use Tutorials/Assistants (Main menu), 29
View Graphs (Main menu), 28
Write/Print Checks (Main menu), 28
ordering Quicken checks, 116
other asset accounts, 38
other liablility accounts, 38
outflows, 195

P

P & L (profit and loss) reports, 205, 283
pasting transactions, 105-106
Payee field, 98, 305
Payment field, 99
payments, recording in payables account, 275-282
payroll, 287-288
  accounts, setting up, 288-291
  assistants, running, 288-289
  categories, setting up, 288-291
  checks
    memorizing, 294-295
    writing, 291-293
  liability accounts, 290-291
  reports, creating, 295-296
  taxes, paying, 295
Payroll reports, 205, 283
personal belongings, tracking, 304-305
personal reports
  cash flow, 195-197
  itemized categories, 197
  missing check, 202
  monthly budget, 197
  net worth, 199-202
  tax schedule, 202
  tax summary, 199
Personal Reports (Reports menu) option, 194-202
pie graphs, 240
placing account files, 51
pointing mouse, 32
pop-up menus, 26-27
  key combinations, 27
Portfolio Composition (Investment) option, 246
Portfolio Value reports, 206
Portfolio Value Trend (Investment) option, 246
postdated transactions, 96
Price History (Investment) option, 246
Print All/Selected checks (Print/Acct menu) option, 133
Print checks dated through (Print/Acct menu) option, 133
Print to (Print/Acct menu) option, 133
Print/Acct menu
  Forms Leader option, 134
  Number of additional copies option, 134
  Print All/Selected checks option, 133
  Print checks dated through option, 133
  Print to option, 133
  Type of checks to print on option, 134

printers
    horizontal alignment, setting, 133
    setting up for checks, 127-128
    vertical alignment, setting, 129-133
printing
    budget reports, 231
    Category and Transfer List, 73-74
    checks, 28, 114, 133-136
        preparation, 128-133
        problem solving, 136
    graphs, 248
    registers, 110
    reports, 192, 212-214
    to disk files, 213-214
    wide reports, 213
programs
    QuickPay, 288
    tutorial, 29
property management
    reports, creating, 303
    transactions, entering, 301-302
pull-down menus, 29-30

Q

question mark (?) wild-card character, 24
Quick Keys, 30
    assigning to accounts, 45
Quicken, 3-4
    as business-accounting system, 13
    as home-accounting system, 12
    checks, ordering, 116
    customization options, 33-34
    exiting, 29, 35
    hardware requirements, 311-312
    installing, 312-315
        hardware requirements, 311-312
    moving within, 25-26
    overview tutorial, 18
    running, 18
    starting, 15-17
    systematic approach to, 8-10
Quicken Main menu screen, 16
QuickFill feature, 123, 150-152
QuickPay program, 288

R

recalling memorized transactions, 138, 146-147
Reconciliation Summary screen, 160
reconciling accounts, 155
    adjusting unresolved differences, 168-169
    balancing errors, 165-169
    completing, 154, 163-164
    credit card accounts, 172, 179-182
    entering missing transactions, 168
    process of, 155-156
    starting, 154, 157-159
recording
    investment transactions, 191
    invoices (accounts receivable), 273-275, 279
    payments (accounts receivable), 275-276, 279-280
    payroll checks, 291-293
    transactions in registers, 100-103
refinance calculator, 237
Register screen, 31
    navigating, 93-94
    opening, 92-93
registers, 91-92
    accessing, 28
    asset (account receivable), setting up, 273
    editing transactions, 104

Index

fields
- Balance, 100
- C (cleared), 99
- Category, 98-99
- Date, 95-96, 305
- Deposit, 99
- Increase, 305
- Memo, 98, 305
- Num (check number), 97
- Payee, 98, 305
- Payment, 99

liability (accounts payable), setting up, 281
opening, 90-93
printing, 110
recording transactions, 100-103

rental properties, 300-301
- reports, creating, 303
- transactions, entering, 301-302

reports, 8
- budget
  - custom, 227, 230-231
  - generating, 227-231
  - monthly, 227, 227-228
  - printing, 231
- business
  - A/P (accounts payable) by Vendor, 205, 283
  - A/R (accounts receivable) by Customer, 205, 283
  - Balance Sheet, 205, 284
  - Cash Flow, 205, 283
  - creating, 283-285
  - Job/Project, 205, 283, 303
  - Missing Check, 205, 284
  - P & L (profit and loss), 205, 283
  - Payroll, 205, 283
- creating, 192
- customizing, 209-210
- investment
  - Investment Income, 206
  - Investment Performance, 206
  - Investment Transactions, 206
  - Portfolio Value, 206
- payroll, 295-296
- personal
  - cash flow, 195-197
  - itemized categories, 197
  - missing check, 202
  - monthly budget, 197
  - net worth, 199-202
  - tax schedule, 202
  - tax summary, 199
- predefined, creating, 206-208
- printing, 192, 212-214
- tax, creating, 265-267
- viewing, 207-208
- wide, printing, 213

Reports menu, 193-194
- Account Balances option, 194, 209
- Budget option, 194, 209
- Business Reports option, 205
- displaying, 28
- Investment Reports option, 205-206
- Memorized Reports option, 194
- Personal Reports option, 194-202
- Summary, 194, 209
- Transaction option, 194, 209

restoring backed up account files, 61-62
retirement planning calculator, 235
reviewing checks, 124
running
- payroll assistant, 288-289
- Quicken, 18

S

saving files, 29
Screen Colors (screen setting), customizing, 33
Screen Patterns (screen setting), customizing, 33
screens
- Assign Transactions to Group, 294
- budget setup
  - displaying, 218
  - key combinations, 219

layout, changing, 220
menu options, 219
transfers, displaying, 226-227
budget setup, displaying, 218
Create Budget Report, 230
customizing settings, 33-34
Describe Group, 294
Help, scrolling through, 21
Monthly Budget Report, 228
Quicken Main menu, 16
Reconciliation Summary, 160
Register, 31
    navigating, 93-94
    opening, 92-93
Transaction Settings, 271
unreadable, 17
Welcome to Quicken 6.0, 16-18
Write Checks, 118
scroll bar, 31
scroll box, 31
scrolling Help screens, 21
searching
    for tax-related categories, 261-262
    for uncleared transactions, 162-163
    Help topics, 22-25
    with wild-card characters, 24
Select Account (Main menu) option, 28
selecting
    account files, 52-53
    accounts, 28, 36, 43-45
    options, 25-26
        from pull-down menus, 30
selection bars, 69
selection key, 25-26
Set Preferences (Main menu) option, 28
Set Preferences menu, displaying, 28
setting up
    Backup Reminder Frequency, 59-60
    credit card accounts, 178-179
    horizontal alignment, 133
    printers for checks, 127-128
    vertical alignment
        daisy wheel or dot-matrix printers, 129-130
        laser printers, 131-133
single-sheet checks, 116
split transactions, 140-143
    deleting, 143
    editing, 143
    entering, 141
    memorizing, 147
splitting transactions, 138
stacked bar graphs, 240
standard categories, 66
Standard Categories dialog box, 40
standard checks, 116
starting
    Quicken, 15-17
    reconciliation, 154, 157-159
subcategories, 7, 78
    creating, 80-81
    deleting, 81
    editing, 81
    naming, 80
    payroll expense, 289
subclasses, 87-89
Summary (Reports menu) option, 194, 209

T

table of contents, Help topics, 20
Tax column, 68
tax files, printing to, 214
Tax Schedule menu, 259
Tax Schedule Report, 265-267
tax schedule reports, 202
Tax Summary Report, 265
tax summary reports, 199
taxes
    accounts, setting up, 262-264
    categories, 255-258
        marking as tax-related, 260-261
        searching for additional, 261-262
        setting up, 259-260

Index

payroll, paying, 295
planning for, 253-255
reports, creating, 265-267
text, displaying in graphs, 248-249
tracking
   accounts payable
      accrual method, 281-282
      cash method, 277
   accounts receivable
      accrual method, 278-280
      cash method, 272-276
   business inventory, 296-299
   home repairs/improvements, 306-308
   personal belongings, 304-305
Transaction (Reports menu) option, 194, 209
Transaction Settings screen, 271
transactions, 65
   categorizing, 98, 270-272
   classifying, 98
   cleared, 156
      marking, 154, 160-161
   copying, 105-106
   credit, 99, 107
   debit, 99, 107
   deleting, 90, 104
   Depreciation, 187
   editing, 104
   entering, 90
      for rental properties, 301-302
   filtering, 199
   grouping
      by categories, 7
      by classes, 7-8
   investment, recording, 191
   memorized, 144-150
      creating, 144-146
      deleting, 150
      editing, 148-149
      recalling, 138, 146-147
   memorizing, 138
   pasting, 105-106
   postdated, 96
   recording in registers, 100-103

   split, 140-143
      deleting, 143
      editing, 143
      entering, 141
      memorizing, 147
   splitting, 138
   uncleared
      correcting, 167
      marking, 161
      searching for, 162-163
   voiding, 106-107
transfers, 107
   creating, 108-109
   displaying, 226
   editing, 109-110
tutorial programs, displaying menu of, 29
Two Week (Edit menu) option, 223
Type column, 68
Type of checks to print on (Print/Acct menu) optio, 134

U

uncleared transactions
   correcting, 167
   marking, 161
   searching for, 162-163
updating
   assets, 186-187
   cash accounts, 172-176
   liabilities, 186-187
Use Register (Main menu) option, 28, 93
Use Tutorials/Assistants (Main menu) option, 29

V

vertical alignment, setting
   daisy wheel or dot-matrix printers, 129-130
   laser printers, 131-133
View Graphs (Main menu) option, 28

View Graphs menu, 240
  Budget and Actual option, 245-246
  Income and Expense option, 243-244
  Investment option, 246
  Net Worth option, 244-245
viewing
  Category and Transfer List, 64, 67-68
  Class List, 64, 84
  graphs, 34
  Help related topics, 21
  reports, 207-208
voiding
  checks, 126-127
  transactions, 106-107
voucher checks, 116

W

wallet checks, 116
Welcome to Quicken 6.0 screen, 16-18
wild-card characters, 24
windows, *see* screens
Write Checks screen, 118
Write/Print Checks (Main menu) option, 28
writing
  checks, 28, 114, 121-123
  payroll checks, 291-293

X-Z

zero-based budgeting, 224-225

Common Quicken Tasks and Commands *(continued)*

Task	Quick Key	Task	Quick Key

You can get help by using the following keys:

Task	Quick Key	Task	Quick Key
Context - sensitive help	`F1` or `Alt` - `H`	Help Index	`Ctrl` - `F1`
Select related help topic in help window	`Tab`	Help Table of Contents	`F1`, `F1`
Go to selected help topic	`Enter`	Return to previous help topic	`Backspace`

In the calendar, register, report, or graph, you can use the following keys to insert a date:

Task	Quick Key	Task	Quick Key
Today's date	`T`	First day of this year	`Y`
First day of current month	`M`	Last day of this year	`R`
Last day of current month	`H`		

Use the following keys in an account, category, or class list

Task	Quick Key	Task	Quick Key
Insert a new account, category, or class	`Ctrl` - `Ins`	Select an item in the list	First letter of item's name

Use the following keys to move around in a window or to move from field to field in a transaction:

Task	Quick Key	Task	Quick Key
Next field or column	`Tab`	Next month	`Ctrl` - `PgDn`
Previous field or column	`Shift` - `Tab`	Previous month	`Ctrl` - `PgUp`
Beginning of field	`Home`	Up one row	`↑`
End of field	`End`	Down one row	`↓`
First field in transaction, window, or report row	`Home`, `Home`	First transaction or upper left corner of report	`Ctrl` - `Home`
Last field in transaction, window, or report row	`End`, `End`	Last transaction or lower right corner of report	`Ctrl` - `End`
Next screen or check	`PgDn`		
Previous screen or check	`PgUp`		

Common Quicken Tasks and Commands

Task	Quick Key	Task	Quick Key
From the Main menu, you can perform the following tasks:			
Back up accounts	Ctrl - B	Select account file	Ctrl - F
Back up accounts and exit	Ctrl - E	Update prices	Ctrl - U
Select account	Ctrl - A		
From the register or Write Checks screen, you can perform the following tasks:			
Copy category or memo in splits	"	Find transaction	Ctrl - F
		Repeat Find (Next)	Ctrl - N
		Repeat Find (Backwards)	Ctrl - B
Copy payee name to address	"	Go to date	Ctrl - G
Copy transaction	Ctrl - Ins	Print	Ctrl - P
Paste transaction	Shift - Ins	Record transaction	Ctrl - Enter or F10
Memorize transaction	Ctrl - M	Select account for transfer	Ctrl - C
Recall a memorized transaction	Ctrl - T	Select or set up account	Ctrl - A
Quick recall memorized transaction	Ctrl - E	Select or set up category	Ctrl - C
QuickFill next or back	Ctrl - + or Ctrl - -	Select or set up class	Ctrl - L
QuickFill transaction	Type payee's name	Select or set up electronic payment	Ctrl - Y
Insert blank transaction	Ctrl - I	Split transaction	Ctrl - S
Delete transaction	Ctrl - D	Switch to transfer account	Ctrl - X
Display pop - up calendar	Ctrl - K		
From any of the Investment registers, you can perform the following tasks:			
Change price by 1/8	- or +	Go to next or previous day	Ctrl - → or Ctrl - ←
Select action	Ctrl - L	Go to next month	Ctrl - PgDn
Select or set up security	Ctrl - Y	Go to previous month	Ctrl - PgUp
Investment goal	Ctrl - L	Get price history	Ctrl - H
Security type	Ctrl - L		
Update prices	Ctrl - U		
You can perform the following tasks from most Quicken screens:			
Decrease date or check number	-	Display Write Checks screen	Ctrl - W
Increase date or check number	+	Go to register	Ctrl - R
Display calculator	Ctrl - O	Save transaction information	F10

continues

Reader Feedback Card

Thank you for purchasing this book from SAMS FIRST BOOK series. Our intent with this series is to bring you timely, authoritative information that you can reference quickly and easily. You can help us by taking a minute to complete and return this card. We appreciate your comments and will use the information to better serve your needs.

1. Where did you purchase this book?

   ☐ Chain bookstore (Walden, B. Dalton) ☐ Direct mail
   ☐ Independent bookstore   ☐ Book club
   ☐ Computer/Software store   ☐ School bookstore
   ☐ Other _____

2. Why did you choose this book? (Check as many as apply.)

   ☐ Price   ☐ Appearance of book
   ☐ Author's reputation   ☐ SAMS' reputation
   ☐ Quick and easy treatment of subject ☐ Only book available on subject

3. How do you use this book? (Check as many as apply.)

   ☐ As a supplement to the product manual ☐ As a reference
   ☐ In place of the product manual   ☐ At home
   ☐ For self-instruction   ☐ At work

4. Please rate this book in the categories below. G = Good; N = Needs improvement; U = Category is unimportant.

   ☐ Price   ☐ Appearance
   ☐ Amount of information ☐ Accuracy
   ☐ Examples   ☐ Quick Steps
   ☐ Inside cover reference ☐ Second color
   ☐ Table of contents   ☐ Index
   ☐ Tips and cautions   ☐ Illustrations
   ☐ Length of book
   ☐ How can we improve this book? _____

5. How many computer books do you normally buy in a year?

   ☐ 1–5   ☐ 5–10   ☐ More than 10
   ☐ I rarely purchase more than one book on a subject.
   ☐ I may purchase a beginning and an advanced book on the same subject.
   ☐ I may purchase several books on particular subjects.
   ☐ (such as _____)

6. Have your purchased other SAMS or Hayden books in the past year? _____
   If yes, how many _____

7. Would you purchase another book in the FIRST BOOK series? _____

8. What are your primary areas of interest in business software? _____

☐ Word processing (particularly _____)
☐ Spreadsheet (particularly _____)
☐ Database (particularly _____)
☐ Graphics (particularly _____)
☐ Personal finance/accounting (particularly _____)
☐ Other (please specify _____)

Other comments on this book or the SAMS' book line: _____
_____

Name _____
Company _____
Address _____
City _____ State _____ Zip _____
Daytime telephone number _____
Title of this book _____

Fold here

NO POSTAGE
NECESSARY
IF MAILED
IN THE
UNITED STATES

BUSINESS REPLY MAIL
FIRST CLASS   PERMIT NO. 336   CARMEL, IN

POSTAGE WILL BE PAID BY ADDRESSEE

SAMS

11711 N. College Ave.
Suite 141
Carmel, IN 46032–9839